GUIDE

TO THE CAMINO IGNACIANO

REPORTORIO DE TODOS
LOS
CAMINOS DE ESPAÑA
(HASTA AGORA NUNCA VISTO)

Juan Villuga
(Valenciano)

Medina – 1546

The Eastern half of the map, drawn by Gonzalo Menéndez Pidal, follows the original drawing (1546) by Juan Villuga to illustrate his book, *Los caminos en la Historia de España*, Ediciones de Cultura Hispánica, Madrid 1951 (http://bibliotecadigital.rah.es /dgbrah/es/consulta/registro.cmd?id=13035).

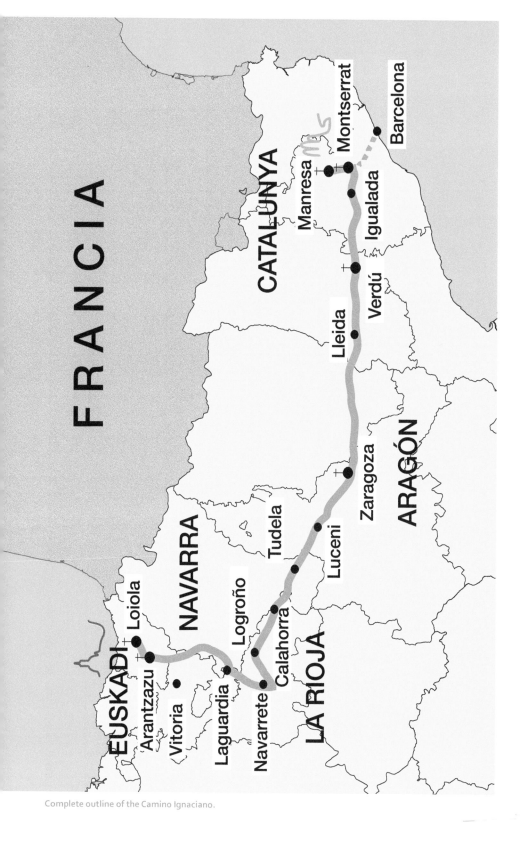

Complete outline of the Camino Ignaciano.

José Luis Iriberri, SJ
Chris Lowney

GUIDE

TO THE CAMINO
IGNACIANO
SECOND EDITION

Original title:
Guía del Camino Ignaciano

© Ediciones Mensajero, 2015; 3rd Edition, 2016
Grupo de Comunicación Loyola

Translated by
Manuel Elliot Jensen
Milton Elliot Jensen

© Ediciones Mensajero, 2017
Grupo de Comunicación Loyola
Padre Lojendio, 2
48008 Bilbao – Spain
Tel.: +34 94 447 0358
info@gcloyola.com
gcloyola.com

Cover design by
Magui Casanova

Printed in the United States
ISBN: 978-1944418731

Published and distributed by
Cluny Media LLC
www.clunymedia.com

Designed and typeset by
Rico Adrados, S.L. – Burgos
www.ricoadrados.com

CONTENTS

We present this guide to offer pilgrims an instrument to help them advance on their way. Both Chris Lowney and José Luis Iriberri are themselves pilgrims, not only of the Camino Ignaciano but, long before, of the well-known Camino de Santiago. The two of them have collaborated in the creation of the Camino Ignaciano since its inception and not only know it very well but are committed to its promotion, offering discussions and participating in conferences of Religious Tourism and Pilgrimages. Chris is a well-known writer, formed in the Ignatian tradition by American Jesuits. José Luis a Jesuit and professor on the San Ignacio Faculty of Tourism and Hotel Management, at the Ramón Llull University in Barcelona. This text incorporates the respective influence and input of both authors.

PART ONE
Getting into it

Welcome, pilgrim!

In 1522, Ignatius of Loyola travelled from his home in Loyola, in Euskadi, to Montserrat and Manresa, near Barcelona. This pilgrimage changed his life. His subsequent undertakings changed the world.

This guide invites you to walk, bike or drive—or simply imagine—the same route that Ignatius took. Get going! Begin your Camino to give thanks for all you have, to know yourself better, to test your stamina, to reflect on your future, or simply for fun. The route is a living cultural and historical treasure. Through the course of the centuries, first the Roman Empire, then the Islamic world and finally diverse, conflicting, Spanish kingdoms and devout Christians have left their fascinating marks on the architecture, the churches, the sacred objects and places that you will see along the Camino. We are sure that this itinerary will strengthen and motivate you; it is very possible that, just as Ignatius did, you will find inspiration to improve the world and you will commit yourself to such a laudable task.

In 2022, the five-hundredth anniversary of Ignatius's extraordinary pilgrimage will be celebrated. This guide has been written to nourish Ignatian pilgrimages as we approach this important commemoration in the history of the Jesuits, the Church and the world. The Camino Ignaciano will have fully taken on life when it has been travelled by even a small fraction of the millions of people who have been educated in Jesuit schools and universities, have made the Spiritual Exercises or have been inspired by the Jesuit tradition to work for a more just and faith-filled world. ¡Buen Camino!

How to use this book

The guide is divided into three parts. The first is an introduction to pilgrimage and to the world of Ignatius, all of which can help you place your own pilgrimage in perspective. The other two parts are intended to be used simultaneously. The second part is the practical guide: the route, distances between cities, lodging choices, and worthwhile places to visit along the Camino. The third part is a spiritual guide. The daily meditations will transform your physical journey into a spiritual itinerary.

If you are still wondering whether or not to make the Camino Ignaciano or if you are in the planning stages, consult the web page www.caminoignaciano. org, where you will find everything you need to best plan your experience. The Camino Ignaciano has something to offer each person: whether walking, cycling or driving, you will always find an itinerary which fits your interests; you simply have to design it yourself, using your creativity.

If you are an «armchair pilgrim», who wishes to traverse the Camino Ignaciano virtually, from home, by reading this book, a heartfelt welcome! As you travel your Camino, day by day, with the aid of this practical and spiritual guide, look at the Camino Ignaciano web page for photos which help you to visualize the landscapes seen by Ignatius or check them out with Google Maps on the web page.

1. THE PILGRIMAGE:
an itinerary of hope and desire

For millennia, we human beings have been going on pilgrimage to sacred places and we are likely to keep doing so for as long as we walk this planet.

Why do we go on pilgrimage?

The impulse to go on pilgrimage spreads across continents, cultures and creeds. Yearly, some thirteen million Christians visit Lourdes and Fatima; millions of Muslims visit Mecca and millions of Hindus go down to Benares to bathe in the sacred Ganges. Many millions more set out, year after year, for sanctuaries of all kinds, large and small, too numerous to be counted, on every inhabited continent. The World Tourism Organization (UNWTO) calculated that in 2012, more than 300 million people travelled exclusively for religious purposes.

At first glance these pilgrimages may seem to have little in common. Buddhists visit Bod Gaya, the place where Buddha experienced enlightenment; Hindus hope that the visit to the *char dham* (four holy sites) of their faith will free them from the cycle of rebirths; Catholic pilgrims who go to Lourdes seek healing for themselves or for a loved-one. What possible relation is there between the Buddhist who serenely meditates under the bodhi tree, the Catholic who implores to be cured of cancer in the grotto of Bernadette or the Hindu who seeks liberation from the wheel of reincarnations?

In fact, the relation is quite strong, for, underlying the diverse interests which compel pilgrims is the bedrock of shared human experience. Whatever our beliefs, whatever the historical era of our birth, we human beings continue to set out on the way because pilgrimage is a lasting metaphor for life. And there are at least three human themes which bind pilgrims of all religious traditions together:

- **Desire**: we are lacking something; we know the world is not perfect; there is some problem to solve or some need to satisfy.

- **Hope**: we hope for something better.

- **The Journey**: human life is a journey and pilgrimage is the metaphor that represents it.

Desire: something lacking

Few (too few) pilgrims get underway simply to give thanks for all that they have received. It is more likely that we go on pilgrimage for the opposite reason: because we want or need something. The sick seek a cure, the mentally anguished sigh for peace and the unreconciled long to fix broken relations with God, family or friends. We seek an answer to troubling dilemmas, we long for spiritual illumination, we pursue a deeper relationship with the Creator, we are drained by the pace of modern life or we are just bored and want to try something new.

We are lacking something, so we go searching for it. After all, if we enjoyed perfect happiness, why would we want to go anyplace? If we already had everything, why would we be looking for something else?

We human beings have longings for more than noble goals and saintly desires. Once, during a pilgrimage, I noticed a young fellow accompanied by an attractive young lady who was limping from a swollen knee. A week and many kilometers later, I was surprised to meet that fellow again in the company of a different lady. So much for chivalry! It seems that the young man had sent his lame companion home on a bus and continued ahead on his pilgrimage with his very human, earthy, motivations.

Regardless of whether your appetites run through sublime or more mundane channels, philosophers recognize something profoundly spiritual in our insatiable desire, in the unquenchable sense that «we are lacking something.» We human beings are permanently restless because, at bottom, we are more than what we have, or eat, earn or possess; the end of life is not in work, the house, or the bank account; neither is it in the sexual conquests that we make. It does not matter what we own, how famous we are, how much we make, with whom we sleep, or which car we drive: we will always feel incomplete in some way, vaguely unsatisfied, desiring more.

Our state of want, the perennial restlessness of the human condition, may mean that we have been innately programmed for something more than earthly life is able to offer, whether we admit this fact or we toil ceaselessly from one quest to another, stumbling, dissatisfied, in the vain hope that fulfillment will come with the next possession. St. Augustine, the famous 5th century bishop, put it in the following words: «Our heart is restless, Lord, until it rests in you» (*Confessions* I, 1, 1).

No amount of money, honor or pleasure will satisfy us forever. These worldly pleasures may content us for a time but sooner or later we will again feel the uneasiness. Just as Augustine saw, our ever-restless heart will not be satisfied with any finite good because it is sensitized for peace, joy and the infinite love that is God.

Because we are restless, we never feel completely at home in the world. In the New Testament, the Letter to the Hebrews states that we are all «pilgrims and strangers on earth» (Heb 11:13). Granted, the sentiment sound too strong. I do not feel «stranger», «exiled» on this lovely earth; in fact, I am glad to be alive and to be (as a rule) quite happy. But it is also true that I do not feel—and suspect that I will never feel—completely fulfilled. So then, we ever-restless human beings set out in search of healing, illumination, answers or experiences that might fulfill us.

This brings us to the second great human impulse for pilgrimage:

Hope: we hope unshakably for something better ...

All pilgrimage is an expression of hope. We hope to reach a destination and to return home, safe and sound. But we also wish the experience of pilgrimage to enrich our lives. We long to find peace, reconciliation, forgiveness, healing, illumination and many other aspirations.

On one afternoon during a long pilgrimage some disheveled pilgrims and I arrived, one by one, at a small town that was struggling to survive in a modern world dominated by large cities. The 38° C temperature (100.5° F) had transformed the village into a ghost town; if we had been gunslingers dodging tumbleweeds, the street scene would have fit perfectly in a cowboy movie.

At dusk, the church bells rang, announcing the evening Mass. Three or four elderly women came out of their shuttered houses and headed for the cool church where we pilgrims were resting. At the end of Mass, the priest prayed for the safety of us pilgrims and, closing the prayer book, improvised: «I know that you pilgrims are exhausted by the heat and are tired, but persevere on your way. If you seek answers, you will find them. If you seek peace, you will find it. If you seek God, he will find you.»

Right! That is it, is it not? That is what we human beings do. We go on pilgrimage full of hope. We hope for peace, answers, a second chance. We hope to find the perfect job, or the man or women of our dreams. And we do not give up hope. We hope unshakably, even against all hope. The diagnosis of a terminal illness does not dissuade us from hoping that some miracle or great medical advance may yet save our beloved spouse or child. We cling to the extraordinarily hopeful stories of our traditions. It consoles us, for example, that Jesus visits a dead girl and says: «*Talitha qum*—Little girl, I tell you, get up!» (Mk 5:41). And, incredibly, the girl gets up.

It is possible that the first, famous, human pilgrim was the biblical patriarch Abraham who, at God's insistence, set off for the Promised Land. The letter to the Hebrews reflects on Abraham's caravan, on the road such a long time and observes: «For if they had felt nostalgia for the [homeland] they left, they could have gone back there. On the contrary, they aspired to a better one, that is, a celestial one» (Heb 11:15-16). In effect, we keep going on our pilgrimage to Lourdes or Montserrat the same as on our pilgrimage through life. We hope for something better and hope spurs us on.

The journey: our life is a journey and pilgrimage is the metaphor that represents it ...

Sometimes our hopes are met and sometimes not. However, we persevere. We often learn something along the way; in this sense, the pilgrimage that one makes to Lourdes or Montserrat is an appropriate metaphor for life itself. Most pilgrims discover the truth of the old saying: the journey is more important than the destination. This is not entirely true of course; no trip will seem finally worth while it if it leads in a totally absurd direction. Ask any person who laments a life wasted in frivolous and empty pursuits.

Still, much of life does concern the journey itself: whom we meet along the way, what we see and savor, how we behave and deal with others, what we learn ... and much more: when all is said and done, that is what constitutes a life well-lived and a pilgrimage well travelled. Nothing magical will happen by the mere fact of reaching a destination like, for example, Manresa, just as nothing magical occurs by the mere fact of reaching the presidency of a company or a comfortable retirement. More often, the magic takes place along the way and those who are on pilgrimage through life would do well to keep their eyes and hearts wide open to whatever discoveries await them along their journey.

I learned this pilgrim's lesson through my own experience on the Camino de Santiago at the price of a bit of suffering. Walking six or seven hours a day during that pilgrimage, I encouraged other pilgrims daily (or they encouraged me). Most of us limited ourselves to exchanging a «¡Buen Camino!» and kept on walking, each content with his own solitude. On occasion we maintained an identical pace and were confronted with a delicate dilemma. Would we continue being silent travelling companions for the next three or four hours, each ruminating over his thoughts to the rhythm of the other's footsteps? Or would one or the other stop to rest unnecessarily, so as to create both the literal and figurative distance between us which we both desired?

Notwithstanding, pilgrims sometimes long for company, not solitude. Someone who has been pondering in silence for an hour or two may want to share his inisghts and afflictions with another person. I have learned aspects of my fellow pilgrims' lives that not even their bosses, their best friends or their lovers knew. An intelligent, young, computer scientist wondered, as he walked, if his life and career should not have had a wider horizon than computer science. In another case, a woman had long been resisting her husband's pleas to start a family: she asked herself if her refusal to have children said something about herself or about her marriage. She hoped to receive some insight into the problem in the hundreds of kilometers that separated her from her destination.

And me? In my case there were no such motives. I love to walk; I love to travel. I'm a religious person. I studied medieval history in university and savored the opportunity to see the Spanish Romanesque and gothic churches. I enjoy solitude and the possibility of fleeing once in a while from the crazed round of meetings, phone calls and e-mail which dominate modern life. Is that not reason enough to go on pilgrimage? I did not have any burning enigma to resolve and no illumination to seek. For the first days of my pilgrimage, I blithely ignored the oft-heard, much-repeated, mantra: «Everyone has something to learn on the Camino.»

But it is true that we all have something to learn and very often we learn it along the way rather than when reaching the end of the pilgrimage. A German pilgrim wrote me an e-mail once, after returning home from a pilgrimage that he had begun simply as a long holiday excursion. In the first days of our respective wanderings, we coincided occasionally. I would arrive sweaty and exhausted at a town and find him already there, relaxed, enjoying a beer on the terrace of some bar. He had arrived two hours before me and was already showered and had hung out his walking clothes to dry in the afternoon sun.

After a few days, I did not see him anymore. I kept putting in my twenty or thirty km a day (grateful to be able to keep up this pace), but he had begun to demand more and more of himself, increasing his daily distance, first from twenty to twenty-four km, then to twenty-eight and even more. His e-mail told me that he had returned safe and sound to Germany at the end of his pilgrimage: «I felt great on the way, my physical condition could not be better,» he wrote. «Most days it was no problem for me to walk long distances. I really enjoyed finding out what I'm capable of, pushing myself to the limit.»

To his surprise, however, these holidays had caused questioning ideas to blossom within him. It is true that he had been excited to stretch his limits and discover his strength but, as he walked, he had also become aware of something disturbing regarding the life that awaited him back home: «I rarely exploit my full potential. Or, to say it with an analogy to the Camino: I only walk twenty km when I could have walked thirty-five. Now I'm convinced that it's good to test one's own limits from time to time. To feel the energy that pulses inside of you. I have still got a great deal to discover.» Everyone has something to learn on a pilgrimage.

As for me? Unexpected ideas dawned. First, I felt a profound solidarity with the millions of Christian forerunners who had travelled that same route before me, throughout centuries and centuries. I thought particularly of the thousands of forgotten people who died while carrying out their pilgrimage and were buried in improvised, unmarked graves along the route. This fact can shock our modern minds but many medieval pilgrims were already worn out peasants when they began their pilgrimages: liberated from their feudal obligations to undertake the trip of their lives, thanks only to the fact that they were no longer considered fit for any productive labor. In the year 1000 A.D., if a peasant died five hundred km from his home, there were neither the resources nor the disposition to send the corpse back home. I began to see myself completing, metaphorically, the itinerary that they were not able to see through to the end, taking on their hopes as I advanced.

But then I became the one who could not finish. Having traversed half of the eight hundred km of my route, nine kilos lighter than the day I set out, feverish, burdened by a respiratory congestion that required antibiotics, with a bleeding blister on one heel and a merely painful one on the other, I felt defeated. I threw in the towel. «No more.» I changed my plane reservation from a telephone booth in a small Spanish town and caught a bus to the nearest

city. The bus paused for a moment next to the pilgrim's trail and I saw two or three walkers pushing on to the goal that now I was not going to reach. I knew that on a pilgrimage of eight hundred km all kinds of things can go wrong; even minor problems, for instance, like an ingrown toenail can become a catastrophe. But in my gut I had been sure that I was going to make it to the finish. How could I not be capable of it? I was in shape, I had trained, I was carrying the right gear and was prepared for any type of contingency. That is who I am, a guy who has everything under control, thinks ahead and works thing out.

Except that, in that instance, I did not have everything under control. Everybody has something to learn on the Camino, says the mantra. Now, having blithely dismissed that slogan for several days, I finally had enough humility to learn what I was supposed to learn: the world is not mine, but God's.

Every couple of years I need to relearn that truth; I begin to act as if I were able to control my own destiny, as if I were never going to get seriously ill, or as if a bank account were sufficient to save me from worldly anxieties. Then, fortunately, a new jolt reminds me that I do not have as much control over the world as I like to think.

During that pilgrimage I learned something else: the sheer joy of being alive. I was travelling at the beginning of September, counting on a rapid arrival of Fall but, in reality, I was punished by a late outbreak of summer. The temperatures had regularly risen to 38 and 40 degrees at midday (over 100° F), day after day; so we pilgrims got up earlier and earlier, determined to cover a good stretch of the stage in the cooler early morning. One morning, I left the pilgrim's shelter 4:30 AM, turned on my headlamp and saw, in front of me, four or five other headlamps already moving through the pre-dawn darkness, each light oscillating slightly, according to each pilgrim's manner of walking.

The line thinned out as the faster walkers left the slower ones behind and I became a solitary point of light beneath an ocean of stars. Since we were headed westward, a cloudy grey sky began to pursue us from the east and, little by little, replaced the star-dotted blackness. Orange rays started to warm my back and to color the innumerable stalks of recently cut ears of corn in a field of stubble. I began to discern the diffuse silhouette of a large hill rising in the distance. Hours later I stopped on the top of that same hill while the ferocious sun, now directly above my head, illuminated and painted the landscape. Below in the valley, quite far off, I saw the town that was my goal for the day and I began to descend the other side of the hill. Time passes in a different way when one moves slowly.

The perception one has of life's priorities can also change. I know a Spanish pilgrim whose daily car commute to work passed close to the famous pilgrim's way towards Santiago. He often saw one or two pilgrims walking while he drove to work. «I used to wonder,» he told me, «what those people were doing and why they were doing it.» Once retired, he decided to do the Camino de Santiago himself. When he had been walking for a few days, he noticed that he was on the same stretch of Camino that he had passed by in his car thousands of times on his trips to and from work. He halted, looked up towards the freeway and contemplated the commuters zooming by in their cars, some of them on their way, without doubt, to the same office district where he had once worked. «I looked at all those cars and I could not help laughing, because I found myself wondering what those people were doing in their cars and why they were doing it!»

Get going. Take your hopes and questions with you. As you advance, you will see some extraordinary things. And you will learn something. After all, everyone has something to learn on the Camino.

2. IMAGINING THE WORLD OF IGNATIUS

Travelling the Camino Ignaciano offers pilgrims the rare opportunity to live in two different eras. Enjoy the present moment and everything that the itinerary offers you. At the same time, imagine the past and imagine what this same trip was like for Ignatius. Begin an imaginary dialogue between the past and the present, taking into account how the world has been transformed, for good and bad, since the time of Ignatius. Tell this man from the 16th century what it is that impresses, excites or disturbs you about the 21st century. Try also to visualize his world: What did the landscape look like? How were food, beliefs, work and habits of that time different from ours?

We might ask, why bother to carry out what could seem to be a silly exercise, conversing with a saint? Well, saints are portrayed too often as pious caricatures: neither sufficiently angelic nor sufficiently human, as if they spent their earthly life in a cloud. This stereotype does not do justice to Ignatius, who valiantly carried out an exhausting pilgrimage of almost seven hundred km without the modern comforts we take for granted. As you come to appreciate his experience, you will transcend those empty stereotypes and encounter more fully his humanity and his spirituality.

Granted, it's not easy for us to imagine Ignatius's time. Our world is everything

that his was not: accelerated, mechanized, noisy, medically sophisticated, scientifically advanced, saturated with information, inundated by social media, secularized, and densely populated. At present, Spain has almost forty-five million inhabitants. That may sound like a lot of people. But, in fact, Spain is one of Europe's least densely populated countries. The Camino Ignaciano crosses regions—for example, the Monegros—in which a few small, dispersed, towns dot vast semi-desert landscapes.

Now consider, in contrast, that the Spain of Ignatius was home to only seven or eight million people, barely twenty percent of the current population. The cities were only a fraction of their present size. Today, seven hundred thousand people live in Zaragoza, whereas, in the year 1500, a mere twenty thousand dwelled there. Barcelona presents an even sharper contrast, between its 1,600,000 inhabitants today and the forty thousand when Ignatius was there. This does not mean to say that it seemed small to him: it was one of the largest cities of Europe and the largest that Ignatius had seen up to that point of his life. Neither would Spain have appeared to him unpopulated or empty: it was the only world he knew.

In fact, these towns and cities might have seemed crowded to an Ignatius whose family home, surrounded by forests and orchards, would have been much more isolated than it is now. His pilgrimage took him through towns where the people lived in small, densely bunched houses, without front yards, soundproof walls, or any of our modern expectations of privacy.

We would consider those towns much more tranquil than the world we walk through today. Disconnect for a moment the «white noise» machine of your brain, the filter that tones down the harsh soundtrack of life. Realize that even small towns nowadays are cacophonic symphonies of car motors, loud speakers and honking horns. Ignatius would hear none of this. He heard different sounds—the wind, the birds, the trot of his mule, the occasional clatter of some horse-drawn cart—while he traversed a landscape devoid of the ever-present bustle of our civilization. Today, trucks and cars pass close by, billboards announce restaurants, and plastic bags litter even the most solitary back roads.

While Ignatius walked to the rhythm of his thoughts, undistracted by music or calls from a smartphone, he contemplated a landscape unencumbered by all these modern artifacts. His sense of time would be radically different from ours. He knew nothing of «minutes» and «seconds»; the «hours» which towns kept track of were not today's twenty-four identical segments but the medieval «hours», fewer in number and of changing duration according to the season of the year by which monks still determine the times of common prayer, such as the «prime», the hour of dawn, or «vespers», the hour of sundown.

Ignatius's concerns with time were more basic: he needed refuge for the night and therefore was very attentive to the daily course of the sun, to judge how many hours of light he had left before stopping. (Keep in mind that, in a world without electric light, few travelers dared to traverse unknown routes by night.) Ignatius did not take any map with him, there were hardly any signs at all on the roads (and neither was it possible to make a phone call asking for directions); thus it is likely that, when he met with other travelers on the Royal Highway (Camino Real), which covered a large part of his route, he would inquire about the distance to the nearest town, about possible lodging along the way, and whether bandits lay in ambush further ahead. A 16th century commentator noted, for example, that, in order to travel safely from Zaragoza to Barcelona, an armed guard was almost essential.

So, the Camino Real that Ignatius followed would not seem at all «royal» to us. There was no governmental department responsible for roads and highways; long-distance routes were in a terrible state of repair, impassible after heavy rains, and bumpy and rutted when it did not rain.

Those on horseback could pick their own way over the rough terrain, but carts often turned out to be useless.

This does not mean that the terrible roads inconvenienced most Spaniards, because most Spaniards simply did not travel. To be sure, some members of the relatively small community of merchants, clergy and nobles were frequently on the move, but the majority of medieval Europeans married locally, never travelled for reasons of work or for vacations, lived and died in the small region around their town, and never ventured more than fifteen km from their houses. Some businessmen dared to travel the roads (or, sent their merchandise by boat along the Ebro River, which runs parallel to long segments of our Camino), but commerce was anything but intense. Large scale economies and mass production are modern concepts. There were no factories with assembly lines churning out torrents of goods to be distributed throughout the country. Instead, local craftsmen provided their neighbors with what they made in their household workshops, while itinerant merchants traded that which could not be produced locally, such as fish from the Mediterranean, cured with salt extracted from its marshes, or spices imported through the port of Barcelona.

Despite the scant volume of commercial activity, townspeople had no trouble furnishing their houses, simply because they possessed so little. As a general rule, they lived in smoky, single-room dwellings without windows. Their furnishings included a table (probably), a bench (maybe) and little more than that except, perhaps, one or two pets. At night, some families laid out a mattress; others simply spread straw to insulate their bodies from the cold dirt floor.

Ignatius surely drew attention when he entered one of these towns. He frequently passed through tiny villages, where only a few dozen families resided; other times, he entered towns with perhaps two thousand inhabitants;only on rare occasions would he come across any larger town. It is true that he was often travelling along the same routes as pilgrims on their way to or from Santiago de Compostela, so his passing as another pilgrim might not have been so unusual. His appearance was doubtlessly unkempt, after so many days on the road and too few baths (and those few baths would have been in cold water). But his clothing, as a minor noble, would contrast with the un-dyed, light, brown, cloth worn by the peasants, just as his language and accent would set him apart.

He was a stranger who crossed through municipalities so compact that the medieval Spaniards would on occasion refer to their home region as «my homeland». The members of any of these communities would not receive Ignatius as a «fellow Spaniard» because neither he nor they identified themselves deeply as «Spanish» in a country that only little by little was beginning to take on a common identity, stemming from the marriage of Fernando and Isabel and the conquests of the previous decades. But if allegiance to an abstract idea like "Spain" was weak, allegiance to the municipality, the ethnic group, the regional kingdom and the language, however, was strong.

Although Ignatius's clothing distinguished him from vagabonds, villagers might still have considered him dangerous for a different reason. On at least one occasion, as he relates in his Autobiography, they forbade him to enter a town, presumably because the local inhabitants feared

2. IMAGINING THE WORLD OF IGNATIUS

he might be infected with the plague. The «Black Death» or bubonic plague had decimated Europe's population in the 14th century, reducing it by half. And the specter of the plague haunted medieval minds. Barcelona alone had suffered half a dozen outbreaks of the plague in the 15th century, and its population in Ignatius's day was much less numerous than it had been two centuries earlier. And plague wrought devastating havoc in smaller towns and cities as well. A priest, after celebrating a funeral rite in a town of fewer than a thousand inhabitants near Zaragoza, wrote with bitter resignation in the parish register: «With this one, it makes forty-eight dead children (from the plague) so far this year.» Think of the heartache: presumably, every single inhabitant of that tiny town knew each one of those children personally.

Thus, when some stranger approached these municipalities, Christian charity competed with caution, though charity usually won; the pilgrims were put up in modest hospices which, as a general rule, also sheltered the town's poor and sick. The risks of that are obvious to us today: sick travelers could infect the more vulnerable natives; and healthy travelers could contract infections and spread them on the course of their journey. But in that era, the criteria of public health were primitive: in the majority of medieval towns, the ill were not hospitalized separately from healthy pilgrims, garbage and human waste piled up on the edge of towns, sewage often flowed freely in the town roads, and the benefits of washing hands before handling food were unknown.

In his Autobiography, Ignatius the pilgrim does not describe the meals these towns offered him, but we can imagine them. To start with, erase potatoes, tomatoes, corn, chocolate, tea, and coffee from the menu: these were non-indigenous crops which at that time were hardly known by everyday Europeans. Scratch out most vegetables and fruits also. Ignatius made the trip during February and March, too early in the year for the gardens and orchards to have ripened, and too early in history for the shipping of refrigerated produce. Elimi-

nate likewise sugar and pepper, products too expensive to have seasoned or sweetened a pilgrim's meal.

In fact, even the word «menu» is deceiving. Travelers did not have a choice; they ate what was put on their plates, and, very likely, at the end of winter, what they were served did not vary much from one town to another. Wheat, olives, and grapes were the typical crops in all the regions Ignatius passed through; so, wine was drunk with most meals and bread was not only a primary foodstuff but sometimes was the improvised «plate» and even «spoon», since all the fellow-diners used a chunk of bread to serve themselves stew from a common pot. Even so, it is possible that Ignatius did not dip too deeply into the pot: his pilgrimage took place during Lent, the liturgical period when medieval Christians fasted almost every day of the week, abstaining from meat and taking only one meal at midday and, perhaps, a light evening snack.

The Lenten diet was, in fact, one of the innumerable ways that the Church influenced daily life. It is impossible to understand Ignatius's historical era without taking into account the Church's broad influence on culture. Consider, to begin with, the visual contrast between Ignatius's surroundings and ours, in which commercial skyscrapers dominate the urban scenery, leaving the churches in shadow both literally and symbolically. In Ignatius's time, the relation was the inverse: the church was invariably the most sophisticated building in any town and occupied a place of honor in the central plaza; against its solid stone walls, flimsy merchant's stalls were set up, its bells announced the changing hours of the day and its spired tower was usually visible from far off, proclaiming the town's identity.

The visual signs of each era transmit a telling message. Skyscrapers dominant the profile of our cities just as commerce drives modern economies; in the Middle-Ages, the Church was an institution of analogous power. There was no big business. Local governments were tiny, they did not finance public schools and hospitals, or civil transportation or garbage pickup or libraries or social aid, or many of the other services which we residents of modern cities take for granted. The Church was usually the principal landowner in the town, the principal employer, the principal supplier of charitable services and, since there were hardly any town halls, the council meetings were normally held in the churches.

And why not? Spain was transforming herself inexorably into a homogeneously Catholic country. In 1492, Jews were given four months to convert or leave Spain forever and, even though Muslims could still practice their faith in Aragón, Islam would be banned about four years after Ignatius passed through that kingdom. Martin Luther had initiated the Protestant reformation only a few years before Ignatius's pilgrimage, but the reformers' ideas took little root in Spain, partly because the agents of the Inquisition kept assiduous watch on the diffusion of suspected heresies among Catholic Christians. In fact, they did somewhat more than just «kept watch»: in the three decades previous to Ignatius' journey, the authorities of the Inquisition in Zaragoza had executed some seventy-five suspected heretics. Though Christians who suffered the Inquisition's sting were relatively few, almost everyone felt the Church's vigilant gaze in one way or another: many priests kept track, family by family, of the attendance at Easter services in their parishes.

In short, religious identity was a public matter and Catholic Christianity was fast becoming the only religious identity allowed. Outside the Church awaited not the freedom to stay in bed on Sunday morning or to believe what one wanted, but the twilight of exile and, in rare cases, the threat of interrogations. In fact, the authorities of the Inquisition detained Ignatius on two occasions in the years following his pilgrimage, suspicious that this lay person with little education would share his so-called «spiritual exercises» with other Christians; what Ignatius essentially did was to preach without a license in an

era long before the free expression of one's own religious opinions began to be easily tolerated.

And, although medieval Christians were, without doubt, as holy or pious as any one of us, the majority of them knew no more than the rudiments of their faith. Books were expensive and, in any case, Europeans of the time, for the most part, did not go to school. More or less eighty percent of the Spaniards were peasants who did not own the land they worked. Many knew how to read simple words, sign their name and, if they were merchants, understand basic contracts; but very few were sufficiently educated to be able to read a religious text. In fact, the only books in the majority of the towns that Ignatius went though were those used by the clergy and civil functionaries.

Thus, the parish priests concentrated on the essentials. Christians abstained from working on Sunday, paid tithes on their meager income, attended the weekly liturgical celebrations, and confessed and received communion once a year, as a general rule on Easter Day. The majority knew the Our Father and the Hail Mary; many also knew the Creed, the Ten Commandments, and the Seven Deadly Sins.

It should not be surprising that the seven deadly sins would form part of the very brief catalogue of essential knowledge. To the Christians of the 16th century, hell seemed a much more real possibility than it does to us nowadays, people who, for the most part, take the inexhaustible love and mercy of God for granted. One of Ignatius's spiritual exercises describes hell as follows: «To hear with the ears, cries, screams, shouting and blasphemies against Christ our Lord and against all his saints. [ ] To smell with the nose smoke, brimstone, sewage and rotten things» (Spiritual Exercises [67-68]). Get the idea?

Since hell seemed a much more vivid possibility, avoiding it became a more pressing concern and also a principal motive for going on pilgrimages. Granted, pilgrims set out for all kinds of reasons. Some wanted to see the world, others sought healing for

sick family members, or a cure for their own chronic ailments.

After all, our medieval ancestors had an acute awareness of sickness and death; up to a third of conceived children died at birth. Even those who were born healthy had a life expectancy of only a little over forty years; people watched their loved ones die at home, not in hospitals. We, children of a scientific age, can question skeptically whether miraculous cures truly occurred as frequently as is recounted in medieval chronicles. But it is probable that Ignatius's contemporaries took even the most outlandish miracle stories literally, because they believed God was present in their world in a more active way than we would typically believe nowadays. Ignatius believed that God worked miracles and sent plagues as punishment, just as related in the Old Testament. Ignatius also believed that God touches the human heart, consoles us, and guides receptive people towards good life choices. We cannot understand Ignatius or his world vision without appreciating how actively and in-

timately he saw God working among us and within us.

Of course, even if we believe God guides us, we human beings do not always heed God's guidance. This explains another prime motivation for pilgrimage: contrition. Some pilgrims did not decide for themselves to visit this or that sanctuary; they obeyed the orders of their confessors. One pilgrim, for example, stumbled into Santiago de Compostela with an iron chain around his neck: a chain forged from the iron of the weapon with which he had murdered someone.

Ignatius seems to walk with one foot inside the pilgrimage tradition of his time and the other foot outside. Throughout his Autobiography, he calls himself «the pilgrim», but he does not cite any of the motives which traditionally moved pilgrims. He was not seeking a cure for his deformed leg, although it was often swollen and painful. Nor did he make the trip at the orders of a confessor, though he certainly saw himself as a penitent sinner. As much as anything else, Ignatius was turning over a new leaf and trying to transform himself, to begin to role model a new set of values. He was essentially reinventing himself (although he would neither have used nor even imagined such a concept, anachronistically modern).

As would later become manifest, the Catholic Church was also on the verge of a reinvention, but a humiliating reinvention, one that would be more imposed than chosen. Ironically, a central element of the Church's impending crisis would stem from pilgrimages and their abuses.

See, the Catholic sacrament of penance purifies the soul of sin, but the sinners must still «amend» (hence the expression to make amends) the wrongdoing, by means of doing penance, works of charity, and through devotional acts, such as a pilgrimage. Those who do not make sufficient amends on earth are faced with a purifying stay in purgatory, hardly an attractive prospect to medieval minds. The Italian painter Botticelli, for example, portrayed the envious in purgatory with their offending eyes sewn shut with wire, while the lustful were tortured by flames. Who would want to spend time in a place like that?

Fortunately for Christians disinclined to endure purgatory, their eyes sewn with wire, an alternative lay at hand: any pilgrim who had confessed and, as penance, visited a designated shrine, was granted an «indulgence» which guaranteed a shorter sentence in purgatory. Abuses arose however. The shrines, which represented a vital source of income for innumerable towns and monasteries, competed to attract pilgrims by offering more and more extensive indulgences and by exhibiting relics, on occasion of doubtful origin. Pilgrims could, for example, venerate the head of John the Baptist in Amiens (France), but also in Constantinople. God knows how!

Abuses multiplied. Itinerant prelates wandered Europe, peddling indulgences in order to raise construction funds for new ecclesiastical buildings. Swindlers issued false indulgences and simply kept the earn-

ings for themselves. Plenary indulgences granted full remission of the punishments of purgatory, so that the wealthy—without even giving up the comforts of hearth and home for an arduous pilgrimage—could basically buy express tickets guaranteeing a detour of purgatory and a direct entrance into heaven.

In light of all that, it's unsurprising that a scandalized Martin Luther demanded reform of the Church in his famous 1517 proclamation. Ignatius began his pilgrimage five years later. While Ignatius slowly wended his way towards Montserrat, the Catholic Church was rolling full speed towards crisis. In the course of a generation after Luther's opening volley, the dominion of Roman Catholicism over western Christianity slowly crumbled, as a third of Christians deserted Rome's sway and fled towards reformed (Protestant) Churches.

Ignatius could not foresee the reform trauma that awaited the Catholic Church, though his Jesuit companions would later become the Church's front line response to the reformers. In fact, it may be that as Ignatius set out on his pilgrimage, he knew little or nothing of Luther's slowly building challenge. And Ignatius probably knew little of other events which were profoundly reshaping the world at that time. Surely he had heard that a new world had been discovered by explorers like Columbus, but Ignatius could not have imagined that the world known by Europeans had basically tripled in size since his birth, that Spain was initiating its «golden age» as a world power, that his own Catholic Church was gravely threatened, and that he himself would one day found a religious order that would play a crucial role in all of these developments that were transforming the world.

Rather, at the end of winter, 1522, he walked and rode through the mountains of Euskadi, along the Ebro river, swollen with melting snow, across the semi-desert Monegros, where fifty-to-seventy km per hour gusts of winter wind blew dirt and dust for endless days over plains lacking any kind of shelter.

We can feel solidarity with Ignatius to the extent that we, too, face the headwinds of change all around us as we make our way into an unknown future. The difference between us and Ignatius? He did not have access to the information that would have helped him appreciate the magnitude of the change. He could not hear the news on the radio or television, or read the newspaper. He probably knew less about the world beyond Europe than a modern fourth grader today.

Ignatius seems small and alone as we imagine him crossing the deserted winter landscape with his mule. Even his world can seem small and isolated: He never saw an Asiatic face or knew a Sub-Saharan African or spoke with a native North or South American.

Still and all, he was on the way to developing a remarkably open attitude towards the world, an openness that distinguished him in his day. His openness, courage, and adaptability enabled him to face not only the challenges of his long pilgrim journey, but also the challenges of a world entering shakily into the Modern Era. A few years later, he would enthusiastically send his Jesuit companions to the edges of the earth as known by Europeans and, by the time of his death, he probably knew more about the world beyond Europe than the most informed monarchs of his era.

As you yourself walk in Ignatius's footsteps, stop occasionally to contemplate the world through his eyes and to build a closer contact with this 16th century man. Try to cultivate the same brave, resilient, and open attitude with which he faced the world. Adopt it as your own formula for living in the 21st century.

PART TWO

A practical guide for your pilgrimage

1. PLANNING AHEAD

A great pilgrimage begins with great advance planning. Don't improvise: take the time to inform yourself and prepare well.

Granted, you can't prepare perfectly. Problems will invariably arise. You may get lost one day, suffer a blister on another, or be buffeted by bad weather on a third. The restaurant may be closed when you arrive, or the hostel may be full. Bottom line: every pilgrimage will call upon your resiliency to solve unexpected problems on your own.

All the more reason to inform yourself in advance and prepare well! Frequently consult the Camino Ignaciano web page (www.caminoignaciano.org) to be up-to-date on modifications or news regarding the Camino Ignaciano. Likewise, this Guide can help you plan what stages and modifications you wish to incorporate in your itinerary. Many permutations are possible, depending on the time you have available and your interests. Hence, please take all the thoughts and suggestions that follow as helpful advice from someone who has walked the Camino Ignaciano before you. But do not feel obligated to do

it in exactly the same way. Rather, do the Camino in your own way.

Adopt the pilgrim spirit and use it to create your own journey. It is not a matter of walking the most kilometers or at the fastest speed or visiting every church along the route. In this guide, the first stages are shorter, to enable you to start with accessible distances and work your way into a better walking shape. Go faster and further if you wish; less so if that is best: Walk at your own pace. As Ignatius of Loyola reminds us: «There is no rush, it is not the walking distance that fills and satisfies the soul, but the inner savoring of each step.»

The Camino Ignaciano pilgrimage, however, does have its «rules». For those who wish to receive an end-of-pilgrimage certificate, we advise you to consult the web page on the subject of credentials and certificates.

Also on the web page you will find the average temperatures of each region the Camino Ignaciano passes through, although the precise weather is impossible to predict. Be that as it may, protection from the sun will be necessary on many parts of the Camino, where trees are scarce. And extra care should be taken in the mountainous zones of Euskadi whenever fog or snow appears: It is necessary to come prepared for rain. But who can predict the weather: Some Australian pilgrims complained, in October, 2013 of having carried the recommended warm clothes and rain gear throughout their 30 day pilgrimage—which they did not use once!

Physical preparation is important, but does not need to be overdone. There are pilgrims who have never trekked in their life and who walk their way into shape as the days go by. A Dutch pilgrim who came in the summer of 2014 explained that she had never been a walker but that her father, when she finished her studies, had told her: «Now is the moment to have an experience» and sent her to the Camino Ignaciano. All by herself, following the directions on the web page, she walked the 30 plus days of pilgrimage, arriving at Manresa completely happy and proud of herself, having discovered many limits that had helped her to better understand herself and to be grateful for her father's advice. On a pilgrimage, it is not a question of physical fitness but of desire, like someone who decides to do the famous Spiritual Exercises of St. Ignatius: it is not a matter of knowledge but of desire. That said, remember to bring well-fitting, flexible footwear, already broken in. A waterproof cover is necessary in case it rains and a change of clothes for resting between stages. Check out the web page of the Camino, where you will find more details, not only about footwear but also about the kind of gear most recommended for a pilgrimage.

It is very advisable to download the maps offered on the Camino Ignaciano web page. Each stage is described with its GPS tracks. Several pilgrims have told us, however, that it is best to take the Google Maps indicated on the web. Non-residents of Spain can assure a steady internet (and GPS) connection by buying a Spanish SIM card in your city of arrival. Prices vary, but as of June, 2018, there were offers for 15-20 Euros per month.

The way-mark arrows for the Camino Ignaciano vary according to region. Normally, the orange arrows will guide you along, but taking this guide with you will solve many problems. In Euskadi, the Camino Ignaciano has been recognized as the Great Route or Great Road 120 (GR-120), but we do not always follow its exact markings. The same thing happens in other regions, where we encounter routes which coincide in part with ours but not exactly. The route followed at present by the Camino Ignaciano was conceived to help the pilgrim, always keeping in mind the shortest distances between towns and minimum steepness of the roads that frequently pass through them, in case assistance is needed.

Regarding the financial cost of making the pilgrimage, it depends to a great degree on the preferences and orientation of the pilgrim. A Basque pilgrim told me that he had done it all for 450 Euros, often buying his food in the supermarkets and sometimes sleeping out in the open. Other pilgrims have invested 3,700 Euros in their personal experience. Personal style is up to each person. But overseas pilgrims should inform themselves in advance about bank

commissions applied to their credit or debit cards in Spain. There are ATMs all over the place, but find out first what you will be charged for each transaction. In general, it is sufficient to bring cash for the first week and then, withdraw cash little by little thereafter.

Last but not least, recall that the phone number for any kind of emergency in Spain is 112. If you run into any problems, call this number and they will find the best way to help you.

As for pilgrims on bicycles, we are happy to say that there are many facilities for them, making it possible to do almost the entire Camino on the same paths as the foot pilgrims. But in a few stages, it will be necessary to detour to secondary asphalt roads because the trail is too difficult for bicycles. In the descriptions of each stage that follows we will give some

more details on these cyclist variants. If you have any concerns about bicycling, know that in August, 2014 the mayor of Verdú and his 13-year-old daughter did the complete Camino with no previous experience of long bicycle trips. A feat? No. All that is needed is a great desire and the physical will to put in the effort. This is the lesson that every pilgrim must learn.

2. DAILY PRACTICAL GUIDE: stages, lodging and places to visit en route

With this book, you have a route guide of the entire Camino Ignaciano, divided into 27 stages, each for one day of walking. Each entry sets the spiritual tone of the day with an Ignatian aphorism, gathered

by Gabriel Hevenesi, a 17th century Jesuit, together with a Bible verse relevant to the theme of pilgrimage. Then comes a brief overview of the stage, followed by a detailed description of the day's walk/ride. You will also find logistical information and notes about important churches or buildings. Also included are references to relevant passages from Ignatius's Autobiography or from other works.

The distances between towns are approximate. According to a group of Australian pilgrims who did the Camino with their own GPS, it appears there are at least 689 total km. Our own GPS system gave us a total of 658 km, and that is the mileage we will be using throughout the guide.

Finally, remember that you need not follow this structure of 27 stages: you decide how far to go each day! We can only hope that you thoroughly enjoy it and live an unforgettable experience. Perhaps your unforgettable experience will begin the first day of your pilgrimage, attending the Mass celebrated in the chapel of the Conversion at 8:30 a.m. in Ignatius's house. If so, do not forget to ask a special blessing for your personal Camino.

The twenty-seven stages of the Camino Ignaciano may/could be these:

1st stage:	from Loyola to Zumarraga	(18.2 km)
2nd stage:	from Zumarraga to Arantzazu	(21.4 km)
3rd stage:	from Arantzazu to Araia	(18.0 km)
4th stage:	from Araia to Alda	(22.0 km)
5th stage:	from Alda to Genevilla	(24.0 km)
6th stage:	from Genevilla to Laguardia	(27.3 km)
7th stage:	from Laguardia to Navarret	(19.6 km)
8th stage:	from Navarrete to Logroño	(13.0 km)
9th stage:	from Logroño to Alcanadre	(30.6 km)
10th stage:	from Alcanadre to Calahorra	(21.5 km)
11th stage:	from Calahorra to Alfaro	(25.6 km)
12th stage:	from Alfaro to Tudela	(25.6 km)
13th stage:	from Tudela to Gallur	(39.3 km)
14th stage:	from Gallur to Alagón	(21.7 km)
15th stage:	from Alagón to Zaragoza	(30.5 km)
16th stage:	from Zaragoza to Fuentes de Ebro	(30.2 km)
17th stage:	from Fuentes de Ebro to Venta de Santa Lucía	(29.6 km)
18th stage:	from Venta de Santa Lucía to Bujaraloz	(21.3 km)
19th stage:	from Bujaraloz to Candasnos	(21.0 km)
20th stage:	from Candasnos to Fraga	(26,8 km)
21st stage:	from Fraga to Lleida	(33.0 km)
22nd stage:	from Lleida to El Palau d'Anglesola	(25.7 km)
23rd stage:	from El Palau d'Anglesola to Verdú	(24,7 km)
24th stage:	from Verdú to Cervera	(17.0 km)
25th stage:	from Cervera to Igualada	(38.6 km)
26th stage:	from Igualada to Montserrat	(27.0 km)
27th stage:	from Montserrat to Manresa	(24.6 km)
	Total km (approximate):	658.2 km

LOYOLA

Tower House of Enparan and bridge over the Urola river in Azpeitia.

Our Camino Ignaciano begins in this lovely sanctuary. Tourists and pilgrims mingle inside Casa Loyola but, upon visiting the home and birthplace of one of the most novel, original and influential personages of history and the surroundings where he reoriented his life, perhaps, from inside the curious mind of an everyday tourist, a pilgrim's spirit will find a way to peek through.

We begin our pilgrimage here in hills of the northeastern Iberian Peninsula. In the old tower house of Guipúzcoa, where Íñigo López de Loyola was born in 1491, we can begin to feel the experience of the holy pilgrim and to confirm that intimate truth that fills us with joy, which is the conviction that our life comes from God and goes to him. Many things happened to Íñigo here in 1521 when, at age 30, he was still «a brazen and vain soldier,» «very fond of women and playing with weapons.» The things that happened

to him here began to mold Ignatius of Loyola into a pilgrim: he came home as a soldier, wounded in body and heart after the defense of Pamplona, and left as one converted into a pilgrim of God. Don't rush to begin your Camino! Rather, a time of spiritual gathering, a time of inner preparation in this countryside between Azpeitia and Azkoitia, will help us to better take on the challenge of the Euskadian mountains and to discover their inner secrets. May St. Ignatius prepare us for the journey we are about to undertake.

Azpeitia (which in Basque means «under the rock») is a small and very pretty city, situated next to the Urola river, retaining the Ignatian aroma that wafts from the houses, streets and the stones in the river which Ignatius contemplated in his childhood and adolescence. Its population is almost 15,000 and it is located only 44 km from a large city: Donostia/San Sebastián. The municipality of Azpeitia

is the birthplace of Ignatius of Loyola and
the family home is perfectly conserved as
part of the large complex of the Sanctuary
of Loyola, which for centuries has been
an important attraction for both tourists
and pilgrims. At the other end of town,
across from the charming old parish
church where Ignatius was baptized, we
find the old Hospital of the Magdalene
where he lodged on his return trip home
after finishing his studies in Paris. This
site has been restored to cherish the fond
memory of the saint's sojourn in Azpeitia
where a veritable moral revolution took
place. Azpeitia is located at the foot of
the massif of Izarraitz, which rises above
it and the town is often frequented by
the inhabitants of the nearby towns. The
town hall's web page can be consulted for
visits to its monuments and for learning
its history (http://iraurgiberritzen.eus).
The Office of Tourism of the Urola is an
excellent source for obtaining maps and
information for finding the Ignatian sites
mentioned here, as well as other tourist
information for the area
(info@iraurigiberritzen.net). Available
lodging can range from pilgrims' shelters,
be it that of the Sanctuary of Loyola
(visitas@santuariodeloyola.org;
albergue@santuariodeloyola.org.
Tel.: 943 025 000) or that of the nuns of
Jesús-María (http://www.jesus-maria.net/
loyola/), to the many hotels and pensions
of the area (among them the Hotel
Arrupe, run by the Society
of Jesus, http://www.hotelarrupe.org/;

Bronze sculpture of the wounded Íñigo
coming back home.

Tel.: 943 025 026). The Jesuits receive
all pilgrims cordially and are available for
counsel, limited only by their multiple
personal occupations. Both in the
Sanctuary and in the Hotel Arrupe, the
pilgrim's credentials can be stamped
on the day of departure.

Tower House of the Loyola family.

LOYOLA – ZUMARRAGA
(18.2 km)

«The man who begins by wanting to make others better is wasting his time, unless he starts with himself.»

«May the Lord, your God, show us the path that we must follow and what we must do» (Jer 42:3).

Church of Aizpurutxo.

In Guipúzcoa, the Camino Ignaciano coincides with the GR-120 in some sections. In Loyola, we find this GR-120 indicated with its typical marks in red and white, pointing in the same direction that takes us to Arantzazu. The pilgrim is to choose if he prefers going by way of the Urola river or through the mountains, following the GR-120. If he opts to follow the GR-120 from here to Zumarraga, he must take into account the 700 m climb before him and the 300 m descent into Zumarraga. In compensation, the mountainous section is shorter, leaving the stage at 15.5 km and taking in the lovely hermitage of Santa María de Zumarraga or La Antigua.

To walk on GR-120 it is necessary to follow the typical red and white signs marked on the lampposts, trees and rocks along the trails. To walk the Urola river route, it is only necessary to follow the old railway which has been converted into a magnificent path, utilized with great frequency by the local inhabitants. Orange arrows, and the white and red signs of this GR-120 variant, mark the whole path up to Zumarraga.

We have chosen this latter route and, therefore, starting from the Basilica of Loyola, we go looking for the river and continue, always parallel to it in the direction of Azkoitia. On a well laid-out road and sheltered by the shade of the trees, we arrive shortly at Azkoitia. We enter the city, always following the river and we leave it, too, next to the Urola. The river is our guide at all times, keeping it to our right. Next to the river, a pleasant fountain with its two spouts of cool water, built in 1831, bring us close to the entrance of the church. Inside we can receive a stamp for our credential and also admire the charming sculptural composition of St. Francis of Assisi surrounded by Jesuits.

We leave Azkoitia and continue on the path or *bidagorri* along the old train tracks. We go through the old tunnels and over the old train bridges which have been restored. We continue following a lovely, slightly sloping, path which is very easy to walk.

Keep an eye out for cyclists, especially in the tunnels. Surrounded by the trees and the green fields, we pass Aizpurucho's church and its houses on the right which tells us that we are now only 6 km from Zumarraga. After a few more tunnels, we first reach the town of Urretxu, entering parallel to the highway. Until now, we have been on same path we took from Loyola and this is where we leave it. It could not be easier. We enter Zumarraga by crossing the Urola River which separates one town from the other. If we ask in the town hall,

the local police have a special stamp for Camino Ignaciano pilgrims. If we have time and strength, it is recommended to walk the 2 km up the mountain to the hermitage of Our Lady of the Antigua, or, if you prefer, you can take a taxi. Ask for information in the town.

Ignatian tip

Ignatius underwent a major inner transformation in Loyola and his family noticed: the Ignatius who arrived from Pamplona had healed externally and by the grace of God had also been granted an unexpected inner healing that he could not disguise. Physically recovered, the time finally came to set off, leave his family home and begin a new life.

«…now feeling somewhat stronger, it seemed to him time to leave, so he said to his brother: "Sir, as you know, the Duke of Nájera now knows that I am well. It would be good for me to go to Navarrete" (where the duke was then). His brother led him from one room to another and with much emotion began to beg him not to ruin his life; to see how the people hoped in him and all that he could do, as well as other such

words, all trying to dissuade him from the good desire that he had. But he responded in a way that, without deviating from the truth, to which he now scrupulously held, left his brother without argument. His brother and some of the household suspected that he wanted to make some great change.»

A great change was underway and this change, although unknown to Ignatius himself, was the force that impelled him

to step out of his «comfort zone» and venture towards the unexplored. Ignatius leaves the past and opens to the uncertain novelty that God offers him. There is great generosity in Ignatius's heart, great freedom, all committed to achieving a new Life in God. Jerusalem is his next objective.

Let us also take advantage of this search for freedom and generosity which can help us to step out of our known, familiar surroundings, though perhaps too constraining for a heart that should never stop growing. All pilgrims carry everyone that they love inside themselves; Ignatius leaves home, but in his enlarged heart takes his whole family with him, with all of its sorrow and glory. We also take all whom we love with us and we walk with them.

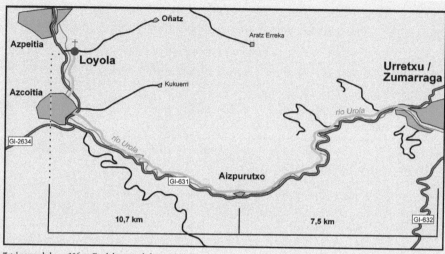

Total upward slope: 306 m. Total downward slope: 13 m. Bicycles: easy.

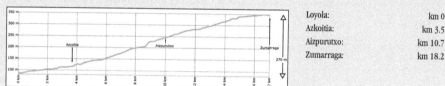

Loyola:	km 0
Azkoitia:	km 3.5
Aizpurutxo:	km 10.7
Zumarraga:	km 18.2

■ Description: The path of the Urola river.

We take our leave of the House and Shrine of St. Ignatius and set off along the asphalt road that begins near the sanctuary parking lot and runs parallel to the river towards Azkoitia. We skirt the edge of the

Sanctuary's gardens, on our left. We continue straight ahead and enter Azkoitia towards the Alameda del Ferrocarril in the direction of the river.

We do not cross the Urola river but we walk parallel to it with the river on our right. We continue straight on and the street meets a cycle lane that leads back towards the river. We continue with the river on our right until we reach some factories and a petrol station. We see a bridge in front of us: we will pass underneath it and go straight on. Once we pass the bridge, a road begins on our left. We take it and

in that way we pass the IBARMIA factory on our right.

We continue going straight ahead along the same path. The road bends to our right at right angles but we go straight ahead onto a secondary road that passes under a bridge. The road brings us across both the river and the GI-631 road by a bridge. We continue straight ahead and, after 800 m, we cross the road once more. We pass through the first of many tunnels.

Continuing straight ahead on the same asphalt path, parallel to the GI-631 road, we reach a new bridge that crosses the road twice. A few yards beyond that we come to a new bridge over the GI-631. We continue on the same path, crossing the road yet again. We pass the little village of Aizpurutxo on our right.

We continue straight ahead and our path meets another path coming up from the road. We continue straight on, looking for the path that is parallel to the GI-631 and a little higher than the roadway and the river.

Still more bridges and another tunnel lie ahead. We continue straight on and we pass a quarry on our right.

The road forks and we take the right branch, parallel to the road and the Urola River. We go through a new tunnel and we approach the houses on our left. We take another tunnel and our path finally leads us to the GI-631, which we take to our left, walking along the path that brings us close to the village of Urretxu. Keeping close to the road, we pass a sewage treatment plant and, following the path parallel to the road, we enter Urretxu and Zumarraga after crossing the river. These two villages are separated by the Urola River.

■ Interesting facts

AZKOITIA: It has a population of over 11,000 inhabitants. Near the Town Hall plaza is the impressive church of Santa María la Real. There are also some medieval tower houses, similar to Ignatius's family home in Loyola. Idiakez Tower or Etxe Beltza's black appearance is due to a fire suffered during the Second Carlist War. This village is known as the «cradle of Basque pelota», because this famous Basque sport's tradition has deep roots here.

AIZPURUTXO: A number of houses are scattered on the mountain slopes. Next to the road there is a bar.

URRETXU: A town of about 6,800 inhabitants. On calle Iparraguirre, you will find well-preserved, stately, 16th century homes which retain their similarities in structure and in the materials used (such as ashlar stone). The church of San Martín de Tours, an austere building of stone and wood, with a mixture of Renaissance, Gothic and Baroque elements inside, is worth mentioning. The municipality is located in a seventeenth century palace. Urretxu has been declared a protected archaeological site; its Fossil and Mineral Museum contains over 1,000 cataloged and classified minerals as well as numerous fossils from the five continents. It offers a wide choice of restaurants, pharmacies, supermarkets and banks.

ZUMARRAGA: A town of more than 10,000 inhabitants. Not until 1660 did it gain the title of town, or its independence.

The building of the magnificent church of Nuesta Señora de la Asunción began in the 16th century. It is built in Basque Gothic style with façades, a tower and a baroque main altar. The town hall building is in the Euskadi plaza where the statue of the Philippines' coloniser Miguel López de Legazpi stands in the center, with the Urola river behind. Do not miss the huge stone that men and women use to test their strength in competitions. As we have already mentioned, the ermita de la Antigua is an interesting visit for ignatian pilgrims. This picturesque chapel stands on a hill on the outskirts of town, following a steep 2 km climb. Did Ignatius pray here at the start of his pilgrimage? We do not know. The chapel has a Romanic façade from the 14th century, a Gothic carving of the Virgin Mary and a 15th century Calvary, which was created during an enlargement of the church, carried out in that century; thus it is easy to imagine Ignatius in this place. The amazing woodwork inside includes beams, ramparts and geometric carvings. In the town there are a wide choice of restaurants, pharmacies, supermarkets and banks. The City Hall has a specific seal to stamp the Camino Ignaciano passport.

■ **TAXI**

Azpeitia

Jesús María Nazábal Eizmendi 943 811 384
Vallina Taxis 943 393 848

Zumarraga
Taxis 943 720 307
Iván Molina 620 511 533

■ **LODGING**
AZKOITIA: Albergue Peregrinos Abaraxka, Altamira 5, Azkoitia. Tel.: 679 464 473

URRETXU: Pensión Juana Elgarresta, c/ Ipeñarrieta, 2-6, ground floor.
Tel.: 943 722 250.
City Hall. Tel.: 943 038 080.
A little more than 4 km away from town, up the hillside, next to the chapel of Santa Bárbara, is the 56-bed Urretxu Hostel at affordable prices. Tel.: 943 723 387.

ZUMARRAGA: Etxeberri Hotel, c/ Etxeberri, s/n (right at the entrance of the village). Tel.: 943 721 211.
Pensión Balentiña, c/ Urola, 6-8.
Tel.: 943 725 041.
Pensión Urola, c/ Antonino Oraá, 2.
Tel.: 943 533 008 / 679 525 259.
Pensión Zelai, c/ Legazpi, 5. Tel.: 670 264 922.
City Hall. Tel.: 943 729 022.

Idiakez Tower House, Azkoitia.

Zumarraga – Arantzazu

(21.4 km)

«We must exert much more effort in disciplining the inner man than the outer; the spirit gives more trouble than the bones.»

«Who can climb the mountain of the Lord? Who can enter the holy enclosure? He of innocent hands and pure heart, who does not turn to idols or swear falsely» (Ps 24:3-4).

Barrendiola dam.

We get up eager for climbing mountains. A steep ascent of 900 m towards Biozkornia makes this stage a challenge to be met with steadfastness and good spirit. We must not get discouraged but take things easy and enjoy the marvelous scenery which progressively opens up before our gaze. Winter pilgrims must be very careful with the snow and intense cold, as well as the fog which will complicate the hike. We leave Zumarraga-Urretxu following the train tracks, keeping them on our left. The long asphalt road will always be parallel to the tracks and in the direction of the mountains which rise steeply in front of us. First we have to go through the industrial zone, with factories all over the place; but then we will arrive at the green meadows and the hillsides teeming with livestock.

There is no getting lost on our path and it keeps us by the Urbia River. Information signs tell us of the local foundries and of the dams which were built to bring water to the factories. We encounter numerous walkers: there is no doubt that the people of these towns stay in good shape. Upon passing, the greeting will frequently be a «kaixo» (hello) or «egun on» (good day) in Euskera.

We come into Legazpi, accompanied by the rhythmic beating of the large metalworks. Until now, our way has been over flat terrain and well marked. In Legazpi, they stamp our credential in the town hall or in some other establishment whose stamp serves to indicate our visit and we continue on our way. We go ahead on a street parallel to the Urbia River. In the river, on our right, trout and ducks share the scene.

Land of iron, the foundries are old and, in another time, were very plentiful. We arrive at the park in Mirandaola, where tradition tells us that in 1580 workers accidently forged a piece of iron that then converted into a cross, an event commemorated on May 3rd, the day of the Holy Cross. Antique foundry objects and an iron handball court are the tasteful decorations. Signposts indicate the way which will take us to Telleriate. We go through town without leaving the route and in a few meters reach the Elorregi Palace. The foundry on our right, behind the chapel, dates from 1384. We continue on the clearly marked, fairly level, route all the way to Brinkola. Entering, we are surprised by the height of a bridge over the river leading to the train station. At the end of town, a sign indicates the direction to the Barrendiola reservoir and also indicates the way of the great route GR-120, which takes us first to the hill of Biozkornia and then to Arantzazu. The entire stretch to the sanctuary is well marked with the red and white GR-120 signs.

Here the first climb begins, staying on the highway until reaching the reservoir. A fountain of cool water awaits us before we get to the top. The reservoir impresses us by its size and its water offers us magnificent reflections of the mountains.

We cross to the other side of the reservoir and skirt it on a relatively flat path. We follow the signs of the GR and begin the ascent to Biozkornia. The path is wide but very steep. Signposts for the natural park indicate the direction. The scenery among the trees is impressive. We go by corrals of livestock and there, the trees end, making way for the pastures and stones.

The climb gets very steep. It is necessary to stop and breathe. The landscape is lovely and provides a spectacular view of the Zumarraga valley that we are leaving behind.

When we arrive at the Biozkornia pass, the signpost indicates the direction to Arantzazu. We always follow the red and white GR-120 signs and the scarce orange arrows. A new valley comes into sight and we descend into Arantzazu. Careful here: boots must be well tied to avoid foot problems. On rainy days we can easily slip in some places due to the abundant mud. The descent is as tough as the ascent: There is no need to rush.

We pass through an impressive spruce forest. It is recommended to spend a few quiet moments in the forest, as its trees seem like the columns of an immense cathedral. Here we can sense what the architect Gaudí thought to portray in his famous Basílica de la Sagrada Familia: nature's architecture could not be more perfect.

At last we arrive at the sanctuary of Arantzazu. The first country house we encounter is an old inn dating from 1500. Tradition would have it that this is the inn where Ignatius stayed during his visit to the Virgin of Arantzazu, or at least his mule did, since he spent the night in a prayer vigil before the Virgin.

Ignatian tip

Ignatius did not want to hurt his family since they were so concerned about his future, yet he knew he must begin his new life. This was confirmed during his very first stop in the chapel of Arantzazu.

«Ignatius left his father's house and set out upon his journey on horseback. His brother wanted to accompany him as far as Oñate, but during the journey Ignatius persuaded him to spend one night in vigil at the shrine of Our Blessed Lady at Arantzazu. Then, after praying for some time at the shrine for strength for the journey, he left his brother in Oñate at the house of their sister. After paying her a short visit, Ignatius journeyed on to Navarrete [to visit the Duke of Nájera].»

What did his brother think about being separated from Ignatius at Oñate? What did Ignatius speak about with Our Lady of Arantzazu during that night in prayer? A new road opened before him, guided only by his desire for greater service to our Lord. We might also ask the intercession of Our Lady, that we might likewise discover the presence of God more deeply as we journey. We ask protection for all whom we love as Ignatius certainly did, entrusting his entire family to the Virgin Mary's intercession.

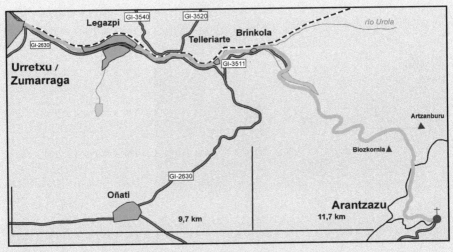

Total upward slope: 896 m. Total downward slope: 555 m.
Bicycles: extremely difficult. The climb is very steep and you have to push the bike most of the way. It may be preferable to reach Arantzazu via the road by cycling first to Oñate; this is a longer route but the climb is less steep. Furthermore it is not clear if cyclists are permitted through the Natural Park, where motor vehicles are not allowed. For pilgrims on foot, in winter precautions are strongly advised and this route is not recommended at all during snow (December – March).

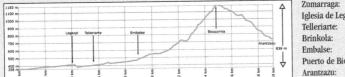

Zumarraga:	km 0
Iglesia de Legazpi:	km 5.1
Telleriarte:	8.3
Brinkola:	km 9.7
Embalse:	km 11.2
Puerto de Biozkornia:	km 16.6
Arantzazu:	km 24.1

■ Description

We leave town from the train station. Facing the façade of the station building, we take the road to our right, looking for the GI-3771 road or Calle de Ipeñarrieta. We follow this street to the end of town. We pass under the bridge that crosses over the railroad tracks. We continue walking parallel to the railway, which is on our left.

We pass a bridge over the Urola River and continue along the railway tracks. At 1.5 km the asphalt road ends and we turn right, at right angles, to reach the GI-2630 road. When we get there, we turn left to enter the town of Legazpi. We continue to follow the same street, lined with factories and, further on, with houses that have gardens. We come to a fork where we go right, down calle Nagusia toward Legazpi parish church.

We head down calle Aizkorri and leave the village.

The football field and sports facilities are on our right. We come to a

Arantzazu.

«Elorregui Palace» Tower House.

roundabout that we go straight across and we take the paved road that runs parallel to the tracks which continue on our left. Our road runs between the river and railroad tracks. We pass factories and homes, going straight ahead without crossing the river by means of the bridges that we pass.

We arrive at a sports area with a court where the Spanish game of pelota is played. It is an unusual «Frontón» because it has walls made of iron rather than concrete. We are at Mirandaola Park. A signpost indicates the way to Telleriarte, to our left. The trail leads to the GI-2630 road which we do not take but, instead, we follow the paved road that begins to our left and leads us into the small town of Telleriarte.

We follow the paved road straight ahead that runs parallel to the railroad tracks and leads to Brinkola. Passing under the bridge leading to the train station, we continue

straight ahead and go through the town along the same street, before going onto the GI-3511 road. A GR-120 signpost indicates the ascent to the Barrendiola Dam (Barrendiola – Aizkorri).

Once we reach the dam, we cross it. On the other side, a dirt road starts to our left that runs along the reservoir and we follow it. The road is marked by red and white GR-120 signs. We reach a fork and we take the path to the right which brings us very close to the trees, almost hiding itself among them. We continue to follow the GR-120 signs. We arrive at a barn which houses sheep and pass by it on our right. We continue our ascent, following the signs that lead us, zigzag fashion, up the slope. We have already passed the trees and, in winter, snow will undoubtedly cover the area.

We arrive at the Biozkornia mountain pass and Arriurdin Mountain (1,273 m) greets us. A

signpost indicates the direction of Arantzazu. We continue to follow the signs which, in the winter snow, can be somewhat difficult to find. The road may be obscured, as is usual in the mountains. Once we have gone over the pass, we take a little break and begin our descent towards the sanctuary. We come to a cylindrical mountain lodge.

We allow ourselves to get carried away by the descent. If we follow the dirt road after leaving the shelter, we will arrive at Arantzazu. In any event, if we want to go a little faster and avoid making a rather long detour, on reaching a bend of 90 degrees to our right, we go straight ahead and take the path (GR signs) that heads towards a wooded area with a few houses on the other side of it. On our arrival at the houses, we turn right and approach other houses about 150 m away and, once there, we take the road that head towards our left. We descend towards Arantzazu which, by now, is just 1 km away. We always follow the GR-120 signs.

Interesting facts

LEGAZPI: Population more than 8,700 inhabitants. Life here revolves around iron and its manufacture. It has an Iron Museum. Near by, there is the beautiful church of Nuestra Señora de la Asunción, dating from the 14th century, and the Bikuña Palace, built in the 16th century. There are restaurants, supermarkets, pharmacies and banks.

TELLERIARTE: A village of scattered houses. Past the village, next to the Urola river we find the tower-house «Elorregi Palace». The chapel and the palace date from the 16th century but the smithy dates from 1384.

BRINKOLA: A village of scattered houses. It does not offer services to pilgrims.

ARANTZAZU: One of the main spiritual centers of Euskadi and a reference point for our Ignatian pilgrimage. The Franciscans have for centuries preserved the tradition that the Virgin, standing on a hawthorn bush, appeared to a shepherd in this place, something that amazed the shepherd, who said: «Arantzan zu?» («You on a thorn?»). From this experience the place became a center of Marian devotion and pilgrimage, as Ignacio de Loyola stated in his autobiography. Between the 16th and 19th centuries the shrine was rebuilt three times due to multiple fires. In 1959 it was decided to build a new basilica. The iron gates are the work of the sculptor Eduardo Chillida. For more information go to the sanctuary website. We can find restaurants and hotels here. The Goiko Benta Ostatua inn was already an inn in St. Ignatius' time (the building dates from 1500) and elders say it was in this same inn where Ignatius stayed during his visit to Arantzazu. Later in his life, Ignatius mentioned Arantzazu in a moving letter. A fire had damaged the sanctuary and he was asked to intercede with the Pope so that the sanctuary would be granted an authorization to celebrate jubilees, for this would bring in pilgrims and allow the sanctuary to gather funds for the much needed restoration. Ignatius answered that he could not lend an active hand, because, «know, my dearest brother, that since two months ago, because of my ills, out of the twenty-four hours of the day, I barely spend four away from bed.» But he remembers the sanctuary fondly, recalling «the devotion of that place and how much God has been served there.» And he points out the importance of the sanctuary in his own spiritual itinerary: «When God our Lord made me a grant so that I could somehow change my life, I remember having found it worthwhile in my soul to spend the night in vigil in the body of that church.»

▉ TAXI
Legazpi

Taxi rank	943 730 021

Arantzazu

Taxi (Arantzazu)	931 780 030
Igorre Taxi rank	946 315 572

▉ LODGING
LEGAZPI: Mauleon Hotel, c/ Nafarroa, 16. Tel.: 943 730 870. Alto Urola Tourist Office (Lenbur). Tel.: 943 730 428. City Hall. Tel.: 943 730 428. The parish church may also offer shelter. Tel.: 636 767 674.

TELLERIARTE: Casa rural Pastain. Tel.: 943 730 672.

ARANTZAZU: Santuario de Arantzazu Hotel. Tel.: 943 781 313. «Goiko Benta Ostatua» Hostel. Tel.: 943 781 305. Sindika Hotel. Tel.: 943 781 303. A large new pilgrim's shelter, complete with kitchen, has opened and is now operating. Contact Joseba at 943 78 05 00 or 656 74 31 48. For Tourist office info: 943 718 911 / 943 796 463. turismo@debagoiena.eus www.turismodebagoiena.com

Arantzazuko Amaren, Virgin of Arantzazu.

ARANTZAZU – ARAIA

(18 km)

«Whoever lives a few moments with intensity is elevated with surprising speed to such a degree of virtue as the lazy will not attain in many years.»

«Because I, the Lord, your God, take you by the right hand and I say to you: "Fear not, myself will help you."» (Is 41:13).

Meadows of Urbia.

Another beautiful but challenging stage in the mountains with a steep climb to the refuge of Urbia followed by a long descent to Araia. A large part of this stage goes through the Aizkorri-Artz National Park where the highest peaks (Aitxuri: 1,551 m) of the watershed between the Cantabrian and the Mediterranean tower above us.

Starting from the sanctuary, we begin to ascend in the direction of Urbia. The climb is challenging but very rewarding: the forest of beech and pines envelops us in pleasant shade and we go ahead feeling the freshness of the green around us. We continue following the red and white signs of the GR.

The path is wide and well laid out; we cannot get lost. We arrive at the Erroiti fountain where, according to tradition, the Virgin of Arantzazu appeared to the shepherd Rodrigo de Baltzategi in 1468. We continue climbing and, after

an hour plus of walking, come to a gorgeous setting of mountains, meadows, trees, shepherds' houses and livestock, a paradise called Urbia.

Through a lovely corridor of trees we arrive at the hermitage of Urbia (1924) and we stop for a moment at the inn, a few meters further on. During the summer, they are open for visitors and it is a good place for a breakfast stop after the climb. We continue always on the dirt path that we have been following: this same path leads directly to the highway and into Araia, so that, in case of difficulty, it is best not to leave this well-marked way.

We exult in the immense meadows and the white rocks that dot the green fields. Horses, cows and wooly sheep share the space, ideal for resting awhile and contemplating the surrounding mountains. The path takes us to the end of the meadows and the descent begins.

In front of us, the whole splendid valley appears and in the distance we see a few towns. We are going down a steep slope so be very careful with the knees if we are carrying much weight. We can keep to the wide dirt path the whole time or we can take some shortcuts, following the GR signs: they all go to the same place.

Araia church.

Here the pilgrim must make a decision: there is a trail through the woods shortening the stage a bit. If there is snow or fog, however, it is better to stay on the wide path; the trail lacks good markings and the ground is wet and muddy, so one must be very careful when wandering into the woods. We recommend following the road; it cannot be missed.

We take one way or the other. Suddenly, we are surprised by the yellow arrows of the Basque Camino de Santiago: we have run across the section that comes from the tunnel of San Adrián, a little higher up; an ancient Roman road which still holds the tracks of cart wheels in its sunken stone pavement. Although we Ignatian pilgrims walk, so to speak, under the inspiration of St. Ignatius, we also feel a kinship with St. James, closely associated both with Spain and with the pilgrimage tradition. In some of the churches along the Camino Ignaciano we will see sculptures of Santiago pilgrims. Perhaps it would be a good idea to ask for St. James' intercession, too!

We follow the arrows and come upon an asphalt highway which we take to our right. This highway now leads us directly to Araia, following the signs. We are not to take the path marked PRA 3012 that shows up to our left or the GR-25 further ahead: it also goes to Araia, but by the long way around, going up and down and making us lose time.

A pretty stage which we will surely remember for the pure contemplation of nature.

Total upward slope: 664 m. Total downward slope: 743 m.
Bicycles: somewhat difficult, riders must dismount on the ascents and push the bike up. For pilgrims on foot, in winter, precautions are strongly advised and this route is not recommended at all during snow (December – March) or fog.
Today there are two options as indicated in the description:

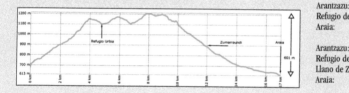

Arantzazu:	km 0
Refugio de Urbia:	km 5
Araia:	km 17
	(following the forest path)
Arantzazu:	km 0
Refugio de Urbia:	km 5
Llano de Zumarraundi:	km 12
Araia:	km 18
	(following the wide path)

■ Description

We say farewell to the Virgin of Arantzazu and follow the red and white signs that lead from the shrine. The Sanctuary remains on our right and we take the road away from it, leading up to the last houses. We follow the signs to Urbia. We continue uphill, straight ahead.
We arrive at a junction of three roads with a fountain nearby. We take the middle road, which bears a signpost indicating the way to Urbia. After walking for a few minutes along the wide and shaded track, we find the spring at Erroiti on our left, which marks the place where legend has it that the Virgin of Arantzazu appeared to the shepherd Rodrigo de Baltzategi.

The road zigzags as we make our way up to the Elorrola mountain pass, following the red and white signs of the main road. We arrive at the mountain pass and start the descent. We come to the Chapel of Nuestra Señora de Urbia (1924), which we leave on our left to follow the dirt road and reach the shelter of Urbia, where in summer we can find refreshments in the bar at the shelter.

Without deviating, we follow the wide, dirt road which is clearly marked. Further on we pass between some shepherds' huts in the meadows. Here we can follow the orange arrows that leave the main road, going inside the forest on our right, or just keep going on the dirt road. The grassy path goes parallel to the road, staying at the same level, while the dirt road descends steeply before it ascends once more to reach the path in the forest two km ahead. Both ways are beautiful, but the forest path is easier. We pass near the Zorrotzari monolith and the nearby Perusaroi mountain shelter. The path and the road come together, and we follow the arrows and the GR signs to our left. After a while, we reach the road and here again **we have two choices**: we can follow the wide dirt road and continue towards Araia, or go to the left, following the path into the wood which is marked with GR on signposts, but also going towards Araia.

The **forest path** is not bad for pilgrims on foot although it can be a bit difficult. First it takes us to the power lines and then, through beautiful forests, it links our path with the Camino de Santiago, coming from San Adrián. Shortly after, it leads to the road, following the yellow Santiago arrows.

If we always keep to the wide dirt road, we will also find the yellow signs of the Camino de Santiago; however, they will not take us to Araia but to Zalduondo, so after some km we will leave them and

continue straight on along the road. Undoubtedly, the wide road is the best for bikes.

We reach the edge of a forest glade called Zumarraundi. To our right, an asphalt road begins that leads to Araia. We continue going down along the well-marked road and reach a fork that we take to our left, in the direction of Araia. We go on walking and pass a country house to our right, named Gartzabal. Keeping to the paved road, we enter Araia after passing a swimming pool complex.

■ Interesting facts

ARAIA: The main town of the District of Asparrena, which is comprised of ten towns in close proximity to each other. With more than 1,500 inhabitants, Araia is a service center for the district. The town hall is built in a Baroque style and bears the arms of the Fraternity of Asparrena. The church of San Pedro is from the fifteenth century and has a neoclassical altarpiece inside. We can find a restaurant, supermarket, pharmacy and bank in this town. Note: in Alda, at the end of the next stage, there are no shops or restaurants, so you have to think about bringing something to eat for the next day.

■ TAXI
Araia

Taxi Elizondo (Agurain)	608 871 820
Juan Francisco González Flores (Agurain)	945 301 113

■ LODGING
There are no low-price pilgrim shelters over the next few pages, and lodging can range from 25 to 55 Euros per night and their room is limited, so it is better to call and book a bed beforehand. The next stage does not guarantee a good night's sleep, so it is better to get it in this one.

ALBEIZ: (on the next stage) Casa de la Iglesia. Tel.: 945 261 676.

ARAIA: In Araia there is a municipal sports pavilion that the city hall will open for a night as a pilgrim's shelter for groups. City Hall. Tel.: 945 304 006 / 945 314 566.

SAN ROMÁN: (on the next stage of the Camino, and a little removed from the Camino route itself): Andamur Hotel, Polígono Otikurri, N-I road. Tel.: 945 314 783. There is also a store. Alojamiento El Ventorro. Tel.: 945 304 372 (next to Adamur petrol station).

EGUINO: Prayer House Haiztur (not on the Camino, some 5 km from Araia), c/ San Esteban, 1. Tel.: 945 314 637. E-mail: mercedariase@yahoo.es

IBARGUREN: (not on the Camino, but not far) Casa rural Legaire Etxea, c/ San Martín, 2. Tel.: 626 895 798.

ZALDUONDO: (not on the Camino, but not far) Casa rural Aizkomendi, c/ Errotalde, 5. Tel.: 679 908 531. Casa rural Eikolara Landaetxea, Arbinatea neighborhood, 30. Tel.: 629 407 767 / 945 304 332 / 945 386 898.

ARAIA – ALDA

(22 km)

«Nothing resists the truth for very long: we can be attacked, but never overcome.»

«I will lead the blind along a road that they do not know, I will guide them along paths of which they are unaware. Before them I will convert the darkness into light, the rough into smooth. That is what I plan to do and I will not fail to do it» (Is 42:16).

Ullibarri, in the Arana Valley.

We leave Araia on a dirt road which takes us in the direction of Albeiz and leads us to the Madrid-Irun railway line. We cross the tracks and, on a bridge over the A-1 freeway, we arrive at the town of San Román, with an impressive church. We continue and, at the end of town, we will find a fountain of undrinkable water. We turn to the left for a few meters and then to the right to begin our hike up to Bikuña and the Opakua pass, at first following the GR-25.

The climb to the ridge of the mountain must be taken slowly, partly because of the steep slope and partly because there is almost always a great deal of mud. But you cannot get lost on the way: always stay in the widest and best-marked parts, always going straight ahead. In a few meters we will leave the GR-25 which separates us from our camino. We continue to be guided by orange arrows and by the white and red GR-120 path marks. We continue to climb on the same path which, at times, is difficult to negotiate owing to the mud. Be careful not to slip. If it has rained recently, the mud grabs hold of our boots; lots of patience.

When we have almost reached the highest point, we come across a signpost for the GR-282 and GR-120. We are going to take it to our right: pay attention because if we follow it to the left it is going to take us back where we started! Further on, the red and white marks

on the stones and trees will guide us
securely but we have to be attentive:
we are walking near the ravine and must
watch our steps closely. The scenery is
gorgeous and stunning, but the distant
view is lost behind the mountains. The
trees shelter us from the sun.

Arriving at the Zezama meadow, the path
disappears and we have to guide ourselves
by the shepherds' houses: we pass among
them, going forward through the meadow
until we come across a new dirt road
which will guide us towards the highway.
Here it is necessary to proceed with much
care to avoid getting lost.

Once on the asphalt road, we must
find the posts for the GR-120 path
and the red and white marks and head
for the Iturrieta mountain pass. There is
a faintly defined path through the woods
that leads us to Iturrieta. There are
some arrows indicating the way but we
have to go ahead carefully. At the top of
Iturrieta we turn left on the wide dirt
road which takes us to Puerto Nuevo.
Pay attention here again: signs are scarce
and we have to be alert to turn to our
right, leaving the road just at the point
where it turns 90 degrees to the left and
goes to some communication antennae.
The turn made, leaving the road, we

descend on a dirt path towards Ullibarri
and then Alda. Beware of the sun and
dehydration: the steep climb and the
length of this stage may keep us on
the road until 4:00 p.m., which can be
pretty rugged. For the walkers, we repeat
that many precautions must be taken in
winter and that it is not advisable to go
when there is snow.

Ullibarri.

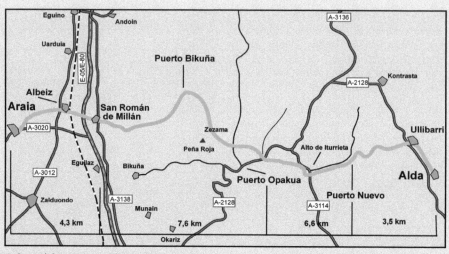

Total upward slope: 723 m. Total downward slope: 515 m.

Bicycles: extreme difficulty. The ascent is steep but the muddy terrain makes it even harder going up. It is not possible to cycle on the paths to Puerto Opakua: you have to dismount and on occasions find other, unmarked alternatives. It is better to take an alternative path to reach the summit of the Opakua hights and from there to Iturralde's hights. So, first follow the A-3138, then take the A-2128, thereby reaching Opakua and Iturralde. The descent from Puerto Nuevo can be a bit difficult for the bicycle, so it may be advisable to follow the asphalt road in order to go through Kontrasta and reach Ullibarri from there.

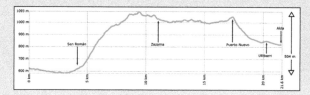

Araia:	km 0
Albeiz:	2.2 km
San Román:	km 4.3
Puerto de Entzia (Bikuña):	km 11.9
Puerto Nuevo:	km 18.5
Ullibarri:	km 20.5
Alda:	km 22

■ Description

We leave Araia by calle Presalde and, once we meet calle Santsarreka, we take a street on our left that heads towards the school and village cultural center. We arrive at a crossroads and we take the road on our right. We always keep to the same road and at the next crossroads we take the one to the left. Another crossroads: we turn to our right and we go towards Albeiz. We can see the town in front of us and we go to it without hesitation.

We cross the road, and we walk behind the church. We head to the train station at the other side of the village and on our left. The station is 500 m from the village of Albeiz.

We cross the railroad tracks and we turn right to find a paved road that leads to a bridge over the E-5 highway. We cross it and we head to the town of San Román. We enter San Román and follow the main street (calle Mayor) which leads to a fountain at the end of the village. At this point we turn left and after a few meters, we turn right, arriving at a wooden cattle gate with signposts marking the GR-25 and the GR-120 which lead us to Bikuña and will be guiding us the whole day's journey.

From here the path we are walking forks twice: the first after approximately 250 m and there we take the left path; the second fork is after another 150 m and once again we take the path leading left. Here we stop following the

GR-25 and we take the road that leads to the Bikuña Mountain Pass. We always follow the same road which sometimes becomes difficult to walk along because of the thick mud. We go through a cattle gate that we close behind us and continue our ascent. We come to a crossroads and we see a GR-282 and GR-120 signpost in front of us. We turn right and here the path levels out. We follow the GR-282 and GR-120, arriving at another chained gate which we have to close behind us. A signpost reads «San Vicente de Arana, 17 km.» We follow the red and white marks but proceed cautiously, especially on foggy days, because we are walking near a cliff. There is no road, only an indistinct trail in the woods, so we are constantly alert, looking for the GR marks on trees and stones.

We arrive at the level Zezama meadow. Here we stop following the GR-282 and we make a 90 degree turn to the left in order to pass very close to a wooden fenced cattle barn with a wooden fence on our left. We follow the traces of the tractor tracks. We try not to lose the GR-120 trail: we must be watchful for there are few orange arrows. We cross the Zezama meadow and we head to a sheep barn that has a small wall by the door and that appears behind some trees. After this barn we turn right and head for a white earthen road in good condition, some 150 m ahead of us. We follow it and cross a paved road. In front of us we see some cattle fences and behind them there is a trail which we take. We are in the Parzonería of Entzia and Iturrieta. We always follow the tractor tracks. The road is eventually lost in a field in which we turn right, climbing up to a white dirt road which we take to our right. We reach the asphalt A-2128 road which goes to the Opakua mountain pass. We take it to our left and in 50 m, next to a weather station, we take the path that starts on the right. We walk down some narrow trails, and we try to maintain the same direction. After 1 km we come to a small meadow within the woods where we turn to our left about 90 degrees and so we head along a well-marked road to the high road that leads us to the heights of Iturrieta.

Once we arrive at the A-3114, we take it to our right 500 m to continue up until we reach the top of Iturrieta and there, take a wide and well-defined road which goes off to the left. Taking it, we thus leave the A-3114. We go straight ahead without leaving the road and, after 1.8 km, we arrive at Puerto Nuevo. We have walked about 18 km from the beginning of this stage and still have some four km left before we reach Alda.

Once we arrive at Puerto Nuevo, we must be very careful: there are no signposts or marks. We have to watch for where the road bears sharply to the left. At this point we must continue straight on towards the Arana Valley by means of the path that is directly in front of us. A livestock gate and the white-and-yellow signs on it help us identify the place. After 1.2 km we come to cultivated fields

Alda.

and to a water reservoir which we leave on our right. We walk straight on without taking any of the side roads and reach the village of Ullibarri. At the entrance to the village, on our left, we find the Hermitage of Santa María.

We go through the village and we pass Ullibarri's church on our right. At the end of calle Mayor is the Hermitage of San Cristóbal. At this point, the road divides and we take it to the right to go directly to Alda, our final destination today.

■ Interesting facts

We cross the valley that connects Vitoria to Pamplona and ascend to the Entzia mountains, the westernmost part of the Urbina and Andia massifs. This stage ends at the Entzia Mountain Pass as we go down into the Arana Valley, a beautiful spectacle. Our accommodation problems remain: we should prepare ourselves to spend the night under the stars.

ULLIBARRI: A small village, with a covered sports hall and a bar.

ALDA: An even smaller village. There are no shops, restaurants or bars, so you have to think about bringing something for dinner and breakfast, or else find a taxi to bring you closer to San Vicente de Arana (next stage); in this town you will find one shop and a

restaurant and they offer a small shelter for pilgrims.

■ TAXI
San Vicente de Arana
Juan Pérez   686 391 355 / 659 641 183

■ LODGING
ALDA: Casa rural Biltegi Etxea, c/ Carretera, 3. Tel.: 945 406 042 / 656 762 793. Call beforehand to make sure there is room. City Hall. Tel.: 945 406 006.
Another option is to reach San Vicente, where there is a recently opened shelter for pilgrims, or, from there, take a taxi to Santa Cruz de Campezo (see next stage). Some may choose to sleep under the stars. Each pilgrim will know what suits him or her best.

ALDA – GENEVILLA

(24 km)

«It is dangerous to have everyone go ahead on the same road; worse to measure others by oneself.»

«Lord, you sound me out and you know me. You know when I sit and when I stand, from afar you perceive my thoughts. You discern my going and my resting, all my paths are known to you» (Ps 139:1-3).

San Vicente de Arana.

This is a stage where we can enjoy some tranquility. We leave Alda, taking a dirt path behind the town hall which runs parallel to the road in the direction of San Vicente de Arana. For the first time, with the sun at our back, we follow our shadows. Before arriving at San Vicente, just to the side of some antennae, we are surprised by a rather tall wooden post: it has some scissors and a weather vane on top. It is the «Maypole of San Vicente». It is a kind of protective amulet for the fields, put up in the town every year between May and September. If we have the chance, we ask for Don Vicente, the church's sacristan and its caretaker for 70 years. He explains the prayer which is recited between May and September every day at 12:30, while the bells are ringing: «Hold off, halt, hold off, dark cloud, do not you fall on me. Guard the bread, guard the wine and guard the fields in flower.» He assures us that in the last 70 years they

have never had hailstones in this town. The prayer and the bells protect them. We leave town on a street marked with the red and white of the GR-120 but at this point we can choose between two equally good alternatives: to follow the official course of the GR or to continue straight on, looking for a mountain bike path (BTT-13) which goes to the town of Orbiso. Both paths are pretty and go through lovely towns, though if the legs are tiring, it might be better to take the BBT path which goes through Orbiso. It is shorter than the GR-120. As in many other things, here the pilgrim is free to decide.

If we are going towards Oteo and Antoñana, this way is not recommended for cyclists because there is a lot of trail in the first stretch, though from Oteo on, it is a wide dirt path which is also easy to walk on. Antoñana is a lovely town that we reach after surmounting a slight climb.

Orbiso.

From Antoñana we go ahead following the old railway, now conditioned for walkers.

If we go by way of the dirt path leading directly to Orbiso, we will have a pleasant walk, with trees shading the path and the reward of the abundant three-spouted fountain at the town's entrance. From there to Santa Cruz we continue on secondary roads without any problem. We come to the pretty town of Santa Cruz de Campezo and perhaps will have the chance to stroll through the flea market, or at least have a cup of coffee in the plaza. Santa Cruz is the largest of the towns in the area and it might be a good idea to buy food for our time in Genevilla where supplies are unavailable. We leave from the back end of town, looking for a route called «Senda de la Torca», which connects us with the GR-1 and GR-120, taking us to Genevilla by way of a pretty oak-shaded lane.

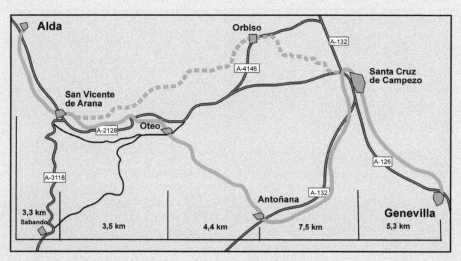

Total upward slope: 303 m. Total downward slope: 437 m (Oteo - Antoñana option).
Bicycles: easy.
Today there are two options as indicated in the description:

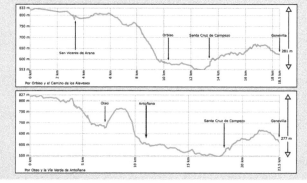

Alda:	km 0
San Vicente de Arana:	km 3.3
Oteo:	km 6.8
Antoñana:	km 11.2
Santa Cruz de Campezo:	km 18.7
Genevilla:	km 24

Alda:	km 0.
San Vicente de Arana:	km 3.3
Orbiso:	km 10.4
Santa Cruz de Campezo:	km 13.5
Genevilla:	km 18.8

■ Description

We leave the town by the dirt road that begins behind the houses near the town hall. At the first crossroads we turn left and continue straight until we reach San Vicente. We go to the village fountain and the 16th century church which is very beautiful indeed. We leave the village by way of calle Uriondo, just behind the church, turning right, following the red and white markings of the GR-282 and the GR-120.

Today's two options take different routes from here: the pilgrim has to choose the best for himself. Both ways take us to Santa Cruz but one takes us through the villages of Oteo and Antoñana and the other takes us through Orbiso. The final destination is the same. To go to Antoñana continue on calle Uriondo and take the first road on the right, just after the last of the village houses. The other option goes straight on the same calle Uriondo and will be explained later on.

The way to Oteo and Antoñana is not very clear at the beginning, but is well marked since it follows the GR-282 and the GR-120 paths. We follow the red and white signs. We are going through the fields to find a dirt road which will be a little clearer in some meters. We climb to our right until we find the A-2128 which is

below us. We always follow the same path, parallel to the road. We reach a point that leads down to the paved road and we cross it. We follow the GR signposts to Oteo.

Our path runs parallel to the road but below it and leaving it on the left. Coming into view of the village of Oteo, we cross the fields to the other side and go directly to the town. We pass Oteo by the calle de Abajo and we take a dirt road that rises towards the horizon. We follow the red and white markings of the GR. Soon we take a first fork to the right, following the way we are heading. A road joins from the right but we continue straight ahead. Our path is well marked and we take no deviation until we come in sight of Antoñana. At that point, we take a deviation to the right that leads to the town center. We pass behind the church and turn right to approach the A-132 road.

At the road, we turn right to go up to the pedestrian bridge that leads to the old train station of the recently restored Vasco-Navarro train. Some train cars remind us that, until we reach Santa Cruz de Campezo, we are going to follow the old railway route. We leave the station on our right and we head to the paved road, A-3136, which we take on our left. We go straight ahead and in 500 m we take a dirt road on our

Oteo.

left that leads to a small bridge. It is signposted, but in the direction that is opposite to ours. Walking this way we reach Santa Cruz de Campezo.

Straight along the same road we come to a bridge that crosses the A-132. Continue straight, now, with the road to our right. We arrive at a crossroads: here we meet the pilgrims who took the option of going through Orbiso. Now we are together on the same route, going into Santa Cruz by calle del Arrabal.

The way that goes through Orbiso, called the Alaveses Camino, follows the paved road that leaves San Vicente de Arana from calle Uriondo. This alternative is signaled by orange marks and bike tourism BTT signs. A road joins us from the left, but we continue straight towards the fields. We leave an agricultural farm on our left and we climb the well-marked road. At the end of the road we turn left and take another

dirt road that goes into the forest. We follow the Mountain Bike (MTB-13 www.paisvascoturismo. net) circuit signs, directed toward Orbiso.

We always continue straight without taking other paths that cross ours. We head straight to Orbiso. We pass through the village at calle Mayor and at the end, we turn to our right and then left onto the exit road to Santa Cruz de Campezo.

Two hundred meters from the village, we leave the road in order to take a paved road that starts on our right. At the first fork we take a left. We leave a farm on our right and we continue always straight along the same path. After some houses, we approach the A-2128 main road. We take a left and we head to the roundabout at the entrance to Santa Cruz. Here we find the pilgrims coming from Antoñana.

We arrive at the entrance to the village of Santa Cruz de Campezo. We cross the A-132 and enter the village by calle Arrabal which leads to the main plaza. The church is at the rear. Our path continues beyond the village: on calle Yoar, we ask for the «Senda de la Torca» (Path of Torca), a dirt road that takes us to Genevilla. A GR signpost and its typical red and white signs show us the direction we have to take. Two hundred meters from the village we leave the wide dirt road and take a less defined one that starts at a right angle on our right. We follow the GR signs through the woods without difficulty. After 4.5 km, the road bears right and we reach the paved NA-743 road, which brings us into Genevilla.

■ Interesting facts

SAN VICENTE DE ARANA: A small village. From May 3rd to September, in the park at the entrance of the village, stands the «guardian tree» for the fields. This tree is taken from the top of the mountain. The men of the village ritually place a weather vane on the trunk that directs the winds in summer and stick a pair of scissors into the trunk to defy the clouds that want to bring adverse weather conditions to the fields. An embedded wax cross symbolizes the effort and work of the townsfolk fighting for their crops. To increase the protective power of the symbolic tree, the men tie the corporal used at the most recent Easter Mass around the trunk of the tree. The chairman in charge of guiding the whole ritual, Don Vicente, says that in the last 70 years there has never been a misfortune due to adverse weather in the valley. The church contains an impressive Renaissance altarpiece. There are also a bar/restaurant; a shop in the village has some provisions but not the makings of a meal.

ANTOÑANA: A small village belonging to the municipality of Campezo. Its forests are harvested and cultivated for truffles. It was founded as a fortified village in 1182 by Sancho the Wise, the King of Navarre. Its urban structure preserves the historical presence of ancient stone buildings, like the Tower House on calle Arquillos, attached to the old wall, and dating from the 18th century. The parish church of San Vicente Mártir was built to replace the original church-fortress. The portico and the frontage are also from the 18th century and the tower is neoclassical. At the edge of town we find the Museum of the Vasco-Navarro Railway, linking the town of Estella with Vitoria. Today, this is a green route of about 25 km and is popular with cyclists.

ORBISO: A small town with its golden age in the sixteenth century. A Palace House with the coat of arms of Ochoa de Alda (1790) sits next to the church. There is a beautiful public bath, from 1806, with a good source of drinking water. The parish church is in honor of San Andrés and has a beautiful baroque tower with two figures, an ovoid dome and is topped by a cylindrical lantern which comes from the second half of the eighteenth century. The church was constructed in the sixteenth century and has an altarpiece inside, dedicated to Santiago, (St. James), which calls to mind, the tradition of pilgrims passing through and sharing of their devotion naturally. There are no services for pilgrims although there is accommodation.

SANTA CRUZ DE CAMPEZO: Center of a district which includes 5 different villages. The Campezo region was already inhabited in the year 18 B.C. by the Várdulos tribe. In 823 the Arab general Abd-Al-Karin Campezo swept through the valley, destroying villages and burning crops. The valley was rebuilt during the reign of Alfonso VI of Castile. In the 12th century, the town was a walled in fortress. Because of its strategic location, the town was hotly contested by the kingdoms of Navarre and Castile. It was under the crown of Navarre until 1200 when it was conquered by Alfonso VII for the kingdom of Castile. In 1368 it was returned to Navarre but in 1377 it was re-taken by Castile. Some remains of the fortifications may be found in the main plaza but they were completely demolished in the Carlist wars (19th c.). The church of the Asunción de Nuestra Señora is a Euskadi Historical Monument. Although the church is Gothic (17th c.), its first construction dates back to the 13th century. The front door is from the 16th century and on the capitals of its columns we see reliefs of St. John and the Virgin Mary at the burial of Jesus. The church choir is Gothic Renaissance from the 16th century. We can also find restaurants, a supermarket, a bank and a health center.

GENEVILLA: A small town, but with a beautiful church dedicated to San Esteban. It was built in the 12th century and modified in the 16th century, with architectural elements of the Gothic-Renaissance style. The interior has a magnificent altarpiece considered one of the two best altarpieces of its style in Navarre. The Duke of Nájera gave money in 1549 to build this magnificent altarpiece and probably others, like the one in Lapoblación. Genevilla is known for delicious white beans, prepared by the locals in a traditional way. But you'll need luck to sample them: there is no bar-restaurant or shop in town, so you have to take your food (lunch – dinner – breakfast) from Santa Cruz or take a taxi to Santa Cruz before returning to Genevilla to sleep.

■ **TAXI**
San Vicente de Arana
Juan Pérez   945 406 064 / 659 641 183
Santa Cruz de Campezo
Taxis   661 830 677
Genevilla
Taxi Genevilla   931 780 030

■ **LODGING**
Lodging is, in general, scarce. It is still advisable to book the rooms beforehand.

SAN VICENTE DE ARANA: City Hall. Tel.: 945 406 006. There is a nice shelter for pilgrims.

ORBISO: Agroturismo Mariví, c/ Herrería, 7-9. Orbiso. Tel.: 945 415 030.

SANTA CRUZ DE CAMPEZO: In the Hermitage of Our Lady of Ibernalo (1.5 km away from the town) we find the Ibernalo Hostel (capacity for 19 people), but there is no restaurant open throughout the year, so we have to bring our dinner and breakfast. Carretera Ermita de Ibernalo, s/n. Tel.: 945 102 271 / 647 911 484. There is another cottage house, but it may only be rented as an entire house. City Hall. Tel.: 945 405 443.

GENEVILLA: Casa rural Usategieta (10% discount for pilgrims, four extra beds available for pilgrims). Tel.: 649 851 602 / 948 378 926. Casa rural El Encinedo, c/ Norte, 2. Tel.: 948 444 016. City Hall. Tel.: 948 444 130. The municipality is also preparing rooms in a building directly opposite the Casa; at least one pilgrim has already stayed there; worth asking.

Genevilla – Laguardia

(27.3 km)

«If you want to be useful to others, start by accepting yourself; the fire lit for others must be already burning at home.»

«Show me, Lord, your way, guide me on the path» (Ps 27:11).

Church of San Roque (Roch), Lapoblación.

We arise, aware that we are now reaching the end of the hardest stages of our Camino Ignaciano, at least as far as the mountains are concerned. We leave in the direction of Cabredo, by the dirt path which takes us straight there, following the GR-1 with its red and white markers. Our dirt path runs parallel to the asphalt road. Entering Cabredo and passing through the town, we have to be careful not to make a mistake. We will be following the GR-1 for a long while, heading towards Marañón but, after the town comes into our sight, we are going to turn sharply to our left to take a path up to the heights above Lapoblación, no longer following the GR-1! The climb is not difficult though, at the end, the path gets narrow and steep. Going up on bicycle, you will have to get off and push, for sure! Better take the asphalt road straight to Lapoblación.

Once on the road, in a few meters we take a path that goes up on our right and brings us directly to Lapoblación, without taking the road. Some impressive windmills serve as our reference on the left. In the town of Lapoblación, if we are lucky, we will be able to contemplate a magnificent, well-conserved altarpiece, a true jewel. We are pleasantly surprised to see the pilgrim's symbols carved into the stones of the entrance to an old house:

the staff, the shell, the gourd: Could it be an old pilgrim's hostel on a medieval route through here? That seems to be the theory. It is thought that this secondary pilgrimage route fell into disuse due to the perils of the mountains: pilgrims were easy prey for bandits and thieves and sometimes even lost their lives. It would not have been so dangerous in Ignatius' day but, even so, it was necessary to keep an eye out on these roads.

From this height, the whole valley of La Rioja and Álava opens up to view. In the distance, we can even make out the city of Logroño. Before that, however, we see the village of Laguardia, perched high up, although it is far below us. We go through the town and head for the road to Meano. Just before reaching the town we take a dirt path going around it from above.

Once around the town, we take a dirt path rising on our right, very well defined and including stone benches where we can sit and rest. Always on the same path, we pass through a lovely woods of holm oak and cork trees; quite different from those we saw in Arantzazu! Climbing and descending, especially descending, the path takes us to Kripan, walking by the wheat fields as we approach the town. To our right, a great rock reminds us of a sleeping snake's head. We enter Kripan where we can quench our thirst in the fountains and gather strength for the second part of this long stage. Behind the church, a paved road leaves the town perpendicularly and steeply

San Andrés, statue on the main altar, Lapoblación.

downhill. After going by some gardens and a sharp curve to the left, we leave the road and the adventure begins: we take an old, very abandoned path that we can hardly see. It goes up and then down to some fields which we must cross in order to reach the road in front of us. We are looking for the prehistoric dolmen, Los Llanos. We have to be «pioneers» here, a bit, because the path all but disappears at this point.

At Los Llanos, we keep on the same path until arriving at the first crossroads. We go to the left and then to the right, directing ourselves towards the «Parque de Unueva», which at times has fresh water in the fountain and shade from its few trees. We are still far away. From here begins the long trek to Laguardia: we walk along seemingly endless farming roads, up and down, turning and crossing. We have to be alert so as not to miss the signs, though the town of Laguardia is in plain sight before us and we know that by one road or another we will finally arrive there.

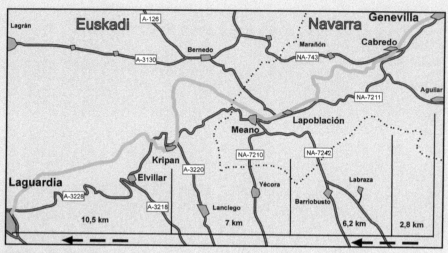

Total upward slope: 729 m. Total downward slope: 733 m.
Bicycles: no outstanding difficulties, although on two occasions we strongly recommend taking the asphalt road.
Leaving Cabredo to go up to Lapoblación it is best to take the road, because the foot path has a 500 meter stretch where the bike
must be pushed uphill. Afterwards, from Lapoblación, it is better to go directly to Kripan by road, although the dirt road
is accessible for mountain bikes.

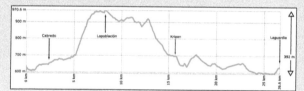

Genevilla:	km 0
Cabredo:	km 2.5
Lapoblación:	km 8.7
Kripan:	km 16.5
Laguardia:	km 27.3

◼ Description

We start off, knowing that we are nearing the end of the hardest stages of our Camino Ignaciano. We leave Genevilla in the direction of the Cabredo Mountain Pass. We take a dirt road that goes straight to Cabredo and runs parallel to the paved road. From Genevilla's main plaza, past the church, we turn right and then left to go down a well-marked dirt road. Be careful, because our road begins on the left after only 50 m and is not as broad and well-defined as the other one.

A GR-1 signpost indicates the way to Cabredo. We continue straight on this road until we reach Cabredo, following the red and white signs.

We go straight through the village and, at the last of the houses, on reaching the fork, instead of taking the road to the right that would lead us to Marañón, we take a road that goes off to the left (and which soon becomes a dirt road). At this point we are following the GR-1 towards Marañón, on a track parallel to the paved road. The red and white signs guide us and

we follow a path with trees that runs along the fields. One km after Cabredo, we can see a milepost showing the direction to Marañón: we follow the path to the right and leave the main route on the left. We follow the descending path which fades into the bushes: the path is marked with red and white signs but the way is hindered by the undergrowth. In one km we reach open field. A road joins us from the left, but we continue straight, for just 100 m.

We see the town of Marañón in front of us.

Attention here because the GR leads directly to Marañón and we have to turn left on a path that makes an angle of 45 degrees. There are no signs here to help you, so you have to be careful not to miss it. This road climbs towards the mountain pass that leads to Lapoblación. We might see the electric generators or windmills up above, which serve as a reference. Soon a fork shows up and we take a right. The road goes up next to the fields. On our left stands a farm house. Our earthen road ends in another well-marked road coming from Marañón. We turn left and we continue climbing. The road climbs up to a trail on our right. We take it. The trail is well marked but it is a very steep mountain path. We follow it up to the hill and onto the NA-7211 roadway. Once we reach the asphalt road, we turn right and in 50 m, again, we take the first road on our right. We walk up this road and at the first intersection we take a left. This dirt road leads directly to the town of Lapoblación.

We go through the village following the paved road and continue straight on downhill. After 600 m we take a dirt road going off to our right, which leads us to the village of Meano. We do not enter the village, but at the first fork, we keep left and later on, follow it as it bends right.

Walking out of town, we head for a fairly large grain farm but we do not take this way. We look for another way that begins on our right. We can recognize the good road because it has stone benches for people to sit on. We must not leave this path, going up to a stone quarry with a good view of the valley. A road joins from the right, but we always go straight ahead. Later we come to a crossroads; a little house of Aguas de la Rioja is on our right. Continue straight on the same road. We reach a sharp curve to the left and, ignoring the upward path, we continue our descent. Within a few meters there is a new branch and we go to the left. We continue to Kripan.

We continue straight on until we reach some fields and the paved A-3220 road, which we take to our right. At the fork, we go right and we enter in the village of Kripan. We head to the center and reach the City Hall where we turn to our right going closer to the church. We come up behind the church and we go straight on the paved road leading away from the village.

Please pay attention here: at 800 m from the village, on a curve that turns to our left, we leave that route and go onto a poorly marked trail to our right. The trail has no signs so you have to be careful crossing the fields. The reference point we seek is the A-3228 asphalt road that is high in our right. At 700 m, we reach the road at a point

Cabredo.

where a path begins with a sign indicating the Dolmen de Los Llanos.

We cross the asphalt road and head to Los Llanos. We leave the prehistoric dolmen on our left and we continue straight until the first crossroads. We turn at a right angle and descend to our left. At the next junction we, take a right onto the paved road and head to the Unueva Park (there is a water source, but it is sometimes dry). After 400 m we cross another road and follow the asphalt. After two bends, we arrive at a crossroads where we turn left. At the next crossroads we turn right. At a fork in the road, we keep left. We go straight and we ignore the path that comes from our left. We go straight on but at the next fork, we bear right. We go straight over the next crossroads before taking a left at the following intersection. We reach a paved road after passing a house on our left. We take the road to our right, always following the same path until we get close to Laguardia. We cross the road and continue to the left to enter the village.

■ Interesting facts

This is the first long stage but it is justified by the need to find good accommodation for the night. We can encourage ourselves by thinking that we have entered the famous «wine region» and are following the Wine Route. The pilgrim must take care not to exceed the due measure!

CABREDO: A small village which offers a shelter for pilgrims.

LAPOBLACIÓN: Population of 160 inhabitants. No services on offer. The church contains another memorable renaissance altarpiece dedicated to San Roque. The ancient Camino de Santiago pilgrims' hostel in the street behind the church is also worth mentioning. Engraved on the stone at the door of the hospital we can still see the typical pilgrimage insigniae that identified the place as a refuge for pilgrims.

MEANO: A small village which offers a bar-restaurant and a pharmacy.

LAGUARDIA: A charming town with about 2,500 inhabitants, which we come to just as we reach the banks of the Ebro river. Its walls and its fortified main plaza bring us back to the past and the history of Ignatius of Loyola. It is said that in the subsoil of this region there are numerous wine cellars in which the wine matures. The church of Santa María de los Reyes was started in the 12th century and completed in the 16th century. An outstanding feature is its monumental Gothic doorway, made of stone in the late 14th century. Its many perfectly preserved colors date from the 17th century, like the altarpiece which is the work of Juan de Bascardo. The Jesuit José Cardiel (there is a beautiful monument near the church of Santa María) was born here. He was sent to the famous Jesuit missions in South America but died in Italy, banished from Spanish crown territories by the king, along with all other Jesuits, in 1782. The church of San Juan Bautista is from the 18th century. Surrounded by walls dating in part to the 13th century, this town offers modern pilgrims a great taste of what the late medieval world would have looked like. Walled medieval towns were usually built on high ground to make them more easily defendable: it was possible to see the enemy coming from afar and, when he drew close and began climbing the hill, a rain of arrows, debris, stones, boiling oil and even excrement would pour on him. Walls were also a protection against other endemic medieval threats. One such threat was the plague, which sometimes ravaged whole regions: the councilmen would close the city gates to travelers suspected of carrying the plague. Another threat was vagabonds, who came into town at night and sacked the houses, which lacked today's elaborate safety meassures. Here we can find restaurants, pharmacies, supermarkets and banks. Tourist Office, Tel.: 945 600 845.

■ TAXI
Genevilla

Taxi Genevilla	931 780 030
Taxis	661 830 677
Laguardia	
Taxis	627 700 409

■ LODGING
CABREDO: A "nice" pilgrim's shelter. Tel.: 948 444 009 / 667 521 264.

MEANO: Casa Rural Atalaya: 660 90 51 13 / 660 22 23 81.

LAGUARDIA: Agroturismo Larretxori, Portal de Páganos, s/n. Tel.: 945 600 763. Villa de Laguardia Hotel, Paseo de San Raimundo, 15. Tel.: 945 600 560. Casa Rural Legado de Ugarte. Tel.: 945 600 114 / 699 621 841. Castillo El Collado Hotel, Paseo El Collado. Tel.: 945 621 200. Biazteri Hostel, c/ Berberana, 1. Tel.: 945 600 026. Posada Mayor de Migueloa Hotel, c/ Mayor, 20. Tel.: 945 621 175. Marixa Hotel, Sancho Abarca, 8. Tel.: 945 600 165. Casa Rural Legado de Zabala 945 600 114/699 621 841. Los Parajes inn, c/ Mayor, 46-48. Tel.: 945 621 130.

Laguardia – Navarrete
(19.6 km)

«We are never to say or do anything until we have asked ourselves if it is going to be pleasing to God, good in itself and edifying for our neighbor.»

«The Lord is my shepherd, I shall not want. He makes me lie down in green pastures; he leads me beside still waters and restores my strength; he guides me in the paths of righteousness for his name's sake» (Ps 23:1-3).

Laguardia and Cantabrian mountain range.

We leave Laguardia in the direction of the system of lagoons of Carravalseca, taking the paved road which leads to the Ubide Winecellars. The lagoons are a bird refuge and, owing to the salinity of the rocks, when the water evaporates the white and pink of the precipitated salt can be seen. It is a lovely setting for contemplating the mountains that we descended yesterday, with Laguardia in the background and the lagoons in front of us.

The path is very walkable, quite flat and with the vineyards spreading out before our eyes, be it the tender green of spring or the red of autumn. We easily reach Lapuebla de Labarca, surprising us around a bend. A magnificent view awaits us, bringing us now the Ebro river. We enter the town near the church, crossing through the center to find the street which descends to the bridge crossing the Ebro.

Called «Iber» by the Romans, the source of the Ebro river is in Cantabria and its length is 910 km, making it the longest river in Spain, flowing into the Mediterranean. On occasion the Ebro overflows its banks and, in certain places, we can see the high-water marks from the most serious floods. Throughout history, this vitally important waterway has been utilized for shipping; on the other hand, at present, it continues to carry sediment downstream, creating an enormous and fertile delta at its mouth. In fact, Amposta, a port city in times of the Roman Empire, is now located substantially inland, due to the huge volume of sediment deposited by the river, century after century.

We cross the Ebro and continue on the road towards the tunnel under the train tracks. Just before reaching it, we turn left to move away from the road, looking for a dirt path, parallel to the tracks, which crosses them some 600 m further on. At this point, we cross the tracks and go straight in the direction of Fuenmayor, ahead of us. We are on the old road which joined Lapuebla with Fuenmayor. At one time, the river had to be crossed by barge. Certainly Ignatius, in his visits to Navarrete travelled along this road several times, negotiating the stream and passing by the ancient settlement of El Tormenal.

We continue, parallel to the road, never crossing it. We come into Fuenmayor and head to the Church plaza, an amiable space with stores and bars in which to take a breather. We contemplate the palaces of La Rioja's nobles, distinguished by their coats of arms. We leave, looking for the road to Navarrete. Upon arriving at the N-232, we look, 150 m on, for a water canal on the left and a signpost: «Camino Viejo a Navarrete». We take this dirt path and pass by vineyards until coming to the freeway AP-68. We go through the tunnel and to the left look for the dirt path which passes close by the tollgates. We take it and, at the first fork, go to the right. This path takes us first to the tunnel under the freeway A-12 and then, directly to Navarrete.

■ Ignatian tip

Ignatius wanted to change his life. To accomplish this he decided to settle his accounts and put his affairs in order:

«*Later, Ignatius remembered that an official in the Duke's*

Navarrete.

palace owed him some money and so he prepared a written account for the Duke's treasurer. Ignatius got his money and left word for it to be distributed to several persons to whom he felt indebted. He also devoted part of the money to restore a statute of the Blessed Virgin which was poorly attired. He then dismissed the two servants who had accompanied him, mounted his mule and set forth alone from Navarrete for Montserrat. From the day he left Navarrete he practiced daily penances.»

It was not money that mattered to Ignatius, but rather practicing works of charity and assisting those who had some particular need. Thus, restoring the image of our Lady seemed an important gesture. As Ignatius' inner transformation took place, he began to externalize this change in religious gestures. He did this in his practice of penance, scourging himself every night. No wonder then that we also do penance for our own past mistakes as a preparation to better receive the gift of new life God offers. Follow Ignatius in this process: perhaps we are also being invited to begin a new life.

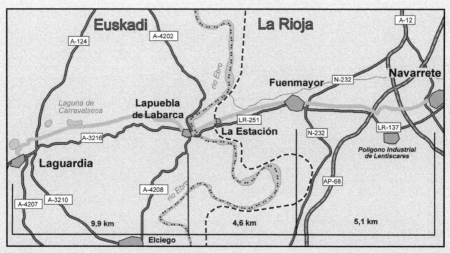

Total upward slope: 241 m. Total downward slope: 342 m.
Bicycles: easy.

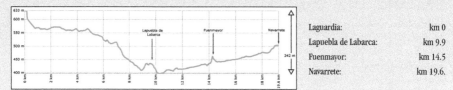

Laguardia:	km 0
Lapuebla de Labarca:	km 9.9
Fuenmayor:	km 14.5
Navarrete:	km 19.6.

■ Description

We leave this beautiful town descending towards the Laguna del Prao de la Paúl. We descend to the road and follow straight ahead along the dirt road that begins just in front of us. We head straight to the lagoon. When we get to it, we go around it taking the way to our right. At the end of the water, we take the dirt road away from the lagoon and toward the road. Our destination is the lagoon known as Carravalseca. We turn to the left and then right

making a Z to reach the A-124 road and cross it. A few meters to our left, there is an asphalt road and a sign saying «Bodegas Ubide» and «Laguna de Musco». We take that road which will continue over the next 3.3 km. We pass the Ubide Wineries on our right and continue straight ahead on our asphalt road without any deviation. Another asphalt road joins ours on our right but we continue straight ahead. A dirt road crosses ours. We continue to follow the asphalt to the edge of the Carravalseca Lagoon.

At 500 m from the Lagoon, we find a fork. We take the right (a house is on the road to the left, which we do not take). At 1.5 km we reach another fork and this time we leave the asphalt and we take the dirt road to our right. From here we will always follow this road without taking any side turns or deviations. Within 3 km we see the town of Labarca and we head for it. We carry straight on our wide and well-defined way until we reach Lapuebla de Labarca. We go through

but avoids the traffic. We recognize it because it runs beside a canal. We take it, turning right, and we follow it straight ahead. A signpost says «Camino Viejo a Navarrete».

We are walking with the canal on our left. When we reach the end, in front of us the AP-68 road forces us to turn to our right to reach the asphalt road to Navarrete. We pass under the bridge and, after 250 m, we take a dirt road on the left that takes us close to the motorway toll booths. We pass the barriers on our left and we continue straight on the dirt road.

the village until we reach the church which is near the Ebro river. We go down the road beside the river because we are going to cross over the bridge towards the industrial area of La Estación.

After going over the bridge, we continue straight on the LR-251 road which rises towards the train tunnel but, before we reach it, we take a dirt road on our left that runs parallel to the train track for about 600 m. We cross the tracks and continue straight. We are on the old road connecting Lapuebla

with Fuenmayor. At the first fork we turn right and then take the second left. We continue straight on. We reach Fuenmayor, still walking on the same paved road, arriving at the main plaza and the church of Santa María.

We cross the town and find National Road 232 where it meets the road to Navarrete (LR-137). Go straight on and after crossing the N-232, we turn left and try to find a dirt road close to us (it starts 130 m from this point) that runs parallel to the Navarrete road

We pass a canal and, at a fork, keep right. We continue straight ahead and go under an overpass which carries the A-12 overhead. We walk on, getting closer to Navarrete. Finally we reach this town, so closely linked to Ignatius's life experiences.

▪ Interesting facts

LAPUEBLA DE LABARCA: With more than 850 people, this town was founded in the year 1369 and has its origin in the boat that used to cross the Ebro river to connect the two provinces on its banks, Navarre and Castile. The church of Nuestra Señora de la Asunción (16th c.) used to receive all the passage money from the boat on Sundays and feasts of the Virgin. A sense of how long wine has been produced in the area can be seen in the neighborhood of Las Cuevas, where cellars dating from the 17th and 18th centuries are set into the hillock that rises west of the town.

Here we can find restaurants, pharmacies, supermarkets and banks.

FUENMAYOR: Its history seems to have originated in a castle tower that could supervise the distribution of irrigation water from the abundant spring from which the town derives its name, which means The Great Spring. In 1363, Fuenmayor was already a settled village which had its own church and a number of inhabitants. In that year, the monastery of Santa María la Real (the Royal) sold the village of Fuenmayor with its 27 neighboring homesteads to Navarrete. In 1521, during the Battle of Pavía, Charles V defeated and captured the French king, Francis I. A certain Antonio de Leiva, a native of Fuenmayor, who took the French king prisoner, won new privileges for the town. It is good wine country, which is reflected in its monument to grapes in front of the church of Santa María (16th c.). The church tower was destroyed and rebuilt in 1981. We pass the Palace Fernández-Bazán (18th c.) with its wonderful coat of arms on its façade. Here we can find restaurants, pharmacies, supermarkets and banks.

NAVARRETE: A city famous for its pottery workshops and the scene of battles between Castile and Navarre. Built on a hill, the houses, with their coats of arms, show the importance of the town where the Dukes of Nájera had a palace. King Alfonso VIII of Castile had asked the villagers to gather around the fort to protect and defend its borders from the kingdom of Navarre. In 1482, the Catholic monarchs granted the noble title of Duke of Nájera to the father of Duke Antonio Manrique de Lara (also viceroy of Navarre from 1515 to 1535), who knew Ignacio de Loyola very well. Ignacio, on his way to Montserrat, came to the Duke's palace in Navarrete to settle an outstanding account with him. The parish church of the Asunción is built in stone with three vaulted naves. Its construction was begun in 1553 by Juan Vallejo and Hernando de Mimenza and there were masons of the caliber of Juan Pérez de Solarte and Pedro de Aguilera who finished it in 1645. In the transept, we can see an altarpiece of St. Francis Xavier, painted in 1720 by Brother Matías de Irala (from Madrid). In Navarrete we may meet pilgrims on the so-called «Camino Francés» on their way to Santiago in Compostela. There is a wide choice of restaurants, pharmacies, supermarkets and banks here.

■ TAXI
Navarrete
Taxis   656 684 950

Lapuebla de Labarca.

■ LODGING
Finding ourselves on the Camino Francés, after following the Ebro Camino and the Catalan Camino, the first pilgrims' shelters start to appear. Besides being able to share our experiences with the Jacobeans, we are lucky to find much cheaper lodging, such as the Navarrete shelter, at 7 Euros per bed, or the one in Calahorra at 12.

LAPUEBLA DE LABARCA: Casa rural Barkero Etxea, c/ Mayor, 25. Tel.: 945 627 218. Casa rural Kandela Etxea, c/ María Cruz Sáenz Díaz, 14. Tel.: 669 217 711. City Hall. Tel.: 945 607 051.

FUENMAYOR: Labranza Hostel, Avenida Estación, 1. Tel.: 941 451 028. Pensión Fuenmayor, Avenida Ciudad de Cenicero, 7. Tel.: 941 450 152. Pensión Úbeda, c/ Úbeda, 15. Tel.: 663 779 629 (special price for pilgrims). City Hall. Tel.: 941 450 014.

NAVARRETE: Posada Ignatius . Plaza del Arco, 4. Tel.: 941 124 094. Municipal shelter (40 beds), c/ de la Cruz, s/n. Tel.: 941 440 776. Albergue La Casa del Peregrino, c/ Las Huertas, 3. Tel.: 630 982 928. Albergue Turístico El Cántaro, c/ Herrerías, 16. Tel.: 941 441 180. Villa de Navarrete Hostel, c/ de la Cruz, 2. Tel.: 941 440 318. City Hall. Tel.: 941 440 005. Rey Sancho Hotel, c/ Mayor Alta, 5. Tel.: 941 441 378. Hotel San Camilo, Carretera de Fuenmayor, 4. Tel.: 941 441 111.

Navarrete – Logroño

(13 km)

«Nothing is difficult for a man whose will is set on what he has proposed, especially if it is something he does for love.»

«The ways of the Lord are smooth, the righteous walk on them» (Hos 14:10).

San Miguel Park, Logroño.

During this entire stage we will be running into pilgrims on the Camino de Santiago, who will ask us about our own way. Thus we are crossing the paths of saints.

We leave from our arrival point at Navarrete on the previous stage and, at the place where we find the yellow arrows of the Camino de Santiago, we take the asphalt path on our right. Further ahead we will come upon the remains of the old pilgrim's hospital of San Juan de Acre (1185).

The asphalt path takes us up to the height of La Grajera and then brings us down towards a big artificial pond. We cannot get lost because we keep passing by the pilgrims coming from Logroño. From above we see the big city, not far away.

We descend towards the pond and go around it. It is a natural reserve of flora and fauna and a recreational center with a public bar and restaurant. We continue along, following the markings indicating the way, directly to Logroño, where we arrive easily, entering through the San Miguel Park. We cross the entire park, looking for the grand Avenida de Burgos. Once on it, we keep the same direction, crossing Logroño almost from one end to the other.

Arriving at the plaza of the Alféreces Provisionales, we are now very near the cathedral and calle Ruavieja where Logrono's most important pilgrim shelter is located. It is worthwhile dedicating a day to visit this pretty city and rest up on our Ignatian pilgrimage.

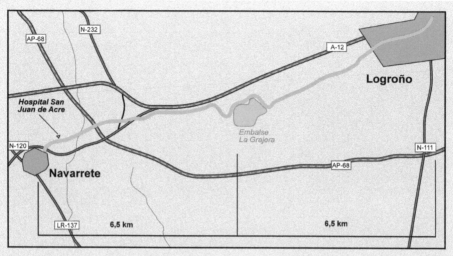

Total upward slope: 169 m. Total downward slope: 294 m.
Bicycles: easy.

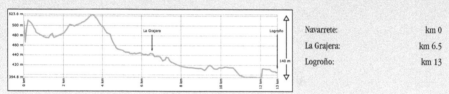

Navarrete:	km 0
La Grajera:	km 6.5
Logroño:	km 13

■ Description

Today we follow the arrows on the Camino de Santiago but in reverse direction. After departing your hostel, find the calle de la Cruz which follows the curvature of the city as it circles the hillock that crowns it. We reach and cross the carretera de Burgos and continue on, looking for an asphalt trail that begins on our right after a curve.

We arrive at the ruins of the old pilgrims' hostel of San Juan of Acre (1185). A sign indicates the location of the hospital church. A bridge enables us to cross the AP-68. We continue along the same road that leads us across an exit (side road) road of the Motorway A-12 towards Navarrete. We move ahead until we find the road to Burgos, which we take to our left.

After 250 m, we can leave the road and go onto an asphalt trail that runs parallel to the road and enables us to avoid the pressure of the traffic. We continue to walk parallel to the road until it separates and makes us go around bordering fields.

Co-cathedral of Logroño.

We follow the signs to Logroño. At the entrance to La Grajera Park, turn left on the dirt road: here we find a fountain and benches for a welcome rest. We move along a dirt trail that winds and brings us to the artificial lake and to the Alto de La Grajera.

We continue straight on in the same direction until we find a dirt trail that

skirts the lake. We take the trail on our right and enjoy the view of the lake. The arrows indicating the Camino de Santiago remind us that we are going «against the tide». We reach a road that we are going to take towards our left, but only for 100 m, as far as the next bend. At that bend, we take the road straight in front of us which is bordered by a neat row of trees.

A bridge brings us to the other side of the road and, after a little while, it brings us to the other side of the motorway through a tunnel. On the other side we continue to our right through a park until we reach the first street, «Prado Viejo». We cross it to go straight up into San Miguel Park.

Following the signs to the park, we look for the grand Avenida de Burgos, which we take to our right and, after 2 km, that will take us in a straight line through Logroño. The name of the street changes to calle del Marqués de Murrieta but not its direction. We go through the Gran Vía de Juan Carlos I and arrive at the plaza de los Alféreces Provisionales; then we go down calle de Los Portales until we reach the cathedral of Santa María la Redonda (15th c.) with its Baroque towers. We take calle Herrerías to calle Travesía del Palacio which we take to our left. The pilgrims' hostel of the St. James Way Rioja Associations is located just 100 m away (200 m from the cathedral).

Navarrete.

■ Interesting facts

LOGROÑO: With more than 130,000 inhabitants, it is the capital of the Province of La Rioja and holds the junction of the French Camino de Santiago (which we have been following since Navarrete) and the Ebro Camino de Santiago (which we will follow

from now on). A visit to the tourist office will provide information about all the monuments and sights we might like to visit (Edificio Escuelas Trevijano, c/ Portales, 50. Tel. 941 273 353). One highlight is the church of San Bartolomé (12th-13th centuries, restored in the 15th c.) with its barrel vaulted ceiling and classic Romanesque style. The facade is Gothic and the tower is Mudejar. The church of Santa María del Palacio was built on the ruins of a palace donated by Alfonso VII of Castile, which is why it is called «la Imperial». It was the first headquarters of the Order of the Holy Sepulcher in Castile. The main altarpiece is by Arnao of Brussels, a Spanish Renaissance sculptor. The Gothic church of Santa María de la Redonda is founded on the remains of a XII century Romanesque church and was proclaimed «co-cathedral» in 1959. Take note of architect Martín de Berriatúa's twin Baroque-style towers which frame it. Logroño offers us the facilities of a bicycle shop, restaurants, pharmacies, health centers, supermarkets and banks.

Jesuit Fathers: In the parish of San Ignacio we find the Jesuits who work there and they will kindly stamp the credential provided we call in during parish office hours.
C/ Huesca, 39 (near calle de los Duques de Nájera and plaza del Primero de Mayo). Tel.: 941 203 504.

Santa María la Redonda Church, Logroño.

■ **TAXI**
Logroño
Radio Taxi 24h   941 505 050
Francisco Javier Sáenz   660 590 912

■ **LODGING**
LOGROÑO: Pilgrim's shelter (100 beds), c/ Ruavieja, 32. Tel.: 941 248 686. Albas Pilgrim's shelter, Plaza Martínez Flamarique, 4. Tel.: 941 700 832. Pilgrim's shelter Check in Rioja, c/ Los Baños, 2. Tel.: 941 272 329. Logroño shelter, c/ Capitán Gallarza, 10. Tel.: 941 254 226. Santiago parish shelter, c/ Barriocepo, 8, 1.°. Tel.: 941 209 501. Santiago Apóstol shelter, c/ Ruavieja, 42. Tel.: 941 256 976 / 670 993 560. Asociación Juvenil Ayedo, Plaza Alférez Provisional, 1. Tel.: 941 229 014. Entresueños Hostel, c/ Portales, 12. Tel.: 941 271 334. La Numantina Hotel, c/ de Sagasta, 4. Tel.: 941 251 411. El Camino inn, c/ Industria, 2. Tel.: 606 735 862 / 941 206 314. City Hall. Tel.: 941 277 000.

Santa María la Redonda, Logroño.

LOGROÑO – ALCANADRE
(30.6 km)

«We can be sure that the progress we make in spiritual things will be in proportion to the degree of our distancing from egotism and concern for our well-being.»

«Good and just is the Lord; for he shows sinners the way; he directs the humble with his law, to the lowly he shows his way. The paths of the Lord are kindness and faithfulness for those who observe his law and its precepts» (Ps 25:8-10).

Aradón, Alcanadre.

Today, approaching the banks of the Ebro, we part from the French Camino de Santiago and enter on the Camino de Santiago of the Ebro, walking «against the flow» of the yellow arrows. We leave the city, following the path on which the Santiago pilgrims coming from Zaragoza enter it. There are not very many pilgrims on this Camino del Ebro. We head to the neighborhood of Varea and, following the bank of the Ebro river, we come across the orange arrow signs of the GR-99. The Roman port was located in Varea and, from here, the boats came and went utilizing the Ebro as a transportation artery.

We make easy headway on asphalt paths through fields and farms. Upon arriving at a bridge over the national highway, N-232, we continue straight on an asphalt path going to a military base. The GR tells us to go up to the bridge but we continue straight ahead some 400 m to an abandoned path appearing on our right. On this path, we approach the train tracks which we cross to enter alongside highway N-232, now in the town of Recajo.

Be careful now, because there is heavy traffic on the road. Unfortunately there are no alternative routes and we have to traverse the next 2.6 km on this unpleasant national highway until reaching the bridge over the Leza river. The highway is well marked with the signs of the Camino de Santiago which we can identify if we look back at them. We have to approach the Leza river in order to go over the bridge and descend to our left to the town of Agoncillo. In Agoncillo, the town hall offices are located in a pretty and very well conserved castle: the Aguas Mansas castle. The plaza with the church makes a very attractive and inviting setting, highlighting the beauty of the castle. We leave the town on the road behind the church to our right. At the end of town, we take a street to the left which is going to bring us, through the fields, to the next town, Arrúbal. We always keep to the marked direction, taking no forks.

We go up to Arrúbal, in the direction of the church. Next to it there is a very well set up pilgrim's shelter: it might be worth considering ending a stage here! We cross the town on calle Calvario and find ourselves facing the valley of the Ebro,

Castillo de Las Aguas, Agoncillo.

with its plentiful fields and trees along the banks of the river. The path brings us near the train tracks, which are going to serve as our guide until reaching the end of the stage in Alcanadre. Signs of the GR-99 will also orient us along this stretch, though we will not follow them exactly since they take a bit of a longer way around, unnecessarily lengthening our stage. Keep an eye out for the orange arrows.

Before arriving at Alcanadre, passing by the impressive rocks of Aradón, we contemplate the vultures that nest in them. These birds weigh up to 8 kg with a wing span of 2.5 m. Continuing always near to the train tracks, we arrive at the station of Alcanadre, which is also the pilgrim's shelter.

Entering the town, on the first street that goes up to the center, after some stairs, we find the first fountain and, continuing straight ahead, we get to the church plaza.

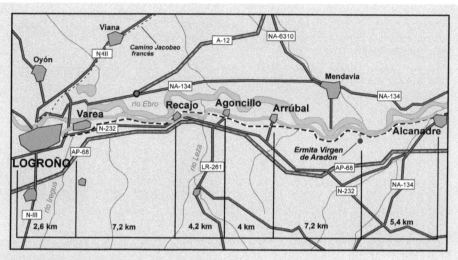

Total upward slope: 87 m. Total downward slope: 126 m.

Bicycles: easy, but take care along the 2.6 km section of the N-232 between the towns of Recajo and Agoncillo. Pilgrims can walk along the left hand side of the road and so they do not need to cross over, but the bikes have to be ridden along the right hand side of the road and it is not easy to cross. It is best to use pedestrian crossings on the way into the towns.

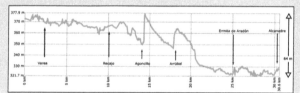

Logroño:	km 0
Varea:	km 2.6
Recajo:	km 9.8
Agoncillo:	km 14
Arrúbal:	km 18
Ermita de Aradón:	km 25.2
Alcanadre:	km 30.6

■ Description

From the pilgrim's shelter at calle Ruavieja 32, we head to calle de San Francisco, behind the Hospital de La Rioja. We continue straight on the calle de la Madre de Dios. After passing under the A-13, turn left and then right to cross the park and approach a bridge over the Iregua River. Having crossed the river, we turn left and follow the Ebro River which flows along on our left. We are in the neighborhood of Varea.

Varea was the site of the old Roman port for boats which used the Ebro as a transport route. We walk straight along the paved road, with no deviation. We follow the GR-99 signs. As we reach an intersection with another paved road, we will see a cattle ranch on our left. We cross through the intersection by continuing straight ahead but shifting a few meters to the left.

We do not leave the paved road until reaching an obligatory curve by an irrigation canal. We will have passed a store on our left. We follow the GR-99 signs.

We cross the canal without a problem and continue on the paved road which will take us near the train tracks in a short

Church of El Salvador, Arrúbal.

while, after going under a highway. We cross another tunnel under the highway and turn right. We reach the road, which we take to our left, leaving the climb to the bridge behind us. Here we stop following the GR-99 signs.

We approach a military base: we continue on the road just 400 m and turn right to cross the train tracks on a level crossing in order to get onto N-232 which we will take to our left. Unfortunately, we cannot take any other route and this national road is unpleasant. We have to walk approximately 2.6 km until we reach the bridge over the Leza River. We enter into the town of Recajo, walking along the N-232.

After crossing the bridge on the Leza River, we at last leave the national highway. Right after the bridge we take a paved road to our left which leads away from the N-232. This road takes us under the train tracks. We continue straight along the same road until we come upon the chapel of Nuestra Señora de los Dolores. Since we are going «against the flow», the main door is not on the side along which we are walking; the Santiago arrows reminds us that we always have the Camino de Santiago at our back. Again we find GR-99 signs.

We enter Agoncillo and walk along calle de La Ermita. As we reach the center of the town, we make a 90-degree turn to our left to find

ourselves before the majestic Castillo de las Aguas, completely restored with a broad plaza which brings out all its beauty.

We pass by the church of Nuestra Señora la Blanca on our left and we turn to the right onto a wide avenue behind the church. We continue in the same direction until reaching the end of town where we will find a trail which we will take to our left. As it winds among farms and fields, the trail crosses other roads twice at right angles but we continue straight ahead at each crossing. About 3.5 km after leaving Agoncillo, our road ends at another road. The town of Arrúbal is just in front of us. We pass over the bridge and go up to the Church of Arrúbal.

We walk through the town along calle Calvario. We leave the town on a paved track which runs parallel to an irrigation canal, which we can see at about 60 m to our left. We follow the track which bends to the right to take us to the train line. Later we pass some houses and a tunnel on our right, always travelling straight ahead.

The path continues parallel to the train line which is to our right. We come near the Ebro River, at one of its frequent bends, so that we are walking between the river on our left and the train line. Right at the point where the river seems to want to run into the train line, we find a bridge across the tracks and end up with the Ebro and the train line both on our left. Walking parallel to the train tracks, we reach a paved path which bends rightward at a right angle and, after 100 m, we see above us the white Chapel of Aradón. We will almost certainly see the huge vultures that nest in the Peñas de Aradón cliffs.

At this point we descend to pass under the railway line. For awhile we follow the GR-99 but, after a well-drawn curve, when the GR signs go straight on, we continue walking along our road that keeps us close to the railway line. From this point, we will always travel with the railway on our right, until we reach the Alcanadre train station which is also a refuge for pilgrims.

Alcanadre.

■ Interesting facts

AGONCILLO: Small town. Worthy of mention are the Castillo de Aguas Mansas (Gentle Waters), built of stone masonry in the 13th-14th centuries, and the church of Nuestra Señora la Blanca. At the main door of the castle can be seen the shield of the cruz de Calatrava. The town offers restaurants, pharmacies, stores and bank

ARRÚBAL: The church of El Salvador was built mostly in the 16th century and finished in the 17th. The town has a restaurant, a pharmacy, a supermarket and a bank.

ALCANADRE: Town of about 750 inhabitants. Its name is of Arabic origin: Al-Cana-Dre, referring to the «bridges» or «arches» of an old bridge over the Ebro River whose ruins are near the town. The church of Santa María (16-17 c.) preserves the Romanesque image which was in the chapel of Aradón (12th c.). Typical of the town is the 1st century Roman aqueduct. Before reaching the village, you can easily see the vultures nesting in Aradón. Some of them weigh 8 kg and measure 2.5 m. The town has a restaurant, pharmacy, supermarket, bank and a health center.

■ TAXI
Logroño

Radio Taxi 24h	941 505 050
Francisco Javier Sáenz	660 590 912

Alcanadre

Taxis Pachicho	948 693 055
Taxis Pradejón	619 964 141

■ LODGING
AGONCILLO: El Molino Hostel, Carretera de Zaragoza, km 12. Tel.: 941 431 316. City Hall. Tel.: 941 431 007.

ARRÚBAL: Pilgrim's shelter (accommodating 30 people) beside the church. City Hall. Tel.: 941 431 103.
Reservation: 941 431 223.

ALCANADRE: Pilgrim's shelter (accommodating 8 people) at the train station. Call in advance to the Town Hall. Tel.: 941 165 004. Agroturismo La Casa Azul. Tel.: 686 730 187 which accepts pilgrims. Hostal Cedipsa, Ctra Estacion, 0. Tel.: 948 693 183. If all else fails, you can always take the train to Logroño or Calahorra, or you can petition the Town Hall for permission to overnight at the sports center.

ALCANADRE – CALAHORRA

(21.5 km)

«Better great prudence and common holiness than great holiness and minimal prudence.»

«Although I walk through dark valleys, I fear nothing: you go with me; your rod and your staff sustain me» (Ps 23:4).

Santa María Cathedral, Calahorra.

On this stage we are going to encounter many signs of the Camino de Santiago but we will not always see them since the markings will be behind us. Today our way is characterized by loose dirt and rocks but is also quite straight, with hardly any trees.

On leaving Alcanadre, be sure to take the middle path which takes us towards a solar energy center (panels very visible) which we will leave on our right. After the climb, a pilgrims' bench allows us to sit and contemplate the fields.

We approach the freeway and we cross it; then we follow a track that runs parallel to it. Vineyards and grain fields roll by. It is easy going but if the sun is high it can be hot. Watch out for sunburn; these areas are very hot in summertime.

We cross the freeway and, further on, also the railway which from this point on will be on our right until reaching Calahorra. We continue straight ahead, on a clear path and there is no getting lost. The electrical generating windmills show us the way to Calahorra.

Once in Calahorra, we look for the Raso plaza; the pilgrim's shelter is found some 300 m behind the plaza, next to the church of San Francisco. The center of the city is pretty and merits a good stroll.

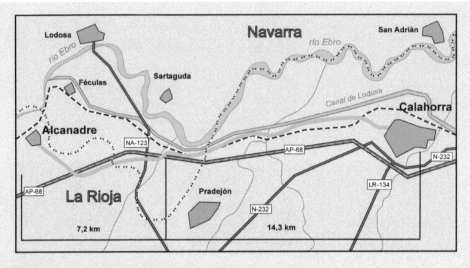

Total upward slope: 314 m. Total downward slope: 264 m.
Cyclists: medium difficulty. There are no steep steps to climb but there are some sections with loose rock that hinders progress.

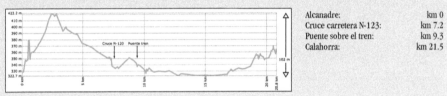

Alcanadre:	km 0
Cruce carretera N-123:	km 7.2
Puente sobre el tren:	km 9.3
Calahorra:	km 21.5

■ Description

We go left as we leave the hostel and walk toward calle de Los Pilares. We follow this street, which curves slightly to the left and then to the right. In this way we cross through the town and reach the LR-260 which we cross at a right angle. We leave the asphalt and enter onto a roadway. We continue straight along that road, passing a warehouse on our right.

We pass a solar power station on our right. In 1.3 km from that point, we arrive at the highest point of the road. Here, the road divides: we take the road to the right, which goes more straight on. This road then turns to the right and we continue to follow it without taking any side road.

We cross highway AP-68 by an overpass. As we come off the overpass, we turn to the left and take the dirt road which runs parallel to the highway. We continue walking parallel to the highway. We come to the N-123. We cross it, turning to our right on the other side of the road. Just at the beginning of the highway

we turn onto our dirt road again. We keep walking parallel to the highway until reaching a tunnel, which allows us to cross under the highway to the other side. We turn right and we go straight on, parallel to the highway until we come

to the train line, which we cross right away on a bridge. Right after the bridge we take a dirt road to our right. The road keeps us walking parallel to the train tracks. We arrive at the Lodosa Water Channel and we turn right.

We reach a paved road, which we cross at a right angle. We take the asphalt road in front of us. Further on, we follow the dirt road until we reach a stone and sand quarry. At the crossroads we keep going on our road, almost in a straight line. The dirt road ends at a T-intersection with another road, which we take to the right and which takes us to a bridge over the train line.

We do not leave the paved road until reaching Calahorra. We cross a

roundabout and continue straight. We enter on the road called Carretera de Murillo and then we turn left on calle de San Millán and proceed to the plaza Diego Camporredondo. We keep going straight on calle Ruiz y Menta until we reach the Paseo del Mercadal, which we take to the right. At the end of the paseo, we turn left onto the calle de los Mártires, which then becomes calle Grande and finally calle Mayor. We walk across the interesting plaza del Raso and, 300 m further on near the plaza de la Doctora García, we find the convent and the church of San Francisco, the location of the modern pilgrims' hostel, which is a total luxury.

Cathedral's bell tower, Calahorra.

■ Interesting facts

CALAHORRA: Two-thousand year old city, point of contact with the Roman highway from Asturica to Tarraco. The city was called Calagurris by the Romans and Kalakoricos by the Iberian Celts. The old Roman Forum was located in the plaza del Raso. For Christians, it is remembered as the site of the martyrdom of two Roman legionnaires, Celedonius and Emeterius (300 A.D.). Calahorra has had a bishop from the 4th century onward. As a result it was able to exercise great influence over the vast extension of its diocese for several centuries. In 714, it was conquered by the Muslims who strongly influenced the region's agriculture and urban life. The city has a long pilgrim tradition, as can be seen in the baptismal font of the Cathedral of Santa María (16th c.), which is covered with shells, gourds and the image of St. James. Also worth mentioning is the chapel of Cristo de la Agonía and another one of «Cristo de la Pelota [football]». This important city has 23,000 inhabitants and offers restaurants, bicycle workshops, drugstores, health center, supermarkets, banks and a tourism office (calle Ángel Oliván, 8. Tel.: 941 105 061.

Open from Tuesday to Saturday, a.m. and p.m. Sundays only in the a.m.).

■ TAXI
Calahorra

Taxis	941 130 016
Taxi Miguel	618 019 156

■ LODGING
CALAHORRA: Pilgrim's shelter San Francisco: c/ Rasillo de San Francisco, s/n (18 plazas), beside the convent of San Francisco. Tel.: 941 590 511 / 637 736 108. Youth Hostel (for groups of 15 people or more), Paseo de las Bolas, s/n. Tel.: 941 105 071. Reservations must be made in the Local Youth Office. Tel.: 941 146 511. Gala Hostel (10% discount for pilgrims carrying credentials), Avenida de La Estación, 7. Tel.: 941 145 515. Ciudad de Calahorra Hotel, c/ Maestro Falla, 1. Tel.: 941 147 434. Parador de turismo Marco Fabio Quintiliano. Paseo del Mercadal, s/n. Tel.: 941 130 358. City Hall. Tel.: 941 105 050.

City Hall, Calahorra.

CALAHORRA – ALFARO

(25.6 km)

«The workers in the Lord's vineyard should have one foot on the ground and the other lifted to continue the journey.»

«Strengthen the weak hands; steady the trembling knees. Say to the cowards: "Be strong, fear not; look at your God who brings satisfaction and vengeance; he comes in person and will save you."» (Is 35:3-4).

San Miguel's Collegiate Church, Alfaro.

From the cathedral we head to the bridge over the Cidacos River which may be dry. After crossing the bridge, we turn left towards the cemetery and, past the train tracks; take a path to our right which will keep us parallel to the tracks for a great part of our way. As has been the case, and will be throughout many stages, the railway will accompany us from town to town.

We pass by extensive fields of grain, fruit trees, olives and vineyards. Agriculture is very prosperous thanks to the proximity of the Ebro River and the Lodosa canal. We go over the canal once and along it for a while in this section. The path changes from asphalt to dirt and then back to asphalt. We cannot lose our way: always in the direction indicated by the train tracks which we approach here and there.

The paths that we take are quite important ones and we continue on them straight ahead. The same road leads us to Rincón de Soto but we are going to make a detour on a dirt road, to avoid so much asphalt: upon coming to a house in runs on our right, we take the dirt path which begins right there. We continue always straight ahead on this path and, at the second track crossing we encounter, we cross the tracks and keep parallel to them into Rincón de Soto. We enter

A meeting of paths in Alfaro. Two pilgrims: the young Ignatian and the elderly Jacobean.

walking on asphalt and dirt, without any shade trees. If we go by here in spring or summer, we might see numerous storks in the fields and flying overhead. On a right angle bend to our right, the path ascends a little to a bridge over the canal and the train tracks. After crossing it, we head to the highway N-232 and continue on its left side. After a long, straight, stretch, coming into Alfaro, we encounter the chapel of the Pillar, impressive on a small promontory above the highway.

At the end of this stretch, we cross the round-about and approach the bus station. Then comes the bullring and, going left, we arrive at the Paseo de la Florida, where we find the pilgrim's shelter, close to the police station. We can find the keys at the tourism office or at the town hall and they will happily stamp the credential. If both places are closed, then pilgrims must find a lodging in one of the hotels in town.

It must be said that in this town pilgrims are received warmly and amicably. It is a good idea to take advantage of the opportunity to visit la Colegiata church, as well as to stroll through the streets, letting ourselves be surprised by the «stork's paradise» represented by this charming town.

town next to the rails and, on the first street, we again cross the tracks to go to a promenade. Behind it and on our right, we find the town hall.

We leave Rincón de Soto by the Avenida del río Alfaro. We follow it and in 1 km, we go through a tunnel which avoids the highway. We go parallel to a water canal on our left. We still have 6 km of

Plaza de España, Alfaro

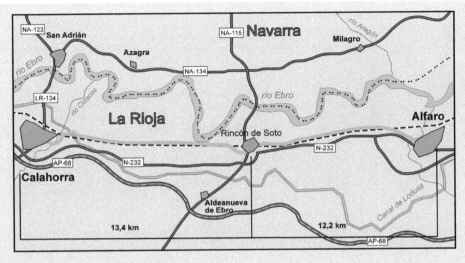

Total upward slope: 142 m. Total downward slope: 172 m.
Bicycles: easy.

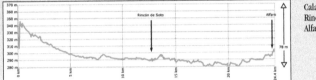

Calahorra:	km 0
Rincón de Soto:	km 13.4
Alfaro:	km 25.6

■ Description

We leave the hostel and walk toward the Cathedral and then cross the Cidacos river which, hopefully, will be flowing. About 150 m after the river we turn to the left onto a paved highway which leads to the town of Azagra (LR-486) and Calahorra's cemetery. We follow it until it takes us to a tunnel under train tracks. About 150 m after the bridge, we leave the highway and take another paved road to our right, which meets up with the train line. As has been happening repeatedly and will continue to happen in future stages, the train line keeps us company from town to town.

We pass over the waters of canal de Lodosa and we keep on the road, leaving the railway behind. A fork in the road shows up; we take the left. After 4.5 km of paved road, next to a demolished house, we take the dirt road to the right. We always walk straight on, without taking any diversion on the different ways that appear. We come close to the railway and we will follow it in parallel until reaching Rincón de Soto. We pass a railroad crossing that stays on our right, continuing straight ahead until we reach a second railroad crossing, which we do cross. In 100 m we take the path to the left and we will continue straight ahead, parallel to the railway tracks, up to the town of Rincón.

We enter Rincón de Soto and cross the tracks to reach la Avenida de la Rioja. From there we go straight on before turning right to reach the City Hall.

We leave Rincón by means of Avenida Príncipe Felipe and we come to an intersection with a railroad crossing. We do not cross but we turn left onto Avenida del río Alfaro. The street turns to the right and directs us to a roadway bridge which crosses over an irrigation canal. We continue straight on the asphalt, keeping the canal to our left.

We pass under the bridge as we continue to walk parallel to the canal for a short while. The road, camino del Esportal, leads us for 6 km along the train line, parallel to the N-232. We walk straight ahead on the same road. Following a curve of 90 degrees to the right, we first go up to cross a small bridge over an irrigation canal, we cross then the train tracks before finally reaching the N-232 which we will follow to our left until we reach Alfaro.

As we walk toward Alfaro, we will come upon the chapel of Pillar, impressively set on a small promontory over the highway. We enter the town and come to a roundabout, where we keep going straight so that we cross over the Alhama river and arrive at the bus station and then at the Plaza de Toros. We walk along the edge of the plaza, keeping it to our left. Following the avenue which turns to the right, we reach a tree-lined promenade, which appears on our left. This is the Paseo de la Florida, where the pilgrims' hostel is located.

■ Interesting facts

RINCÓN DE SOTO: Church of San Miguel (16th century with later restorations). The town offers the possibility of restaurants, pharmacies, health center, supermarkets and banks.

ALFARO: The Colegiata de San Miguel Arcángel (16th-17th c.) is a majestic sight, with its more than 3,000 square m. It is worth visiting the interior of this building, a national monument since 1976, with its baroque main altar (18th c.), another altar of the same period, dedicated to la Dolorosa «Our Lady of Sorrows», the sculpture of the Virgen Peregrina «pilgrim Virgin»—a tribute to the many pilgrims who pass through this city—and the Gothic Christ in the chapel of San José. In another church, that of San Francisco, a large baroque canvas depicting the apparition of the apostle James in the battle of Clavijo is displayed. Depending on the season, it can be easy to see storks crowning the most important buildings: the city is well known as «the paradise of storks». Alfaro (10,000 inhabitants) welcomes pilgrims with its restaurants, pharmacies, health center, supermarkets, banks and an office of tourism (plaza de España, 1. Tel.: 941 180 133.Open Tuesday to Saturday, morning and afternoon; Sundays, morning only).

■ TAXI
Alfaro

Taxis La Esperanza	678 617 029
Taxis Javier Gil	626 310 612

■ LODGING
RINCÓN DE SOTO:
City Hall. Tel.: 941 160 013.

ALFARO: Pilgrim's shelter (12 free places): c/ Paseo de la Florida, 23 (near the local police station). Tel.: 666 041 958. Palacios Hotel, Carretera Zaragoza, 57. Tel.: 941 180 100. HM Alfaro Hotel, c/ San Antón, 32. Tel.: 941 180 056. Alhama Youth Hostel, c/ Puerta de Milagro. Tel.: 941 291 100. City Hall, c/ Las Pozas, 14. Tel.: 941 180 133. Tourist Office: 941 180 133.

ALFARO – TUDELA

(25.6 km)

«Whoever has God lacks nothing, even though he has nothing else.»

«In all your ways keep him in mind and he will smooth your paths» (Prov 3:6).

Plaza de los Fueros, Tudela.

We leave Alfaro, the stork's paradise, by the highway that goes to the cemetery. A lovely statue of two pilgrims symbolizes the ancient Camino de Santiago and the new Camino Ignaciano sharing the route. We continue straight ahead on the same asphalt road which takes us to Castejón. We enter town and go through it on the same road. On our right is the church and on the left, the town hall. If we are lucky, we will see the preparations for the typical bull running which is held during the June festival.

Leaving town, we approach the train tracks and we will be walking parallel to them, to our left, for more than 5 km. A bridge helps us cross them and, just past the bridge, we turn to our left to take the dirt path which leads us next to the Ebro River. If desired, we can continue straight ahead on the asphalt road until reaching Tudela but it is recommended to turn off the road and see the river because here we are offered some of the most spectacular vistas of our entire Camino Ignaciano.

We come up to the edge of the Ebro, which runs deeply at this stage, and we contemplate the beauty of the setting. In some places we can also find a bit of shade to sit and enjoy the moment.

We continue to follow the main dirt path, going by some half-demolished houses. Nearing Tudela, we return to the road that we left before and a large image of the Sacred Heart of Jesus on high tells us that the city is not far off.

We enter Tudela going by the train tunnel and we encounter the Church of Santa María Magdalena (12th c.), in which Ignatius of Loyola surely stopped to give thanks to our Lord. We follow the signs to the center to the city. Tudela is adorned by attractive streets with inviting nooks and many churches that we can visit.

■ Ignatian tip

As a courageous and earnest knight, Ignatius did not set limits. If a particular saint was known for a special penance or service to our Lord, Ignatius had to match and surpass it. We have here an example of an inner experience wherein someone who had been forgiven much felt he also had to be prepared to give much in return. The intensity of such effort corresponds to an inner awareness of being truly saved by God's mercy.

«It will be helpful to recall one event that occurred during this journey as a way of showing just how God directed Ignatius. Although filled with an ardent desire to serve God, his knowledge of spiritual things was still very obscure. He had undertaken extraordinary penances not only to atone for his past sins, but also with the intention of doing something pleasing to his Lord. Indeed he declared that, though filled with the liveliest abhorrence of his past sins, he could not assure himself that they were forgiven.

Yet so intense was his desire to do great things for Christ during his austerities that

he did not think of his sins. And when he recalled the penances practiced by the saints, his whole energy was directed to equal or even surpass these holy persons. He found his consolation in this holy ambition since he had no ulterior motive for his penances, knowing very little as yet about humility or charity or patience. He knew still less the value of discretion which regulates the practice of these virtues. To do something great for the glory of his God, to emulate saintly persons in all that they had done before him—this was the sole purpose of Ignatius in his practices of external penance.»

As Fr. J.M. Rambla, SJ, states in his book «The Pilgrim», the concept of the «MAGIS» is a keynote of the Ignatian symphony. Love always leads to a dynamic excess without measure. Love does not conform to the cold balance of what is just and right. Love always seeks out the «more», surrenders «more», becomes «more», and grows «more». The famous Ignatian motto «Ad Majorem Dei Gloriam» effectively expresses this growing dynamism of committed love. At the

same time, Ignatius also recognized that, during this period of his life, he lacked the discretion «to regulate and measure these virtues» as he evaluated his great desires. It is this discretion that St. Paul identifies as a virtue which helps us in every circumstance of life to «find God's will, that is, what is good and pleasing to God, and perfect» (Romans 12:2). By dint of personal observation and knowledge of God's presence, Ignatius would eventually learn to live by such discretion, and thus to pass it on to his fellow Jesuits. The «greater glory of God» will come about with a good dose of «love for God» and decisive action «to serve God». Ignatius will affirm what St. Irenaeus said much earlier: «The glory of God is man fully alive!» To this goal Ignatius pledged his life.

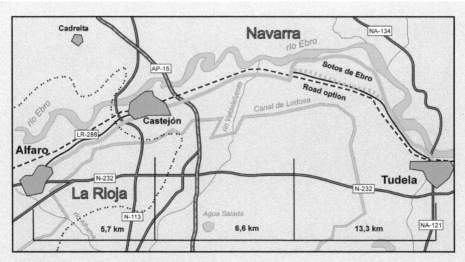

Total upward slope: 121 m. Total downward slope: 188 m.
Bicycles: easy.

Alfaro:	km 0
Castejón:	km 5.7
Cruce del ferrocarril	km 12.3
Tudela:	km 25.6

■ Description

We start out from the pilgrims' hostel, taking the calle de las Pozas toward the plaza de España and, from there, toward the plaza Chica and the calle Araciel y Castejón. We come out by the puerta de Castejón and follow the Avenida de Navarra.

We leave Alfaro by highway LR-288, which leads us directly to the next town, Castejón, which is in the Autonomous Community of Navarre. The train line runs beside us, on our left.

We cross the roundabout of N-113 road and enter Castejón, straight ahead on calle de San José.

We pass through Castejón, almost in a straight line, first by calle de San José and then by calle de Sarasate. Going straight ahead, we reach the end of town and on our left

Tudela.

we see an incline towards the bridge over the railroad tracks. We walk towards the bridge but we do not cross; instead, we turn down the road to the right that leads parallel to the train tracks.

We keep following the train line, which runs parallel to the road on the left. A km further on, we cross under AP-15 highway. We cannot get lost if we keep following the train line. At 5.5 km from the highway bridge, our road passes over the train line. Here we have to decide if we will take the shorter route (2 km less, but over pavement)

or the more picturesque one (farm road near the Ebro River). The asphalt option is clear and there is no way to get lost on it: just keep going straight until reaching Tudela. The other option, which passes near the Ebro and also near a place known as Sotos de Ebro, crosses other dirt pathways, so we should pay attention to in order not to lose our way.

Undoubtedly, the dirt road gives us the best views of the Ebro River that we will find on our Camino Ignaciano. The road that we have to follow to our left is found easily. After crossing the bridge over the train line, we follow a steep curve to our left which turns us back in the opposite direction from the one we were taking on the asphalt road. Having left the main road, the dirt road now takes us around a wide turn to the right and brings us close to the Ebro River. Reaching the river, we keep it on our left and follow it downstream. The track has turnoffs and

alternative routes which lead to the fields being irrigated by the Ebro. We continue straight, staying close to the river and walking parallel to it. We pass behind some houses that are on our right. At the next junction, continue straight ahead. We arrive at some abandoned corrals on our left. Continue straight ahead. At the next junction we turn to our left. We see the city of Tudela in the distance. We arrive at some warehouses and meet the same road that we left a few km before.

Once we reach the asphalt road, we follow it to our left. We will find ourselves with the train line on our right and the Ebro River on our left. We will soon pass a small dam on the river. Some 300 m beyond the dam, we take a dirt road to our left; this continues parallel to the main road. Using this route, we spare ourselves walking on pavement with cars nearby. This path leads us directly to the entrance of Tudela, always parallel with the roadway.

We enter Tudela where we find the Romanesque church of Santa María Magdalena awaiting us. Following the calle del Portal, we approach the Cathedral, the city hall and the tourism office. The pilgrims' hostel (also the Youth Hostel) is found about 1.2 km outside the city, following the Avenida de Zaragoza and the calle de la Caridad.

Interesting facts

CASTEJÓN: An important railroad junction, the city has a museum dedicated to railroads. Also, the modern church of St. Francis Xavier (1944) reminds us that we are now in Navarre, the kingdom upon which that Jesuit saint left a profound mark, as expressed in the many churches dedicated to him. The town offers the possibility of restaurants, drugstores, clinic, supermarkets and banks. City Hall phone number: 984 844 002.

TUDELA: Capital of Ribera de Navarra, it was established in the year 802 by the Muslims and is one of the most important cities of Muslim origin on the Iberian Peninsula. Worth a visit, the Cathedral (Romanesque style in transition to Gothic) was built in 1168 on the site of the principal mosque; it has recently been restored. Walking around behind it, we will find the famous Puerta del Juicio (Judgment Gate). In the plaza de los Fueros (1687) we find the 16th century city hall. A walk toward the Ebro River will take us to the bridge which has its origins in the 9th century. Many historical and monumental buildings are within easy reach of the pilgrim, such as the church of Santa María Magdalena (12th c.) near the Ebro. It would be very useful to visit the tourism office (plaza de los Fueros, tel.: 948 848 058). The city has a bicycle repair shop, restaurants, pharmacies, health center, supermarkets, banks and tourism office.

Note: Churches built over/on top of mosques? Along the Camino Ignaciano we find churches built on land formerly occupied by mosques (for example in Tudela, Alagón, Zaragoza and Lleida); these mosques, in turn, were often raised on top of pre-existing Christian churches. The medieval conquerors, both Muslims and Christians, converted the holy places of their defeated foes. Thus we see a deeply symbolic practice that enacts the total overthrow of a defeated civilization and their religion at the hands of their conquerors. However, more practical considerations also came into play: it was much easier to transform a standing building than to erect an entirely new one; the elegant steeple of «La Giralda», Seville's Cathedral, is the best example in Spain of a minaret turned into a belltower with a spire; the Cathedral del Salvador in Zaragoza is another example of this custom.

Jesuit Fathers: The parish of Nuestra Señora de Lourdes is staffed by the Jesuit fathers, who will be happy to stamp the pilgrims' credentials, provided pilgrims arrive during regular hours. Address: c/ de Arcos Escribano, 34. Tel.: 948 820 297.

■ TAXI
Castejón: 636 471 672.
Tudela
Asociación Taxis de Tudela   948 822 027
Taxi Aranguren   948 821 199

■ LODGING
TUDELA: Youth Hostel (call and make a reservation), c/ Camino Caritat, 17. Tel.: 664 636 175. AC Ciudad de Tudela Hotel, c/ de la Misericordia. Tel.: 948 402 440. Santamaría Hotel, San Marcial, 14. Tel.: 948 821 200. Tudela Bardenas Hotel, Avenida de Zaragoza, 60. Tel.: 948 410 778 / 948 410 802. Bed4U Tudela Hotel, c/ Mañeru, s/n. Tel.: 948 413 413. NH DELTA Hotel, Avenida de Zaragoza, 29. Tel.: 948 821 400. Hostal Pichorradicas. c/ Cortadores, 11. Tel.: 948 821 021. Remigio Gaztambide Hostel, c/ Gaztambide, 4 (next to the plaza de Los Fueros: discount for pilgrims) Tel.: 948 820 850. City Hall. Tel.: 948 417 100.

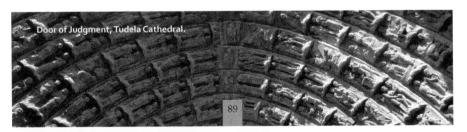

Door of Judgment, Tudela Cathedral.

TUDELA – GALLUR

(39.3 km)

«It is not enough that I serve God alone; I must help all hearts to love him and all tongues to praise him.»

«Sound me out, Lord, and know my heart; put me to the test to know my feelings: see if my behavior is offensive and guide me on the straight path» (Ps 139:23-24).

San Pedro's Church, Gallur.

Today we have a very long stage which must be taken calmly and with preparation and which will see us underway very early and stopping in each town for water. This route under the sun must be traversed in the early hours.

Starting from the pilgrim's shelter, we walk towards the bridge over the train tracks. We go up on the bridge and, after crossing, turn to the right to find the path which runs parallel to the rails. Again today, the train will be the point of reference.

The path goes through the fields some 6 km until meeting El Bocal, which is the beginning of the Imperial Canal. We will follow the canal first on its right side and then, crossing the bridge, we will continue on its left, straight ahead until we reach Ribaforada. If we haven't worn a hat up to now, it is time to put one on: there are not many trees in this stretch and we have 5 km coming up. We cross the bridge to enter Ribaforada and go through it. Just at the town's entrance stands the 12th century church of San Blas and the shields of the Templars, the founders of Ribaforada, are kept in the library in the plaza next to the church.

We come to the train tracks but we do not cross them, keeping to their

left on the street which runs parallel to them. We are going to follow these tracks, staying close to them, until entering the village of Cortes. Heads up here, because there are two short sections of 500 m each where we can lose our way. The first section is when just arriving at a bridge over the tracks, which is easy to recognize by some industrial sheds right where the path disappears. We continue straight, to the side of the tracks and go underneath the bridge, next to the rails. Then our path continues straight ahead. The second section is a bit further on and we have to pay attention to the signs on the ground to identify the point where we are to continue straight, taking a faint trail next to the train tracks. If we get lost, we will have to take the first road to our right which will bring us back, next to the railway. Past these two points and after leaving a tunnel to our right, under the

tracks, our way angles toward some pig farms and now brings us to Cortes.

Cortes is a medieval village with a magnificent castle. We leave on the highway that goes to the train station. We cross the tracks through the tunnel and continue straight towards Mallén. In this town we head to the church plaza and from there we are going to look for a street which takes us down to the industrial park and an abandoned bar-restaurant on highway N-232.

We cross the highway and, at the end of the industrial park, we follow the path which descends towards the train tunnel and the Imperial Canal, which we take to the right, to cross on a nearby bridge. Once across, we follow the Imperial Canal for more than 6 km. Keeping the canal on our right, we contemplate this engineering marvel and the entire Ebro valley which spreads out before us. The pines give off a strong aroma in the afternoon heat and the pilgrim is going to be grateful for the water in the canal that refreshes the gaze. We continue always on the bank of the canal until entering Gallur. A blue bridge over the canal draws our attention: it is the bridge that one can cross to go to the municipal swimming pools and the pilgrim's shelter, which is located next to the train station.

Today we are sure to need a refreshing end of stage and this is it!

Imperial Canal.

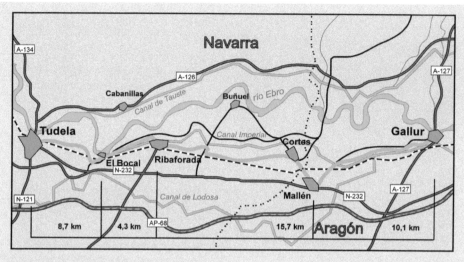

Total upward slope: 103 m. Total downward slope: 160 m.
Easy for cyclists, but there are two points between Ribaforada and Cortes at which you have to take short alternative routes, following dirt roads bordering these points. If you always keep the railway as your reference point, you will not get lost. Pilgrims on foot can travel more easily along the small trails or loose stone paths near the railway, which remains our reference until Cortes.

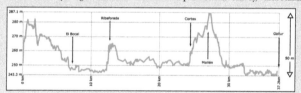

Tudela:	km 0
El Bocal:	km 8.7
Ribaforada:	km 13.5
Cortes:	km 26.2
Mallén:	km 29.2
Gallur:	km 39.3

■ Description

We leave Tudela. We follow the calle Camino Caritat to our left and head to the bridge over the railway lines. Next to the bridge, there is a small path leading from the same bridge which enables us to cross the tracks. In these early morning hours we take the route of the sun which is rising over the distant Mediterranean.

We cross the bridge and, just as we come down, we take a road to the right which curves backward and leads to a power transformer station. Our route is wide and continues straight ahead without difficulty. As we progress, we leave behind farms and small villages. Staying on the wide path, we reach the asphalt road which we pass under, by way of the bridge over the train line; it takes us the long way around. Once we have left that bridge, we come to a crossroads where we take the road to the right, which takes us close to the train lines. After about 1 km, a paved roadway appears. The train line, always on our right, accompanies us until we come close to the main gate of the «El Carrizal» ranch.

Our route continues straight ahead; it is wide and without turnoffs. A little later, we come upon a road, which we take to our left. We then come near the Imperial Canal, which we will follow as we go on. The road continues, with the waters of the canal on our left and the train line on our right.

We reach the bridge called «Formigales». Right after crossing it, we take the road to the right, a wide path that leaves the «El Bocal» buildings behind us. We continue walking, following the course of the water, which is always on our right. If up to this point you have not been using a hat, we recommend that you put one on now: there are not many trees in this part of the Camino and we have 5 km ahead of us!

On our right, we take the first bridge that crosses the canal. Leaving the canal behind, we enter Ribaforada. The same street by which we enter the town leads us directly to the train line which goes through the center of the town. When we come to the train line, we turn to our left without crossing the tracks. A kindly travelling companion, el camino de hierro (the «iron road»), will take us some 10 km, until we reach Cortes. Always on our righ, it will be our trusty guide. After about two km, the road turns at a right angle and begins to separate from the rail line. There can be no mistake because there is a large factory and, at a distance of about 200 m, we can see a bridge. Continue alongside the tracks until just after the bridge and then the road appears again, still parallel to the train lines.

After another, two long kilometers, cyclists have to let the road take them almost 1 km away from the railway line until

they see a very clear intersection to their right which takes them back to the same pilgrim's road which we were walking along, near the railroad. Pilgrims on foot take a different route: they can follow the road straight ahead which runs beside the railway line, although it does become a bit obscure along this 200 meter stretch. At the end of this section, the dirt road that is always parallel with the railway reappears. Cyclists can, from this point, continue along the dirt road. We keep walking with the train tracks on our right. Finally, our route angles off away from the train line and take us further and further away from it, toward the first farms, which indicate we are in the vicinity of the town of Cortes. Our farm road continues straight until we come to a large roundabout, right at the entrance to Cortes. We turn to our right at that roundabout.

As we enter the town, we follow the main road,

which turns slightly to the right, until we reach a narrow street appearing on our left and leading us to a castle and the church of San Juan Bautista. We keep travelling along the same street until it turns into another street toward the right. We should stay on the calle San Miguel and keep walking toward the train station. When we reach the tracks, the road goes under them and so do we.

We stay on our road as it turns slightly to the right. We follow a long, straight stretch of paved highway, which leads us to a roundabout allowing us to pass under the N-232 road. We keep going straight, crossing a second roundabout without turning to either side. At this point we will be entering Mallén.

When we reach a triangular plaza with a garden, we turn left and walk alongside the plaza. This street brings us to the plaza containing the Church of Nuestra Señora de los Ángeles. We take

We go through the train tunnel and in 300 m we arrive at the Imperial Canal. We take the turn to the right and cross the nearby bridge, following the canal on its left side until we reach Gallur. We have almost 7 km ahead of us to walk.

Remaining beside the canal, we enter Gallur, crossing the blue bridge over the Imperial Canal in the direction of the municipal pools. Right in front of us is the train station and in the building next door is the pilgrims' hostel and restaurant.

Avenida de Zaragoza and in 100 m turn left down calle Camino de Santiago which descends towards the N-232. We cross it towards the Mallén industrial park. We go straight down the street that goes through the industrial park and when we reach the end, we take the path on the right. In 50 m, at the first fork, we take the dirt road to the left.

■ Interesting facts

EL BOCAL: Since Aragón's Imperial Canal begins here, the town is called «Bocal Real» or «royal wellspring». The Imperial Canal was commissioned in 1528 by Emperor Charles V and finished in the 18th century, under the direction of Ramón de Pignatelli who died after extending the canal past Zaragoza but without achieving his great goal of reaching the sea. Nearby, we find the Emperor's Palace with Navarre's oldest oak tree in its gardens. Also, after going through El Bocal, one reaches the Casa de las Compuertas (floodgate house), with a new dam, built in 1790. «El Bocal» is well worth a visit because of its tranquility and the beauty of its surroundings. The old dam and the Palace with its gardens are also interesting.

RIBAFORADA: Town of about 3,000 inhabitants. It was founded in 1157, during the reign of Sancho el Sabio (the Wise) of Navarre, by the Knights Templar. Its earliest function was to protect the Christian pilgrims who were travelling on the Camino de Santiago. In 1313 the religious order of

the Hospitallers of Saint John of Jerusalem assumed responsibility for the town. Of special interest is the church of San Blas, built with brick and masonry in the 12th century, with modifications in the 16th and 17th centuries. In the same plaza the Templar shields are visible on the facades of the buildings. The chapel of Nuestra Señora de la Dehesa is also here. The town offers restaurants, pharmacies, health center, supermarkets and banks.

CORTES: In the center of the town, we find the castle and its tower, built in the 12th century and rebuilt in the 16th. The church of San Juan Bautista is Gothic-Renaissance style, with a Moorish tower. The town has 3,000 inhabitants and offers restaurants, pharmacies, a health center, supermarkets and banks.

MALLÉN: This town belongs to the Autonomous Community of Aragón although, originally it served as a wayside spot, marking the road connecting Aragón with Navarre. It has Celtic origins and the Romans built the highway here between Tarraco and Asturica. The order of Hospitallers of Saint John built the Church of Nuestra Señora de los Ángeles in which three styles may be distinguished: Romanesque (12th c.), Gothic (13th c.), and late Baroque (18th c.). Until the 16th century, the town also had a chapel dedicated to the Apostle St. James. It is a small town but offers a bicycle repair shop, restaurants, pharmacies, health center, supermarkets and banks.

GALLUR: Since Neolithic times there have been various settlements in this area, which grew with the Roman occupation of the Ebro valley. The settlements were called pagi (Latin) and one of them gave its name to this little town. It was originally called pagus gallorum, the settlement of the Gauls, since the original inhabitants were from Gallia. Later on, there was a strong Muslim presence but, in 1119, troops from Aragón, under Alphonsus I, transformed the town into a Mozarabic settlement, populated by Aragonese and Andalusians. The church of San Pedro, of Gallic-Roman origin, is located in the upper part of town. It is for the most part a neo-classical edifice (18th c.), with a tower built in the 20th century. An ancient castle, built by Alphonsus I (12th c.), was situated on the site where the church is now. It is worthwhile taking a walk across the iron bridge over the Ebro River, which is joined here by a tributary, the Barba River. With its more than 3,000 inhabitants, the town offers bicycle repair shop, restaurants, pharmacies, health center, supermarkets, banks and a tourism office.

Note: The Muslim influence throughout the Camino Ignaciano. What do the terms «mudéjar» (Mudejar) and «morisco» (Moorish) mean? From the beginning of the 8th century, the majority of the territory through which our Camino Ignaciano passes was governed by Muslim rulers. At first, Córdoba was the capital of Al-Andalus, as the Muslim-ruled part of Spain was known. But, in the early part of the 11th century, Al-Andalus was divided into smaller regional states and a large part of Aragon's territory came to be administered from Zaragoza. Alfonso el Batallador and other

Christian kings recovered most of this territory in the 12th century. Both the conquest of Zaragoza (1118) and that of Gallur and Tudela (1119) were critical turning points in what the Spanish Christians called the Reconquista (Reconquest).

Many Muslims remained in this region once Christian dominance was consolidated and still, in Ignatius' time (1512), in the village of Gallur, the great majority of families were Muslim. The word «mudéjar» designates those Muslims who lived in lands governed by Christians. The term «morisco» designates those Muslims who, though converted at least in name to Christianity, tried to conserve elements of their old culture. In some small populations, Arabic continued to be spoken well into the 16th century.

Mudejars and Moriscos contributed in an important way both to agriculture and to crafts, and their influence is evident in many towns and cities, most notably in Zaragoza. Typical aspects of the «mudejar» style are: the use of brick instead of stone as the basic construction material, glazed tiles, decorated bell towers, elaborate geometrical motifs on both walls and dishware (the Islamic faith prohibits, in essence, the representation of human figures, so that decorative Muslim art developed featuring chiefly geometric motifs instead).

■ TAXI
Gallur
Taxis Zueco   976 857 318

■ LODGING
RIBAFORADA: City Hall. Tel.: 948 864 005.

MALLÉN: Pinocho Hostel, c/ Tudela, 4. Tel.: 976 850 225.
City Hall. Tel.: 976 850 005. Pilgrim Shelter, c/ Paradero, 3 (above the public library). Tel.: 976 850 374 / 618 998 839.

GALLUR: Pilgrim's shelter (32 beds, beside the train station). Tel.: 976 864 396 / 618 833 696. El Colono Hostel (special prices for pilgrims) 976 864 275
City Hall. Tel.: 976 864 073.

GALLUR – ALAGÓN
(21.7 km)

«A man who finds the way of virtue difficult, but enters upon it bravely in order to dominate himself, wins twice the reward of those whose lazy mind and nature do not trouble them at all.»

«But I will always be with you: you grasp my right hand; you guide me according to your plans and lead me to a glorious destination. Whom do I have in heaven? With you, what is the earth to me?» (Ps 73:23-25).

Alcalá de Ebro.

For today's stage we must get up very early: it would be a good idea to do the first 8 km before the sun shows its face. We have quite a few kilometers on asphalt and it is better not to walk on it in the midday heat. On the other hand, this stage is full of culture and of Ignatian reminders, as we will see. We leave by the calle del Camino Real, the ancestral route which took so many travelers, soldiers and pilgrims from one point to the other across the Iberian Peninsula, from the Mediterranean to the Cantabrian and vice versa. Today, this royal roadway is the camino which takes us directly to Luceni. The Luceni plaza, surrounded by handsome trees and the seat of the itinerant market, possesses an abundant fountain from which we cannot drink: it would seem that runoff from the proliferation of hog farms near the town has, in recent years, contaminated the water. But, as pointed out by Jesuit historians, Luceni is likely the scene of one of the most commented upon episodes in St. Ignatius of Loyola's Autobiography: his meeting with the Moor and the subsequent decision he left up to his mule.

Leaving town, opposite number 37, calle Daoíz y Velarde, we find the road to Pedrola which Ignatius did not take, thus saving the life of that Muslim.

Guided by the Autobiography, we continue, like Ignatius' mule, straight ahead on the Camino Real, with no possibility of getting lost, into the next town, Alcalá de Ebro. From time to time we walk alongside the Ebro which again shows itself in all of its breadth and extraordinary beauty.

In Alcalá de Ebro, if we know about Cervantes and his famous work, *Don Quixote*, perhaps we will let ourselves be seduced by the idea that we are precisely on that islet Barataria, promised by Don Quijote to his faithful squire, Sancho Panza, for him to govern. It is not really an island but, when the Ebro floods, a portion of land is left isolated. A charming statue of Governor Sancho can be seen behind the church.

We leave town by calle Cervantes and calmly continue our pilgrimage on dirt and asphalt paths to Cabañas de Ebro. We encounter little shade, though we might be able to go into one of the nearby fields and rest a bit under a tree. We arrive at Cabañas de Ebro and continue along the highway towards Alagón at the end of this stage. Watch the traffic in the last kilometer and a half; it is quite intense.

We happily leave the highway upon finding a tunnel under the freeway which places us now on the last leg of this stage. The bell tower of the church of San Pedro appears on high. We head for it and finish our stage.

Ignatian tip

At this stage of his pilgrimage, the still «very cavalier» Ignatius had an experience that could have changed the course of his life. God was aware of the danger and was ready to teach Ignatius the value of prudence and controlling his impulses, even in what he believed was a good cause.

«As he journeyed on, he came upon a Moor riding a mule. They both fell to talking and the conversation turned to Our Lady. The Moor admitted that the Virgin had conceived without man's aid but could not believe that she remained a virgin after having given birth. He was so obstinate in holding this opinion that no amount of reasoning by Ignatius could force him to abandon it. Shortly afterward the Moor rode on, leaving the pilgrim to his own thoughts about what had taken place. These gave rise to emotions that sorely troubled him and he thought he had failed in his duty to honor the Mother of God. The longer he thought about the matter, the more his soul was filled with indignation against himself for allowing the Moor to say such a calumnious thing about Our Lady. He concluded that he was obliged to defend her honor. As a result, he felt a strong desire to search out the Moor and give him a taste of his dagger for what he had said. This battle of desires lasted for some time with the pilgrim still doubtful at the end as to what course he should follow. The Moor had gone on ahead and had mentioned that he was going to a town not too far distant from the highway. Ignatius, wearied by his inner struggle and not able to come to any clear decision, decided to settle his doubts in the following way: he would let the mule decide, and gave her free reign up to the cross-road. If the mule took the road that led to the village, he would pursue the Moor and kill him. But if his mule kept to the highway, he would allow the wretch to escape and so, he allowed his mule to decide. It happened through God's Providence that the mule kept to the highway even though the village was only thirty or forty yards distant and the road leading to it was broad and smooth.»

We add here an interpretation of this text from the Autobiography, written by José Luis María Vigil. It illustrates quite well the sentiments of Ignatius Loyola at this stage of his journey:

«It happened that, when I [Ignatius] was reflecting by myself, I happened to overtake a Muslim eager

Sancho Panza, Alcalá de Ebro.

to talk. I was not upset at him since courtesy is a habit for someone well-born. We spoke, I do not know of what, until he asked about the purpose of my journey. I said I was going to the shrine since I did not think he would understand my desire to reach the Holy Land. In that guise we spoke about the Virgin since I was filled with the enthusiasm of a new convert. The Moor was composed, even respectful and reasonable. He said he was not opposed to the virginity of Our Lady before her delivery, which for a Muslim says a great deal. But he could not understand her remaining a virgin after giving birth. I gave him many reasons for this, but he refused to accept them. We spoke a lot in vain, without coming to any agreement on the matter. Finally, he declared that he was going to Pedrola, a Moorish village just a few miles beyond the crossroads up ahead.

I remained gloomy and aggrieved and I decided that I had not acted honorably with the Moor. I worried that I had spoken more than necessary about the Virgin Mary and had thus offended her. Had I done well to allow this? But I have to be judged according to the time when I lived. Martin Luther, a competent theologian and not a man of the sword, said, twenty years later, that it was lawful to stab a Jew if he was heard blaspheming. He further confessed that he "would give a blow and pierce him with his sword if he could because, since it is lawful to kill a thief, how much more lawful must it be to kill a blasphemer." Further, more than two centuries earlier, a saintly king of France told his men: "Chevaliers, when you hear someone cursing the Christian faith, defend the faith not with words but with the sword, thrusting it as far as possible into the belly of the infidel."

Is it any wonder then, that I (the pilgrim) entertained thoughts of murder since the honor of Our Lady was called into question? I had a deep craving to search for the Moor and stab him to death, yet I doubted that this was the right course of action. So I decided to drop the reins of my horse at the crossroads ahead. If the horse went towards Pedrola I would find the Moor and slay him. But, if the horse stayed on the highway, then I would leave things alone and find peace. That Moor never knew how close he came to death that afternoon. It pleased God that he lived, despite his blindness in denying the virgin birth of His Mother, Our Lady» (cf. J. L. MARTÍN VIGIL, Yo, Ignacio de Loyola, Planeta, Barcelona 1989, 64).

God saved that Muslim traveler but he also kept Ignatius Loyola from committing an act that could have had severe consequences. God's presence is manifested in our personal history in many ways. We can discover the Hand of God in the simplest and most humble events, letting the mule decide which way to go. If we discern the actions of our lives from the light of a heart open to God, we then become «agents of life» rather than death.

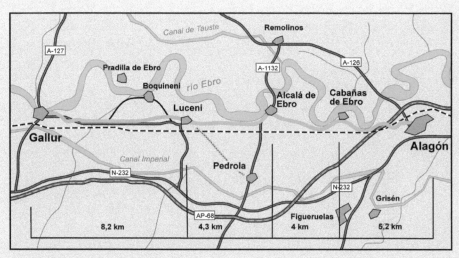

Total upward slope: 45 m. Total downward slope: 70 m.
Bicycles: easy, although there is a section of the CV-911 that carries a great deal of traffic and so care should be taken.

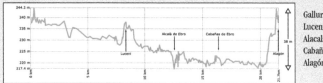

Gallur:	km 0
Luceni:	km 8.2.
Alacalá de Ebro:	km 12.5
Cabañas de Ebro:	km 16.5
Alagón:	km 21.7

■ Description

We take the road by the Parque de Pignatelli next to the canal. From there we take the calle del Camino Real, in homage to the old Camino Real which San Ignacio trod in his time. Today it is the broad, paved, road, VP-24. (Caution: this road can be heavily trafficked).

Walking straight ahead, as always, we will reach Luceni after passing a roundabout at the intersection of the road that goes to Boquineni.

We enter town by calle de Ramón y Cajal, which we follow straight through town with no problem. At one point we will pass the town plaza to our left, with its banks and plane trees. We continue straight and, upon leaving the town, we find a turnoff which would take us to Pedrola, but we keep going straight. After a few kilometers we come close to a bend of the Ebro which tells us we are near the town of Alcalá de Ebro. Turn left to go directly to the City Hall and calle Cervantes, where the road begins which leads towards the town of Cabañas de Ebro.

Walking along calle Cervantes, we leave town after about 500 m and there we find a crossroads. We take the road to the left, toward Cabañas, which becomes a path after a little more than a

San Pedro's Church, Alagón.

kilometer and gradually brings us close, once again, to the Ebro river.

We continue straight ahead, with the Ebro on our left, for about one km until we reach Cabañas de Ebro. With the church on our right, we enter the town and cross through it, leaving by calle Mayor. From there we follow the CV-411 which, after 1.5 km, takes us to the CV-911 which we take to our left. This road has lots of traffic so care is needed. After 1.5 km, we come upon a tunnel on our right which crosses under highway AP-68. We go through the tunnel and also pass under the train line by way of another tunnel. This road takes us directly to Alagón. If we cross the road and follow in a straight line, the Avenida de la Portalada will take us to the center of the town.

■ Interesting facts

LUCENI: The name of the town, which has about 1,000 inhabitants, is evidence of an ancient Roman presence (Lucius); the town was on the road which linked the Mediterranean to the northern part of the Iberian Peninsula. Archeological excavations of the first settlements have unearthed coins and medals of the emperor Antonius Pius (2nd century A.D.), as well as Visigoth coins from the reigns of Wamba and Witiza (7th and 8th c.). The church, dedicated to the Virgin of Candelaria, dates from the 13th century.

Following the Autobiography, we are in all likelihood right at the town where St. Ignatius recalls the time he had to decide on the life or death of a Muslim with whom he had had a discussion. God wanted to guide Ignatius in such a way that it was life that came out victorious. Luceni offers the pilgrim a bicycle shop, restaurants, pharmacies, health center, supermarkets and banks. Unfortunately, for the past few years, water sources in Luceni have not been drinkable owing to contamination from nearby pig farms.

ALCALÁ DE EBRO: The castle ruins give us a hint about the origin of the town's name: it comes from the Arabic, al-calat, the castle. In the impressive baroque church of la Santísima Trinidad (17th c.) there is a picture dedicated to St. Francis Borgia, third superior general of the Society of Jesus. There are two obligatory photos: one of the Ebro River and the other of the statue of «Sancho Panza» on the street behind the church. With just 300 inhabitants, the town offers us a restaurant, a pharmacy, a health center, a supermarket and a bank.

Church of la Santísima Trinidad, Alcalá de Ebro.

CABAÑAS DE EBRO: Small town of 500 inhabitants. A restaurant and a store are available for the pilgrim.

ALAGÓN: This town, situated where the Jalón River flows into the Ebro, has its origins in the Iberian city of Alaun, the most easterly of the Vasconian (ancient Basque) cities. Here coins were minted with inscriptions in the Iberian alphabet. The town was conquered by Muslims in 714. From its Muslim period there is an impressive Moorish work in the church of San Pedro Apóstol. The church, situated on the site of the former mosque, is well worth a visit, especially for its main altar (16th c.). In the old part of town there is a former college of the Society of Jesus, beside the church of San Antonio de Padua. It offers restaurants, pharmacies, a health center, supermarkets and banks. Contact can be made with the tourism office at turismoalagon@hotmail.com or by telephoning 976 611 814.

■ **TAXI**

Alagón

Autotaxi Ferruz	976 854 063
Taxi Ángel	657 529 269
Taxi Aguilar	653 706 707

■ **LODGING**

LUCENI: Hotel La Imperial, Carretera de Logroño, km 37. Tel.: 976 652 111. Pensión Alejandro, c/ Horno, 1. Tel.: 679 441 838. City Hall. Tel.: 976 652 003.

CABAÑAS DE EBRO: Casa rural Guadalupe, Callizo de la Jota, 1-3. Tel.: 637 524 363. City Hall. Tel.: 976 611 086.

ALAGÓN: Los Ángeles Hotel, Plaza Alhóndiga, 4. Tel.: 976 611 340. Baraka Hostel, c/ San Pedro, 13. Tel.: 976 616 011. Pensión Jarea, c/ Méndez Núñez 45. Tel.: 629 489 776. City Hall. Tel.: 976 610 300.

ALAGÓN – ZARAGOZA
(30.5 km)

«If a man wishes to reform the world, be it by reason of the authority
of his position or by the duty of his charge, he must always start
with himself.»

«If I fly to the ring of the dawn or I dwell at the far shore of the sea,
there your left hand sustains me and your right hand holds me firm.
If I say: the darkness engulfs me, around me day becomes night, for
you the darkness is not dark, night is as bright as day: darkness or
light is all the same» (Ps 139:9-12).

Basilica of the Pilar (Pillar), Zaragoza.

Today we approach one of the great
capitals of our pilgrimage. Without doubt
we will make a long stopover and enjoy
the rest and historical and cultural riches
which Zaragoza offers us. But before the
breather in Aragón's capital, we must
complete this rather long stage, quite
possibly under a strong sun.

We leave the town of Alagón, descending
towards the train station, but we turn to
the left in order to take the bridge that
crosses the tracks. From here on we are
going to be walking on dirt and asphalt
alternatively until reaching the end of our
stage.

Awaiting us is a tranquil day, passing
through four small towns, allowing us
to advance, «step-by-step» and with
provisions ready at hand. In addition,
each one of these towns comes with its
own sample of Mudejar art. The pilgrim
is impressed by the discovery of these
bell towers and spires of braided brick,
characteristic of the Muslim influence in
Spain, which was very positive in many
aspects: many of the irrigation canals that
we are going to cross today date from the
Muslim period.

From Alagón we head towards Torres de
Berrellén. We come upon the Jalón River,
with little water. Fields and farms lead

us to the town. We find the same type of path, taking us in the direction of the next town, Sobradiel. We cannot get lost on the asphalt path and it is very easy to see one town from the other, like a rosary which offers us one bead after another. We see Utebo from far off but before, we have to cross the A-68 bridge and pass by some old factories which today are deserted and in semi-ruin.

The proximity of the Ebro River allows frequent sightings of water fowl, typical near our Camino Ignaciano. Following canals from the Muslim era, we arrive at Monzalbarba. We cross town on the calle de Nuestra Señora la Sagrada, which coincides with the ancient Roman road from Asturica to Tarraco, between the Cantabrian northwest and the Mediterranean southeast. Leaving town, we take the road of the Almozara which leads us directly to Zaragoza. We enter Zaragoza and are greeted by a grand reception on the part of the Ebro River: a wide meandering bend in the river embraces within itself what was Expo 2008, featuring water as its theme. We go on, accompanying the Ebro in its great curve to the left and thus direct ourselves toward the Aljafería park with its impressive castle, the seat of Aragón's Courts. From there we head to the center of the city. It is worth spending the whole day, if not more, in this lovely, large, city on the Ebro.

■ Ignatian tip

On our tour through the old city of Zaragoza, we found signs of a figure who is little known but who has extraordinary significance for the Society of Jesus: St. Joseph Pignatelli, SJ, sixth son of the noble family of the Counts of Fuentes.

Born in Zaragoza on December 27, 1737 this child had no idea of the difficulties life would hold for him. First, at the age of four, his mother's death caused the family move to Naples. Then, when his father died five years later, he returned to Zaragoza with his older brother and began his studies in the Jesuit school there. After

graduating, he decided to join the Society of Jesus along with his younger brother, Nicholas.

After entering the novitiate in 1753 and completing his subsequent years of training and studies, he began his ministry educating youth at the Colegio Inmaculada, only to be interrupted with the expulsion of the Jesuits from Spain in 1767. After soldiers entered the school and community residence on April 3, 1767, the path of his life took a very different direction.

After spending a day locked in the house refectory, the Jesuits were expelled

from the city, without their belongings, and sent to Tarragona where they embarked for the Papal States. They were denied asylum in the Papal States and so they began an arduous journey by boat, looking for a place that would accept them. Not until seven months later, in October, did the ordeal end at the port of Ferrara. From there, Pignatelli found his way to Bologna where, working as a diocesan priest, he devoted himself to the fight for the full restoration of the Society of Jesus which, by now, had been formally suppressed by Pope Clement XIV in 1773.

The Pilar.

Pignatelli's biographers point out that it was after his expulsion from Spain when Pignatelli, still a young Jesuit who had not made his final vows, became the primary comfort, support and leader of his brother Jesuits in those difficult times, so much so that his provincial appointed him superior of his companions, accompanying, accommodating, feeding and assisting them in so many ways, men who suffered expulsion, overcrowding, lack of food and, above all, were unable to find a home, travelling from city to city, feeling hated and rejected.

His family and his brother had tried suggesting more comfortable choices for him but he preferred to keep his commitment to the Society of Jesus until the end, together with his suffering colleagues. Joseph Pignatelli died in Rome on November 15, 1811, after a long-suffering and adventurous life, failing to see the restoration of his beloved Society of Jesus for which he had struggled so hard and which took place three years later in 1814. He was, however, able to renew his vows in 1797 along with the rest of the Society, which had been able to continue its existence in Russia.

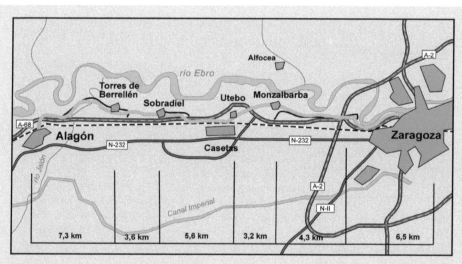

Total upward slope: 204 m. Total downward slope: 203 m.
Bicycles: easy.

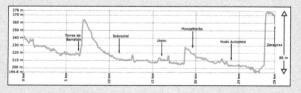

Alagón:	km 0
Torres de Berrellén:	km 7.3
Sobradiel:	km 10.9
Utebo:	km 16.5
Monzalbarba:	km 19.7
Gran nudo de autopistas:	km 24
Zaragoza (El Pilar):	km 30.5

Description

We start from the center of Alagón, going down calle Chacón, in the direction of calle de la Estación, because we are going toward a bridge which crosses the train line outside of town. Going straight ahead, the road takes us over a second bridge, this one crossing the AP-68 highway.

Right after crossing the highway, we turn right, onto a road which is at first paved and then becomes a dirt road. This road runs parallel to the highway which accompanies us on our right for a good stretch. We will reach a bridge over the highway. We do not cross that bridge but swerve left to curve around the bridge, and then take a roadway to our left just past the bridge. This road cuts away from the highway at a right angle.

The dirt road gives way to the asphalt that now marks our path. We keep straight and we come across the Jalón River on our right. We walk close to the Jalón River following it along its left bank. We cross the river and after that, the path takes us further from it in a sharp bend to the right. We always keep straight on the asphalt road until we arrive in Torres de Berrellén.

We enter the town on calle de Garfilán and we head to the City Hall. We visit the church on calle Aragón

and finally we leave town by way of calle Cervantes and camino de Sobradiel. We will find ourselves in open fields. About 600 m further on, we cross an irrigation canal and keep going straight. Many of the present-day canals date from the Muslim period. Two km further on we reach a point where the road divides in two in order to allow a canal to flow down the middle of it. We take the roadway to the left, with the canal on our right and we walk parallel to the canal until we reach the small town of Sobradiel.

We look for the church, which is in the park, and we continue ahead passing the church to our left. Calle del Pino takes us toward the exit from town. We continue straight on the paved road, which, after 1.6 km, turns 90 degrees to the right and leaves us at a bridge which again crosses the AP-68 highway. We cross the highway and find

Aljafería Palace.

ourselves at a roundabout. We take the second exit which leads us toward the industrial area. After about 100 m, we take a paved road (which is later unpaved) which runs alongside the wall of the last company. The Casetas train station is on our right. About 200 m ahead, we find the Magrisa factory which we keep on our right. After about 2 km, this road will take us to Utebo without ever crossing the train tracks

Alfajería.

and without actually entering into the town of Casetas. We see the town of Utebo in the distance and we head towards its church.

We turn 90 degrees to the left on calle de Joaquín Costa which soon becomes calle Miguel Hernández. We head toward the center of town. After passing the plaza and a garden, we turn to our right, entering onto calle Antonio Machado. This takes us out of town and, after a kilometer, it crosses a bridge over the highway.

After crossing the bridge, we walk straight ahead, parallel to an irrigation canal on our right. We cross the canal a little further on and continue to follow it but now it is on our left. The road «jumps» from one canal to another one, which now is on our right. We follow it just 100 m and continue

straight along our route until we come out on a street from which we can already see the next town: Monzalbarba. Turning to our left, we enter the town by calle de Nuestra Señora la Sagrada (an old Roman road) and we walk straight through.

Just as we leave town by the camino de Monzalbarba, we find the small church of Nuestra Señora la Sagrada (Our Sacred Lady). The road turns 90 degrees to the right but we continue straight ahead on the paved road. We are in the path of La Almozara. We continue straight for a few kilometers. We leave a road on our right which leads to a bridge over the highway. We continue straight on our road until we find another bridge which we cross over the highway. After crossing the bridge, we pass through a

tunnel and then cross the last bridge—all of which saves us going through the highway intersection and will announce our arrival in Zaragoza. We continue on straight until we reach the bank of the Ebro River. We make a 90 degree turn to our right and we walk along the riverside path.

We continue on the road, which keeps following the river, which is to our left. In case it is not obvious: what we have before us is what once was Expo Zaragoza 2008, a large international exposition on the subject of water. We enter Zaragoza, where all the roads are fine, as long as we stay near the Ebro River. Located on the river (which we always keep on our left) are the old town center and the plaza de El Pilar, which we find after crossing the Puente de Santiago bridge and before reaching the Puente de Piedra.

The Pillar.

■ Interesting facts

TORRES DE BERRELLÉN: The chapel of Nuestra Señora de Castellar, built in the 11th century, was restored in the 20th. The ruins of a castle speak to us of lands reconquered from the Muslims by Sancho Ramírez y Pedro I in the 11th century. The town offers us restaurant, pharmacy, health center, supermarket and bank.

SOBRADIEL: From 1140–when Ramón Berenguer, Prince of Aragón and Count of Barcelona, granted to his vassal Artal the castle and town of Sobradiel, including its inhabitants and territory–until 1945, the residents of this town had to lease their land from the Counts of Sobradiel. Since 1945, the farmers have been able buy and own the land they work. Beside the palace of the Dukes of Sobradiel (now the town hall) is found the late-17th century baroque church, built of red brick and dedicated to Santiago, the Apostle. The town offers restaurants, pharmacies, health center, supermarkets and banks.

UTEBO: Not to be missed is the amazing Moorish bell tower of the church of Nuestra Señora de la Asunción (the Moorish-Gothic part from the 16th century and the baroque from the 18th). In majestic fashion, the bell tower changes from a square lower level to an octagonal shaped upper section. (Note: Groups may be able to arrange a tour of the church/tower by calling Utebo historical society in advance). The tile adornment is priceless. Just walking around this town of 13,000 inhabitants, visiting the houses and palaces of the 16th and 17th centuries, is a valuable experience. The ceramics and mosaics remind us of its Roman origins. It was situated on the 8th milestone of the road connecting Cesaraugusta (Zaragoza) and Asturica (the villa of Astorga, in the northwest of the Iberian Peninsula). The town offers restaurants, pharmacies, a health center, bicycle repair shop, supermarket and bank.

MONZALBARBA: The impressive Moorish tower of the old parish church greets our Camino. Like the church, the buildings surrounding it are from the 16th century. As we have noticed, the Muslim influence is very strong along this part of our itinerary. This was originally a Muslim Berber settlement, founded by Abdul Jabbar when he encamped on the river island of Santa Catalina. The town's name, «manzil-barbar», means Berber settlement. Pilgrims will find restaurants, a health center, supermarkets and banks.

ZARAGOZA: A striking city, with the Basilica of the Pillar as the beacon of the Camino. In our limited space it is impossible to touch on all that might be visited in this 2000-year old city (from 13 B.C.). A must is a visit to the Virgin, which commemorates St. James's legendary passage through Spanish lands. The basilica holds the honor of being the first center of Marian devotion in Christendom. Bearing witness to the St. James tradition are the many hospitals, which served pilgrims walking on the Camino Real. It is worthwhile just to wander through the old town and visit the Catedral del Salvador («la Seo», as the natives call it, Cathedral of the Savior), built by the Christians on the grounds of the old main mosque, which was in turn raised on top of a primitive Visigothic church, itself built where a Roman temple once stood. The kings of Aragón were usually crowned in this cathedral. A visit to this testimony of

Tower of the Church of the Magdalene.

Roman presence in the city, named by them Caesaraugusta, is recommended to all enthusiasts. It is also recommended to visit the Mudejar Church of the Magdalena and, of course, the Palace of Aljafería, seat of Aragón's autonomous parliament. The town offers bicycle shops, restaurants, pharmacies, health centers, supermarkets, banks and a tourism office next to the basilica (www.zaragozaturismo.com). Tel.: 902 142 008 / 976 201 200.
Jesuit Fathers: At the Centro Pignatelli (Paseo de la Constitución, 6. Tel.: 976 217 221 and 976 217 217) we can find the Jesuit Fathers who work in this cultural and spiritual center and who will kindly sign or stamp our credentials if we come when the center is open, during office hours. Likewise, we can find more information on the places in Zaragoza associated with José Pignatelli or enjoy a Eucharistic celebration.

Nuestra Señora de El Pilar.

Note: Nuestra Señora de El Pilar. Tradition maintains that in the year 40 A.D. the Virgin Mary appeared to the apostle St. James, of whom it is said that he had come to Spain on mission to the pagan tribes of the time (no documental proof exists from the apostolic era of this missionary voyage of James to Spain, and the first references to it are found in manuscripts from the early Middle Ages). According to the tradition, while James rested near the Ebro, discouraged by his lack of success, the Virgin appeared to him on top of a pillar, encouraging him to persevere in his efforts, and asked him to raise a small chapel on that site to preserve the "pillar" or column which she would leave as testimony of her appearance. The chapel evolved into a Romanesque church and was rebuilt numerous times, passing through many styles,

including Mudejar. In 1518, after two centuries of labor, a reconstruction of the church in Gothic-Mudejar style was concluded.

We can imagine Ignatius, in 1522, having heard of the recently finished church, desired to come with affection to visit the new home of his venerated Virgin Mary. We do not have documental confirmation of his visit, but it is difficult to think that, coming through such an important city and in such extraordinary circumstances, he would not wish to enter the sanctuary and prostrate himself at the feet of our Lady, as was his custom.

■ TAXI
Zaragoza

Radio Taxi 24h	976 424 242
Cooperativa de Auto Taxi	976 751 414

■ LODGING
TORRES DE BERRELLÉN: Pilgrim's shelter (8 beds). City Hall. Tel.: 976 653 101. Café Aroa (Avenida Goya, 8) also has the keys to the hostel. Tel.: 976 653 866.

UTEBO: Don Juan inn, San Lamberto, 14. Tel.: 650 770 575. Silvio inn, Paseo Berbegal, 22. Tel.: 976 770 503. Pensión Arade, Las Parras 4. Tel.: 616 997 358. El Águila Hotel, Carretera Logroño, km 13,4. Tel.: 976 771 100. Europe Hotel, Ciudad de Ponce, 4. Tel.: 976 792 900. Las Ventas Hotel, Carretera Logroño, km 10,5. Tel.: 976 770 482. City Hall. Tel.: 976 770 111.

MONZALBARBA: City Hall. Tel.: 976 462 315.

ZARAGOZA: Pensión Iglesias, c/ Verónica, 14. Tel.: 976 293 161. San Jorge Hostel, c/ Mayor, 4. Tel.: 976 397 462. El Descanso Hostel, c/ San Lorenzo, 2. Tel.: 976 291 741. Pensión Manifestación. Tel.: 976 295 821 / 666 114 096. Zaragoza Youth Hostel, c/ Predicadores, 70. Tel.: 976 282 043. Baltasar Gracián Youth Hostel, c/ Franco y López, 4. Tel.: 976 306 690. Las Torres Hotel, Plaza de El Pilar, 11. Tel.: 976 394 250.

ZARAGOZA – FUENTES DE EBRO

(30.2 km)

«Give me only your love and your grace, oh Lord and I will be rich enough; I do not ask for more.»

«Open to me the gates of triumph and I will enter to give thanks to the Lord» (Ps 118:19).

The Cartuja Baja.

Each pilgrim will have probably slept in a different place in Zaragoza, so we will have to decide how to get to the exit point; on foot, by bus or taxi. Depending on where we lodged the day before up to 3 km can be added to the «official» calculation for this stage.

We leave from the Basilica of the Pillar and we walk along the Ebro River, keeping it on our left all the time. We are going to follow the Jacobean Camino del Ebro up to where it reaches the Cartuja Baja, using the so-called «Camino Natural la Alfranca». It is well marked and there are always many hikers. We will not get lost: after passing under the bridge over la Ronda de la Hispanidad (Z-30) bridge and after the beautiful white train bridge, we

follow the signs of La Alfranca and, a few km later, we arrive at La Cartuja, which deserves a short stop and maybe some breakfast in the bar.

We continue along this stage on the dirt paths which keep us next to the A-68. They're a bit elevated so we are able to contemplate the Ebro valley in all of its spacious splendor. We arrive at Burgo de Ebro. Right in the middle of town, the plaza La Paz has a fountain to slake the thirst of the pilgrims. Leaving town, we continue to our left staying on the elevated path which offers us the view of the valley.

Be careful not to lose the correct way since, on arriving at an electrical tower,

We also go close by the archeological site of La Cabañeta where Roman artifacts from the 2nd century have been found. We continue straight ahead, always on the same path which skirts the valley from above until going through a tunnel of the ARA-1 freeway, next to an irrigation canal, and we head towards the industrial park «El Espartal». We go through the park, walking next to the canal and, at the end, we take the road marked «Cañada Real Las Peñas». From this point on, the town of Fuentes de Ebro comes into view in the distance. We take a dirt path which directs us straight towards it. Before crossing an asphalt bridge, we turn to our left on a dirt path which leads us next to the train tracks. We follow the rails until finding a bridge which crosses the tracks and we head to the center of the town. Easy end of stage.

we take a path to our left which follows the edge of the embankment and passes by the chapel of la Virgin de la Columna.

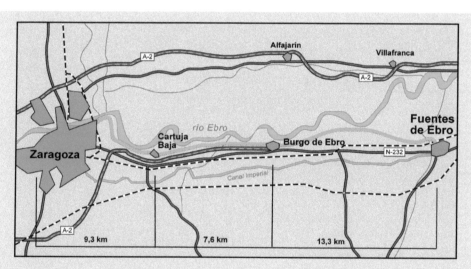

Total upward slope: 144 m. Total downward slope: 292 m.
Bicycles: easy.

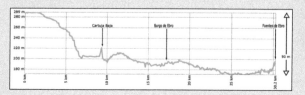

Zaragoza (El Pilar):	km 0
Cartuja Baja:	km 9.3
Burgo de Ebro:	km 16.9
Fuentes de Ebro:	km 30.2

■ Description

The starting point is the Basilica of the Pillar and we head towards the promenade by the Ebro River, keeping it on our left the whole time. We walk along the Paseo de Echegaray y Caballero, under the bridge of Camino de las Torres, until we pass under the bridge of the Ronda de la Hispanidad and then we go straight along the dirt path called «Camino Natural La Alfranca». We are guided securely by the signs marking the GR-99 and the posts pointing towards La Alfranca. Five km from Zaragoza we pass under the Z-40 bridge. We continue by the river, avoiding the side paths. With the river beside us, we reach a crossroads where we turn 90 degrees to our right: it is well marked and the bell tower of Cartuja Baja can be seen just 800 m ahead of us. We reach the main façade of the Cartuja and turn right, taking the Camino de los Muros (Camino of the Walls), which will lead us towards Burgo de Ebro.

We take the dirt road that starts ahead of us and we follow it 500 m until we cross a tunnel.

Continue straight on the dirt track. The road forks: we go up to the right, following the GR signs. Continue straight ahead without turning onto any side roads. After 2 km, we meet the railway and the highway on our right. Pass close to them by a bridge

and then continue straight on. We are in the industrial zone of Galacho.

We go straight on, parallel to the highway. We arrive at a roundabout. If we were to go under the highway we would enter the town of Torre de Barracón but we will not. Rather, we go straight on, parallel to the highway which ends here and becomes the N-232 road. Following it, we reach Burgo de Ebro.

The same Castellón road that allowed us to leave Zaragoza is the one that takes us to Burgo, going through the town from one side to the other. We continue on the same road and, at the exit, next to some sport facilities (swimming pools, football ground), an asphalt track starts on the left, leading to a pinewood park. After that we continue straight up on our right. In 1 km, we come to a fork with an electrical tower: we take the road to the left. We carry on, walking along the

way that turns into a wide bend to go around the residential area of Virgen de la Columna, whose shrine is on our right.

We pass near the archaeological site of La Cabañeta, where Roman remains from the 2th century B.C. were found. We leave them on our left and we continue straight on. At the crossroads we continue straight on. We pass under the bridge that carries the ARA-1 highway across the irrigation canal that is on our left. We enter the industrial park «El Espartal». We follow the canal which is always on our left. When we reach a small bridge over the canal, we take the asphalt road that starts on our right. We are in the «Cañada Real las Peñas».

At the end of the industrial park, the road turns right but we continue straight ahead and we cross the water canal. We can see Fuentes de Ebro ahead of us. We will follow the same dirt road straight ahead to the town until we find a

Chapel of the Virgen de la Columna.

the bridge, on our left, a road begins which guides us directly to the town.

The road leads us to the railway line. We follow the tracks in the direction of Fuentes. We pass between two buildings and approach the bridge over the railroad. We cross it and enter the town.

paved bridge crossing the railway line. We do not cross it but at 250 m from

Continuing along calle Francisco de los Ríos, we find the N-232 which goes through the village.

Interesting facts

LA CARTUJA: At one time a monastery dedicated to the Immaculate Conception (17th c.). Today the galleries of the cloister serve as walkways and the Carthusians' cells have become dwellings. It contains a restaurant, health center, supermarket and bank.

BURGO DE EBRO: In this small town one can find a restaurant, health center, pharmacy, supermarket and bank.

Church of San Miguel, Fuentes de Ebro.

FUENTES DE EBRO: It is worth paying a visit to the church, dedicated to San Miguel Arcángel, with its beautiful 18th century Eucharistic monument to Jueves Santo (Holy Thursday) in the chapel of Nuestra Señora del Rosario. With around 4,600 inhabitants, it offers restaurants, pharmacy, health center, supermarkets and a bank.

Note: Stages 17 to 19: the north wind and the Monegros. A little past Zaragoza, the Camino Ignaciano enters a semi-desert landscape: the Monegros. The name appears to derive from the juniper bushes which, with their dark trunks and needles, give color to the Monegros' «black hills» and, consequently, to the entire region. At present, irrigation is transforming large swaths of the Monegros into arable land but, for the most part, this region is dry, extremely hot in the summer and bitterly cold in the winter and the number of stores and lodging establishments is almost negligible.

Probably, in Ignatius' day, there were not many more people than now. As you walk, try to imagine him next to you, with his mule and his gimpy leg, advancing little by little in this vast and solitary wasteland. Ignatius left his house in Loyola at the end of January or the beginning of February, crossing the Monegros at the end of winter. Nighttime temperatures in this part of Spain would have been around freezing and the north wind could be extremely intense. These strong winds (el cierzo), characteristic of the Ebro valley and already documented during the Roman era, can blow in gusts of up to 100 km/h in the winter and early spring. The peasants build stone barriers to protect crops from wind erosion and pilgrims can easily suffer its rigors.

Pilgrims should not underestimate these inhospitable surroundings. It is highly advisable to carry enough water to surmount the distance between Pina de Ebro and Bujaraloz. It must be remembered that at the end of stage 17 there is no lodging, so it is necessary to sleep on the ground, passing the night under the starlight.

Pilgrims who are not in good physical shape might consider taking a bus from Zaragoza to Bujaraloz and continue on from there. As another alternative, this 16th stage could be completed by taking a bus back from Fuentes de Ebro to Zaragoza and then taking a bus from Zaragoza to Bujaraloz the next day. Another possibility is to do the stage normally and, once in Venta de Santa Lucía, call a taxi from Pina de Ebro or Bujaraloz and take it to the next pueblo to bed down. It is also possible to take a municipal bus (www. agredasa.es) that halts in Venta de Santa Lucía at 15:30, headed for Bujaraloz.

In spite of all these warnings, it is most likely that the pilgrim who crosses the

Monegros on foot will have one of the most remarkable experiences of the Camino Ignaciano, something totally unimaginable for the pilgrims on the bus who whiz by this landscape at 120 km/h. That remarkable privilege will be a profound solidarity with Ignatius, who crossed this region alone when it was much more isolated and desolate than it is now. One cannot but try to imagine the thoughts and feelings that came to him in such a solitary spot. Still, today, pilgrims will be intensely aware of the deep silence which reigns on this stretch of the Camino: excellent surroundings to listen to the most profound thoughts of one's own soul.

■ TAXI
Fuentes de Ebro
Taxi Sonia Rubio   627 574 290

■ LODGING
FUENTES DE EBRO: San Miguel Hostel, c/ de Trinque, 8. Tel.: 976 169 071. Patio Hostel, c/ de los Sitios, 37. Tel.: 976 161 065. Texas Hostel, c/ Mayor, 15. Tel.: 976 160 419. Elena Hostel, Avenida Santiago Lapuente, 9-11 (discount for pilgrims). Tel.: 976 160 267 / 628 478 199. City Hall. Tel.: 976 169 100. (Pool is free for pilgrims).

Fuentes de Ebro – Venta de Santa Lucía
(29.6 km)

«The more desperate a situation seems, the more we must trust in God; when human help fails, God is near.»

«My feet avoid all the evil ways, in order to observe your word. [...] I reflect on your decrees, hence I detest every false path» (Ps 119:101.104).

Plaza de España, Pina de Ebro.

We begin the stage with firm resolve. This may be the most dreaded stage of the entire Camino Ignaciano but we can overcome it with a good pilgrim spirit which seeks austerity and solitude.

We bid farewell to Fuentes de Ebro and, today, we take our leave of the Ebro Camino de Santiago which has brought us from Logroño. Our Camino Ignaciano now follows the Camino Real which Ignatius of Loyola took in his pilgrimage to Montserrat and which coincides also, in inverse direction, with the Catalan Camino de Santiago.

We leave on calle Mayor and go down to the highway on calle Ramón y Cajal. We cross the highway and continue straight to the right and, in a few meters, again turn right on calle Baño. We will continue straight ahead on this street which becomes a path and, on arriving at a stone quarry, takes us under the tracks of the High Speed («AVE») Train. On the other side is the bridge over the tracks of the conventional train. We cross them and continue parallel to these rails for 3 km.

We reach a point where a road crosses the tracks, but we do not cross over the tracks; instead, we move away from the tracks and, with three successive turns to the left, we head to the edge of the Ebro River. Be careful with these turns because there are no signs on the path. In this point the river is once again majestic. In 2015, the river overflowed here and swept away the path, but the path was rebuilt again in 2016: this is an ongoing story with the Ebro. We follow the course of the river to the bridge, which allows us to cross to the town of Pina de Ebro. In the church plaza we stock up on water and something to eat and then continue on our way, going out to the main road on calle Fernando el Católico. We continue up the asphalt road, passing an agricultural co-op and the cemetery behind it.

We take the dirt path which goes to the industrial park. The white hermitage of San Gregorio perches high on our right. We arrive at the park and go around it to the right looking for some electrical towers and a dirt path which ascends towards the hills of the Monegros. A large cut-out of a black bull, on the horizon serves us a reference.

The sparse vegetation bears witness to the harsh climate of this region. We do not find any trees or shelter to protect us from the sun. It is necessary to be prepared for what awaits us. In the summer, the sun heats the earth and the air to more than 40 degrees C (105° F) and we are not going to find any water fountains. In winter, the nights can be very cold. A strong fragrance of rosemary and other aromatic plants accompanies us along the way, and hares and rabbits constantly appear, jumping out, almost from under our feet.

Up on top of the Monegros plateau, and after passing some large sheep corrals which serve as references, we take the path to the left and continue straight. Pay attention during this stretch of stage 17. It can be a bit difficult to keep on the right path since there are quite a few forks and very few signs.

The place we are headed to is next to the national road, N-II, which is always on our left. In case of doubt or straying, it is best to turn to the left and go straight until coming to the highway N-II which, heading to our right, will then take us into la Venta de Santa Lucía.

At last we reach the end of stage 17. There is nowhere for pilgrims to put up so we will have to sleep out, under the stars. We have to find a smooth, level, spot on the ground and lie down, calmly awaiting the moonrise.

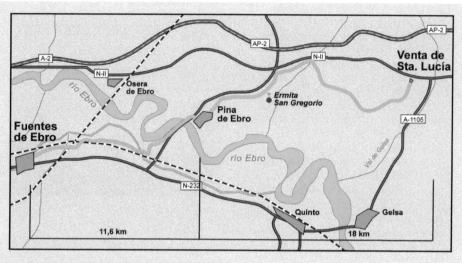

Total upward slope: 266 m. Total downward slope: 186 m.
Bicycles: easy, but the climb to the plateau of Los Monegros is a bit steep.

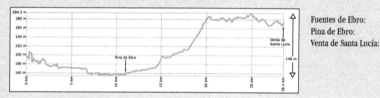

Fuentes de Ebro:	km 0
Pina de Ebro:	km 11.6
Venta de Santa Lucía:	km 29.6

■ Description

From the church door we take the calle Mayor before us and we follow it until we reach calle Ramón y Cajal, which starts on the left, and we follow it. We arrive at the national highway and cross it, following the street straight ahead until it forks. We take the right fork, Avenida Lorenzo Pardo. Pay attention because we have to turn right in 250 meters on calle Baño. Keep going the same way until we arrive at a tunnel which passes under the high speed «AVE» train line. Be alert because, on reaching a stone quarry, we find a fork at which we must turn right to reach the AVE railway line (the path to the left leads to a tunnel under the conventional railway).

After the tunnel, the road takes us to a bridge above the Zaragoza-Barcelona railway. We cross it and turn right to take the dirt road parallel to the conventional railway. Go straight ahead along the tracks for the next 3 km. In a few meters, we pass under a bridge and later we pass a railroad crossing on our right. We always continue straight on.

A road joins us on the right but we keep bearing left. In 100 meters we turn left, entering a new path, and then turn left again within a few meters. Walking straight ahead we reach the Ebro River, and we continue along its shore by turning to our right.

We carry on straight ahead. We reach A-1107 road and there we turn left to cross the bridge. From here onwards, we leave the Ebro Camino de Santiago and follow the Catalan Camino de Santiago. Right after crossing the bridge we take a right turn, and we arrive in Pina de Ebro. We enter Pina de Ebro, looking for the church and the main plaza with its city hall (which is on our right, near the river). Here we need to regain our strength in one of the many bar-restaurants in the plaza. We must pick up water reserves for the section that we still have to walk today and perhaps part of the next stage tomorrow.

To leave the town, we look for calle Fernando el Católico, off the plaza down the street from the church. We take the calle Fernando el Católico to the left and leave the village to find ourselves on the asphalt road, heading for the N-II national highway. A large warehouse belonging to Pina de Ebro's agricultural cooperative serves as a guide: the COOPINA sign is clearly visible. After another 1.5 km, we reach the Agricultural Cooperative and take the dirt road that runs parallel to the motorway.

We pass the cooperative and the village cemetery on our right. The church of San Gregorio appears high up on our right. Our road reaches an irrigation canal and we leave the motorway, taking the dirt road marked «Mirador de San Gregorio». We walk along the dirt road, but

do not take the road to San Gregorio: instead we continue on until we reach the industrial zone's asphalt street which lies ahead of us. We take the downhill road to our right. At the first street we meet, we turn left and follow it towards some large electrical pylons. We see orange arrows on the lampposts along the street.

We reach an intersection next to a high voltage transmission tower. A dirt road opens on our right, next to the tower and we take it. We find electricity poles along the road and, in front of us, the figure of a large black bull, like a billboard-cutout, greets us. We are getting closer to the black bull. We continue straight until we reach the N-II motorway which will now be our new companion along our Camino.

We do not cross the motorway but turn right to take a road which takes us away from the N-II for a while. We go up towards the Los Monegros plateau. We continue straight, following our dirt road that winds through the fields. We make no deviation. At 2.8 km from the N-II, we reach the level of Los Monegros plateau and can see some fairly large livestock stables on the left. On reaching the stables, the road forks: we take the left fork and continue straight on.

Within a kilometer from the stable there is a new fork in the road; we take the right fork. Continue ahead for 1.8 km until the road forks again and take the left. In about one km, there is a new fork in the road; we now take the road to the right to climb the slope. Go straight ahead on the main road, ignoring the side roads leading to the fields on either side. We are getting closer to the N-II. The road brings us into the rear of the village of Venta de Santa Lucía.

Interesting facts

We began with a series of stages that are not the Camino Ignaciano's easiest. The stages near Loyola in the Basque Country were hard, with steep slopes and cold in the winter. Now we face the so-called «Monegros Desert». We must be careful not to fall into the trap of wanting to pass through it «running» as quickly as possible. Parts of it are difficult; you have to go at your own pace, neither faster nor slower than necessary. If at any stage of the Camino Ignaciano you are going to choose to sleep romantically under the open sky, it will be in the «Monegros Desert». Also, water is scarce there and it will be difficult to have a daily shower! Each pilgrim has to find his own way.

PINA DE EBRO: This is the last village on the Catalan Camino de Santiago (the first for us). The Franciscan monastery of San Salvador (16th-17th c.) has the Moorish style which we saw before reaching Zaragoza. In this village of over 2,000 people, one can find a restaurant, pharmacy, supermarket and bank. City Hall. Tel.: 976 165 007.

VENTA DE SANTA LUCIA: Restaurant. There are no accommodations here.

National Highway N-II, km 372.3. Tel.: 976 162 001. It is wise to call from Pina de Ebro to the restaurant to make sure it is open and can provide water and a dinner. If there is no answer, it would be better to buy food and drink in Pina and be ready for dinner and breakfast in the open air. There is a possibility of taking the bus at Venta (at 15:30, www.agredasa.es) and heading to Bujaraloz, skipping the next stage. This bus line reaches all towns between Zaragoza and Lleida, proving very handy for pilgrims.

◼ TAXI
Pina de Ebro
Taxi José María Franco   618 543 767

Bujaraloz
Taxi Carlos   608 782 616

◼ LODGING
PINA DE EBRO: Pensión Los Valles, Magisterio Nacional, 7.
Tel.: 976 165 553 / 675 721 711.
City Hall. Tel.: 976 165 007

VENTA DE SANTA LUCÍA: No lodging available.

VENTA DE SANTA LUCÍA – BUJARALOZ
(21.3 km)

«Guard against condemning the action of any person. Consider the intention of your neighbor, who is often honest and innocent, even when his action seems wrong to you from external appearances.»

«The wilderness and the desert will rejoice, the wasteland will gladly blossom, like the daffodil it will bloom, overflowing with joy and happiness […]. They will see the glory of the Lord, the beauty of our God» (Is 35:1-3).

If we have slept under the stars, it will surely be easy to get up early and get underway, even without sunlight. The path separates us from the highway N-II which has too much traffic for pilgrims. At the same time, however, this highway will serve to orient us. It follows the original pilgrims' Camino Real which has connected town after town, along the route, for centuries.

The Camino Ignaciano always runs parallel to the N-II until reaching Bujaraloz, first following it on our left and then, 5 km after passing the gas station, on our right.

We continue walking towards the rising sun. The aroma of the plants along the path and the hares jumping and running from under our feet help us to enjoy this relatively short stage. We cannot lose our way along this path and our arrival to Bujaraloz comes very easily: a rest stop which helps us replenish the strength which was depleted on the last section.

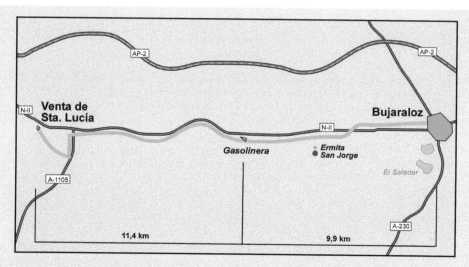

Total upward slope: 191 m. Total downward slope: 135 m.
Bicycles: easy.

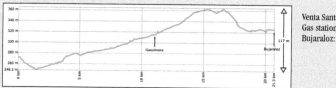

Venta Santa Lucía:	km 0
Gas station:	km 11.4
Bujaraloz:	km 21.3

■ Description

We wake up and we have to make a decision: either (1) to follow the N-II road on our right; or (2) take the road marked with orange arrows which takes us away from the N-II. After 1 km along the N-II, the first option will join with the second; the second option, however, does not reach the same point until after a walk of 3 km. The advantage of the second option over the first is that it avoids the N-II but taking it means we have to walk on asphalt for an additional 1.5 km after leaving the dirt track. It is up to the pilgrim to decide.

If you follow the N-II (1st option), just go straight, being very careful of the traffic. After 1 km, we intersect with those who have come the other way. This is at the junction with a road coming from Quinto to Venta de Santa Lucía.

If we follow the second option along the dirt road, we take the road to our right that brings us away from the national

highway (N-II). We keep going ahead without any deviation until we reach the A-1105 road which comes from Quinto. At this point, we take a left on the A-1105 and we turn back toward the N-II.

After 50 m on the N-II, we take a dirt road on our right and continue straight on, without taking any of the intersections that cross it. If in doubt, we must continue as parallel as possible to the N-II, which serves as a guide, always on our left.

We arrive at a gas station (Gasolinera). Leaving the gas station, we follow

Bujaraloz.

the dirt road in the same direction as before. We walk parallel to the N-II, keeping it on our left. At 5 km after the gas station, our dirt road crosses the N-II and we continue

parallel to it but now with the N-II to our right. Keep on without any deviation, following the N-II as far as Bujaraloz where we take calle Santiago to the plaza Mayor.

◼ Interesting facts

BUJARALOZ: A small town, population of about 1000 inhabitants. Its baroque church is dedicated to the apostle, St. James, although the town's patron is San Agustín. It is said that at one time San Fabián and San Sebastián were the patrons of Bujaraloz. But these holy patrons did nothing when a terrible plague of locusts came from Africa, so the people of Bujaraloz decided to find another patron saint that would defend them from the locusts. They put ballot papers into a box with the names of candidates for patron saints. They pulled out a ballot at random three times and, each time, the name of San Agustín came out. The odd thing is that the name of San Agustín had not been written on any of the papers by the citizens. Bujaraloz is called the «capital» of the Monegros, which comprises 31 municipalities. Its services include a restaurant, supermarket, pharmacy and bank.

About 10 km south of Bujaraloz we find a peculiar landscape dotted with numerous salt ponds (Los Saladares) that in summer due to the effect of evaporation become wide stretches of salt. «Laguna de la Playa» (Lake of the Beach), on the road to Sástago, is the largest lake (an area of 2 by 3 km).

◼ TAXI
Bujaraloz
Taxi Jesús   976 173 104
Taxi Agustín   976 173 551

◼ LODGING
BUJARALOZ: La Parrilla Monegros II Hostel, Carretera N-II, km 390,5. Tel.: 976 173 230. El Español Hostel (reduced fare for pilgrims and breakfast from 6:30 a.m.), Carretera N-II, km 390. Tel.: 976 173 192 / 976 173 043. Las Sabinas Hostel, c/ Santa Ana, 6-8. Tel.: 976 179 328. City Hall. Tel.: 976 173 175.

BUJARALOZ – CANDASNOS
(21 km)

«Do not undertake anything without consulting God.»

«For waters will burst forth in the wilderness and streams in the Arabah. The burning sands will become pools and the thirsty ground, springs of water… A highway will cross there called the holy way… It will be for his people; none shall go astray … for those rescued by the Lord shall return upon it, entering Zion singing songs of joy, crowned with everlasting happiness. Their sorrow and mourning shall disappear» (Is 35:6-10).

Peñalba.

Again, we have a short and easy stage to follow. The farm road which we take out of Bujaraloz leaves the N-II off to our right until we reach the next town, Peñalba.

Our path goes through fields and is far enough away from the highway that we can enjoy the silence and a very relaxed atmosphere. At times we have to climb a slope but, for the most part, we keep to level ground or we descend. We arrive at Peñalba from the rear of town. We approach the church and from it walk down to the canal. We cross the bridge and head to the next bridge which we cross under. Our path keeps parallel to the canal.

We come close to some farms and, after a small lagoon with ducks, some power lines serve as our reference as we take a path to the left going up a steep slope until reaching the N-II. We do not cross it, but follow it, keeping it always to our left for reference until reaching Candasnos.

After passing a small bridge over a stream, we continue straight ahead, but with open eyes because the path is in very bad shape and easy to lose. The point of reference is always the N-II. We cannot get lost and we can always walk this stretch along the N-II, in spite of the heavy traffic.

After this, we come to a fruit store and a source of water. Soon we can see the town of Candasnos in the distance. We go on as always, straight ahead and arrive without problems.

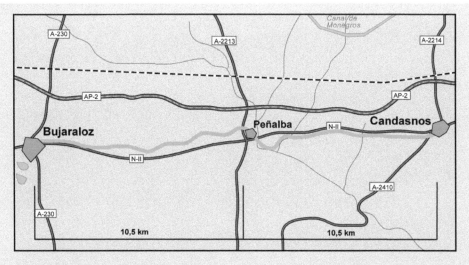

Total upward slope: 203 m. Total downward slope: 258 m.
Bicycles: easy, although there is a small stretch of 300 meters on the Cañada Real between Peñalba and Candasnos where the road almost disappears and becomes a path. Maintaining balance on the bike will be difficult. It is better to take the national road.

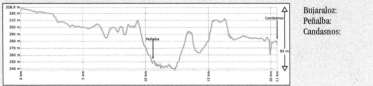

Bujaraloz:	km 0
Peñalba:	km 10.5
Candasnos:	km 21

■ Description

We leave the center of town, reaching calle Baja and passing in front of the Shrine of Nuestra Señora de la Misericordia. We go straight to the N-II. We will continue along an asphalt country road, parallel to the N-II, keeping it on our right. Some industrial buildings are on the left. We go straight ahead.

Candasnos.

We always carry on straight without taking any of the junctions that we frequently come across. Three km from Bujaraloz, the path diverges and we take the left one; the right one climbs upward to some heights. Next to a farm on our left, our path merges with another one which we take to our right. After 250 meters, we come to a fork and we take the one to our left. Two km further we come to road A-2213 and we turn right, just for some few meters, as very soon we take the asphalt road starting on the left.

The asphalt becomes dirt. We go down the hill and, at the bottom, we take a road to the right that goes to the village of Peñalba which we can now see at the end of the road. We reach the village and we take the street that turns towards the left, to the church and the town hall. We take the road to our left and head to another canal and the bridge that crosses it. After crossing the bridge, we turn to our right and follow the canal to the bridge carrying the N-II.

We pass underneath this bridge, crossing the N-ll, and continue straight onto an asphalt road that we take, without crossing the canal. We continue straight on and the asphalt changes to dirt. To our left are farms and the silhouette

of a black bull up on a hill. We continue straight on the level path. We pass a lake which we leave on our right. Soon we come to an electrical pole and we take the road that goes off to our left up to the top of the hill. Electrical poles line the road.

In the end, we arrive at the top and also at the national highway (N-II). We do not cross the highway but we take a dirt

road on our right which parallels it. It descends for a little ways and then starts up again through an area with trees. Our advice for bikers and walkers is to consider avoiding this last climb, especially if recent weather has been wet,because it may not be in great condition (One recent pilgrim found it fine, and better than the alternative road, which is sometimes busy with trucks). To avoid the last climb: after descending the initial slope, you follow the N-II highway back up. This section is about 500 m. Proceed very carefully because of the heavy truck traffic. Once this way up is completed, there is a rest area with a fruit shop. At this point, we can again take the parallel dirt road, next to the N-II highway. The signs will guide us. We arrive at a little bridge over the little river. We cross over it and follow it, always staying on the surface road next to the N-II. Close to the village of Candasnos, we follow the road which enters the town.

Interesting facts

Once again, we will find there are no trees or shade.

PEÑALBA: A small village, in which we can find a restaurant, supermarket, pharmacy and bank.

CANDASNOS: Small population of 500 inhabitants. Its church, which is dedicated to Santa María de la Asunción, was first built in the 12th century in Romanesque style, using cut stone (you can still see the stonemasons' marks on them). This Romanesque style was distinguished by a high nave and semi-circular apse. What is remarkable about this temple is its transition to the Gothic, characteristic of the fourteenth century. More than half way up, the temple's brick construction begins; the apse changes from a semicircle to a polygon, marked by windows with pointed arches. We find a restaurant, supermarket and bank. There is a possibility of taking the bus (bus stop is close to the church) at 16:00 (www.agredasa.es) and heading to Fraga, skipping the next stage. This bus line reaches all the towns between Zaragoza and Lleida, proving very handy for pilgrims.

■ TAXI
Candasnos

Taxi Juan	600 485 020
Taxista Fraga	693 359 450

■ LODGING
PEÑALBA: Casa rural El Balsetón, c/ del Carmen, 24. Tel.: 649 545 450.

CANDASNOS: El Pilar inn (very often closed and sometimes reluctant to accept pilgrims), c/ Zaragoza, 13. Tel.: 974 463 017. No official pilgrim shelter in Candasnos! The City Hall may be willing to suggest a possibility: Tel.: 974 463 001 Alternatively, the bus company Agredasa currently has busses to Fraga at 4PM and 8PM.

CANDASNOS – FRAGA

(26.8 km)

«Let he who is rich strive to possess his goods instead of being possessed by them.»

«I trod a smooth path because from youth I sought wisdom» (Si 51:15).

Fraga.

Today's stage is long but relatively easy since, for the most part, it is flat and we have a long downhill at the end. On the other hand, we will not encounter any intermediate towns so we have to think about carrying enough water and sun protection.

We leave Candasnos, going out by the municipal swimming pools and staying parallel to the N-II. The path is good and impossible to lose. We come to the bridge over the freeway and on the other side we see the Hotel La Cruzanzana. We follow the dirt path which runs parallel to the N-II, always straight ahead. Again the hares jump out as we go by and we see them quickly disappear into their warrens.

At some 6 km from our departure, our path crosses the highway thanks to a tunnel. On the other side of the tunnel,

we turn to the right to go up to a wide dirt path which runs parallel to the N-II, which will now stay on our right until we reach Fraga.

We leave the wide path and continue on another one, less well defined but continuing straight, in the same direction, parallel to the N-II. We pass by a gas station, where we can buy food and water, if needed (there is also a restaurant at the gas station on the opposite side of the highway). We continue on our way, always straight ahead with no chance of getting lost.

We come to the end of the Monegros plateau and we see the Cinca river valley, opening splendidly ahead of us. The N-II begins a steep descent which we are not going to follow; we turn away from it to our left.

Here, we look for some electrical towers and a dirt path which skirts around the height of the mesa. Another electrical tower serves as our reference for following the path which now descends towards Fraga. We cannot lose our way on the path but we have to turn to the left at the first crossroads and, 200 m later, we have to turn right at the next one. We must pay attention to the directional arrows.

Fraga appears imposingly in front of us. We enter on the Avenida de Aragón, which leads us directly to the bridge over the Cinca and to the old quarter. The supermarkets are in this first zone; the church and the town hall in the old section.

Cinca river.

We are sure to feel the taste of victory at the end of this stage, after having crossed the Monegros. But the next stage will also be a bit long and rough-going at the beginning, so we have to get prepared and gather strength.

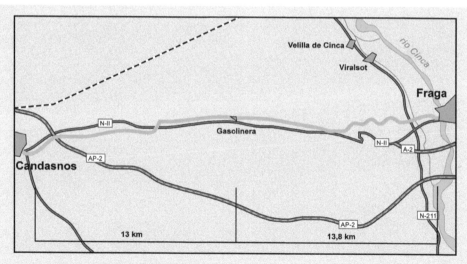

Total upward slope: 214 m. Total downward slope: 361 m.
Bicycles: easy, although the descent from the Monegros plateau is steep and some sections of the road have deep grooves because of the rain.

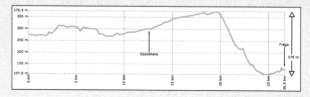

Candasnos:	km 0
Gasolinera:	km 13
Fraga:	km 26.8

Description

From the center of town, we go out by the calle de la Balsa del Tejar, which is next to the church. We pass the city baths on our right and we continue straight, keeping the N-II on our left. We enter the Cañada Real, which begins as an asphalt road and then becomes dirt.

A bridge brings us across the AP-2 or Autopista del Nordeste (Northeast Highway). To our left we see the Hotel Cruzanzana. Continue parallel to the N-II, which is on our left. Three kilometers from the bridge we cross the N-II through a tunnel and climb to the right to find a path and continue walking parallel to N-II, but now it is on our right. We continue straight ahead, at times going a little away from the N-II but always in sight of it. We pass a petrol station and continue straight. A line of electricity poles serves as a guide.

We reach a bar here with food available, El Ventorrillo, and we are back by the N-II. We continue along the side of the N-II and soon take a road to the left which will bring us away from the N-II. It stays on the plateau, while the N-II goes down to the Cinca valley. Our road divides: take the right, leaving the left, next to an electrical tower. The road provides a magnificent view of the valley. Passing a small stone building, we again find a fork in the road at the foot of an electrical tower; we take the right, downhill. A yellow arrow on the left reminds us we are still going «against the flow».

We continue by way of a sharp descent. Just before we reach the plain, our road ends in another one which we take to our left. We continue straight for approximately 200 m and turn right onto another road that starts here and descends to Fraga. Red and white signs help us to follow the right road but be careful and do not forget to turn right because the white and red marks continue straight on which is not the right direction for us. Our road brings us straight down to Fraga. We reach the highway and turn right. After 100 m we find a roundabout which indicates «N-II to Lérida». We enter the city on the N-II which becomes the beautiful Avenida de Aragón. Straight ahead, we reach the Cinca River. The Camino Ignaciano continues across the river, in the old quarter, close to the City Hall.

■ Interesting facts

FRAGA: With more than 13,000 inhabitants, this is the largest population center on the lower Cinca River. Iberian in origin, with nearby Roman ruins, and a clear role in the history of the reconquest of Aragón, Fraga was granted city status by Philip V in 1709. La Torre de los Frailes (Friars' Tower), which has been well restored, was built by the Templars in 1128. Its 12th century Romanesque church is dedicated to St. Peter and was built on the site of an earlier mosque. The town's layout reflects the Arabian tradition with adobe houses which can still be seen in some areas. Near the old docks along the riverbanks, there was a shipyard for building and repairing boats. The town's buildings are very interesting: the casa de Junqueras, the governor's palace, the home of the Piarist religious congregation and many others, all Gothic in the style of the 16th and 17th centuries. It is also worth visiting Fraga's museum, located at the palacio Moncada c/ San José de Calasanz, 12. Tel.: 974 472 533), a 17th century structure that has recently been renovated. You can find everything you need in Fraga: restaurants, supermarkets, health centers, banks, bike shops, pharmacies and an information office (Tel.: 974 470 050).

■ TAXI
Fraga

Taxi Fraga 24h	931 780 030
Taxi Eugenio	690 627 475
Taxi Romera SL	974 471 673

■ LODGING
FRAGA: Aribau Hostel, Avenida de Madrid, 25. Tel.: 974 471 887. Oasis Hostel, Carretera Nacional II, km 442. Tel.: 974 470 654. Trébol Hostel, Avenida de Aragón, 9. Tel.: 974 471 533. Olles inn, Avenida de Madrid, 33. Tel.: 974 453 834. City Hall. Tel.: 974 470 050. With a pilgrim's certificate, available in the parish office (Tel.: 974 470 183 / 974 470 865), or at the sisters who manage the senior citizens home in Fraga, it is possible to have a reduced price in Hostal Trebol or stay for free in bungalows at the Fraga camping-restaurant, which is 1 kilometer outside of town, walking up Soses street.

Fraga.

FRAGA – LLEIDA
(33 km)

«When the devil wants to attack someone, the first thing he does is ascertain which flank is the weakest, or where the defenses are less well disposed, and then brings his artillery to open a breach at that point.»

«As I was with Moses I will be with you; I will not leave you or abandon you. [...] Be brave and of good cheer to fulfill all that my servant Moses commands you; do not swerve to the right or to the left, and you will be successful in all of your endeavors» (Jos 1:5-7).

La Seu Vella, Lleida.

Again we confront a long stage in order to be able to join the two large cities of Fraga and Lérida, or Lleida in Catalan. In effect, we now enter into Cataluña, the last of the autonomous regions we will traverse to reach our destination. The landscape turns much greener, with large numbers of fruit trees which will accompany us in some of our future stages. Likewise, joining the Segre River gives us another reason to be happy after the aridity of the recent days.

We leave Fraga going up towards the N-II and we pass near the cemetery. We follow the national road until reaching a sign which indicates the direction of the «Campo de Tiro Las Acacias». We go up this road to avoid going through the N-II's tunnel. After reaching the top, we go down the other side towards the industrial park which is under construction. We cross a large plot of land which has not yet been built on and, finally, head towards the hotel which we see in front of us. We continue along the side of the freeway, which always stays to our right.

At the roundabout we enter Cataluña and discover the first of the large wooden signposts that will accompany us to Manresa. We climb the hill in front of us and go down the other side to find the freeway once again. The path changes from asphalt to dirt and back to asphalt.

We come to a bridge marked with the sign «Camino Real», which reminds us of the historical route on which we are walking. We cross it and continue on the path to the side and parallel to the freeway, which is now on our right. We approach an industrial park. We follow the signposts which lead us across the fields to the village of Alcarràs, a small but socially dynamic town.

We leave Alcarràs on the Avenida del Onze de Setembre, following the signs which take us to an asphalt path that, crossing the fields, brings us again near the N-II. We come to a shopping zone. Once past it, we take the path which leads us, finally, to the entrance of a cattle farm and, from there, to the town of Butsènit. Just beyond the church, a right hand turn brings us down a dirt path to the Segre River.

We follow the river on its course towards the city of Lleida, feeling the proximity of the water. If it is the right season, storks, ducks and swans will not fail to show up for their date with the pilgrim! We do not cross the river but always keep to the same bank. We enter the city next to the river and, very close to the first bridges we find the parish of San Ignacio.

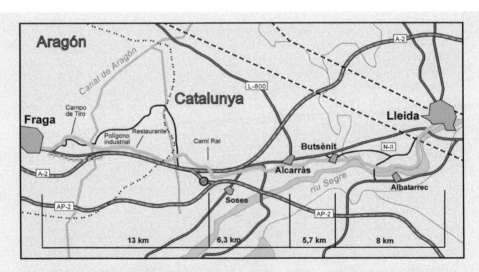

Total upward slope: 265 m. Total downward slope: 233 m.
Bicycles: easy, although the way out of Fraga is very steep and you must watch out for where the highway crosses when going through the «Campo de Tiro Las Acacias» (Acacias Shooting Range). If you go through the tunnel you do not have to cross. Further ahead, you must be careful not to enter the service road in the wrong direction. See the alternatives in the detailed description of the stage.

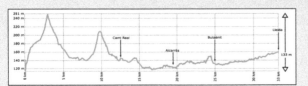

Fraga:	km 0
Camí Real:	km 13
Alcarràs:	km 19.3
Butsènit:	km 25
Lleida:	km 33

Description

We leave Fraga from the plaza de España, where the Town Hall is located. Standing on Paseo de Barrón Segoñe, facing the Town Hall, we find calle Obradores Revolt on our left, going up a steep hill. We take this street up the hill until we reach the N-II. Then we take the white bridge as far as the cemetery and, from there, continue on the road running parallel to the N-II. Our journey takes us up, climbing out of Fraga. We can also continue travelling parallel to the N-II on the right hand side of the highway, without crossing over.

Whichever side of the road we travel along, we reach a sign that reads «Campo de Tiro Las Acacias», indicating an asphalt track bearing left. This track has the advantage of leading us away from traffic, although it rises steeply and then descends back down. Cyclists can continue straight along the N-II for a couple of km, avoiding the climb, until they take, after a small tunnel, the service road indicated by the road signs. We are not to enter the A-2 freeway. We descend from the bridge and, arriving at a roundabout, we turn left, to go through the A-2 underpass. A sign reads «Zona Industrial». Entering the industrial area and taking the first road on the right, cyclists will link up with those on foot. This is where those who decided to walk along the «Campo de Tiro Las Acacias» would arrive. These pilgrims, having followed the orange arrows on the asphalt to the top of the track, would continue the route as it bends left, as far as the fork in the path. From this vantage point, the yellow poles from the gas company ENDESA GAS would be visible to the right and would lead the pilgrims to the industrial zone. On entering the industrial area, they would take the first road in front of them which runs parallel to the A-2 on the right. In 2 km they would come to the roundabout which is the meeting place of the two routes.

We enter the roundabout from the right and exit at the second asphalt path, signed «Service Road». A STOP sign painted on the asphalt indicates the route we must take around the back of a hostel-restaurant. Once there, we approach the A-2 service road which we take turning left. Two red STOP signs tell us, once again, that we are not going in the right direction: we are always going against the tide!

If you are riding a bike, it is not advisable to ride along the shoulder on roads without sidewalks. That is why it may be better to go back about 200 m, crossing a bridge over the A-2 and getting the first road turning on the left. If we follow that way for some kilometers, always next to the A-2, we will end up arriving at the vicinity of Soses and we will get back to the path designed on the map for foot pilgrims.

We go under a bridge that crosses the A-2, continuing straight ahead on the service road until we reach a roundabout. At this point we leave the Aragón region, and we begin our walk through Cataluña. A signpost shows the way. From this point, until we arrive at Montserrat,

these signposts of the Generalitat de Cataluña will be of great help. We take the second asphalt path to our left, a narrow, steep climb. A half-hidden pond appears on our right and we continue up the road on the right, which runs alongside the pond.

Upon reaching the top, our track leads to another asphalt path that we take, bearing left but only for 100 m, because once again we turn right onto a dirt track. The signposts clearly indicate the route. We turn to our right and then left, towards a high voltage transformer and a wooded area. We start a

steep descent, continuing along a very winding road that bears right and left, until we reach an asphalt road which leads us to yet another roundabout back on the A-2.

We do not enter the roundabout but continue straight on, heading for the nearby bridge to cross the A-2. At the beginning of the bridge, we meet

a signpost that reminds us that we are on the «Camí Real», the road that Ignatius travelled on before his last experience at Manresa. Crossing the bridge and arriving at the roundabout, we turn to our left and go towards the A-2, because we want to take the service road on our right that is parallel to the highway. In a few meters we pass the Hostel Cataluña y Aragón and a CAMPSA gas station on the other side of the A-2, on our left. We follow the service road and arrive at another bridge, passing underneath.

Continuing along the service road, after a descent, we enter a large roundabout, taking the first exit on the right. We are now at 448 km along the N-II. We continue along the shoulder of the N-II which separates us from the A-2 and leads us to some warehouses. At a roundabout, we pass near a modern, iron, sun-topped sculpture, as well

as the CEMESA factory. At this point, 150 m from the CEMESA roundabout, there is a track on our right which we take. A signpost indicates the road to Lleida. The asphalt track turns to earth and we reach the road leading to Torres de Segre. We turn right and in 250 m we take the asphalt road to our left, which leads us to Alcarràs. The Catalan government signposts accurately point the way.

We continue along this road without deviating, despite its winding nature, arriving at Alcarràs by way of calle Clamor. Here we find the first signs of the Catalan language along the Camino Ignaciano. By continuing straight, we find the N-II or «Avinguda de Catalunya», easily identified by the heavy traffic and traffic lights. Here, we turn right. After the road bears left, we come to el Passeig del Riu, at which we turn right. We leave Alcarràs's church behind us. On

Passeig del Riu, at the first junction, we turn left onto the Avinguda Onze de Setembre.

Having reached the end of the Avinguda Onze de Setembre, a signpost points us towards the village of Butsènit. We take the asphalt path to the right and soon turn left onto the path that begins while directly facing an agricultural building. We continue along this path without diversions, following the signposts. We take the path to our left, at a right angle. We follow this path that leads us back to the N-II. When we reach a tunnel, we do not go through it, turning right instead, and continuing parallel to the N-II. We pass a large shopping center on our right and come to another roundabout. A signpost indicates an asphalt path on our right that should be taken.

We always follow the asphalt road. At some point we find a signpost indicating a left turn onto a path towards a stream. We cross a narrow bridge and turn left towards a dairy farm. Near the farm gate, we take the path indicated on our right, arriving at some farm buildings. We are now approaching the village of Butsènit. As we reach the road into town, we turn right into the village. We pass a primary school before arriving at the Church of Nuestra Señora de la Asunción. We turn 90° right, to take a road that descends sharply beside the schoolyard.

The road leads directly to the Segre River. We follow the river, keeping it on our right. If the time is right, storks, ducks and swans will not fail to keep their appointment with the walker! We follow the meandering river, passing under the railway line. Continuing straight ahead, walking parallel to the Segre River, we reach an asphalt road and turn right at the signpost. Finally, we reach the town of Lleida, the grand, ancient capital of the province of Lleida. Keep walking along the Segre River, cross the bridge over the N-II and enter the town by the Avinguda Alcalde Areny.

Although not really visible, since it is located on the ground floor of a building, the parish of Sant Ignasi de Loiola, run by the Jesuits, is on our left, only 400 m from the bridge we have just crossed. (Make enquiries after passing the «Gateway of the Marist Brothers».)

Church of Santa María, Butsènit.

Interesting facts

ALCARRÀS: A population of 9,000 people, dedicated to agriculture and livestock. In the time of Ignatius, it had about 80 families. The church of la Asunción (18th c.) was constructed on the spot where an ancient feudal castle had stood. We also find a restaurant, supermarket, pharmacy, health center and a bank. Town Council office: Tel.: 973 790 004.

BUTSÈNIT: Butsènit has undertaken a project to build a pilgrim's shelter very close to the capital city (tel.: 629 312 614).

LLEIDA: A big and beautiful Catalonian city, with unique buildings and museums. If you wish to make the most of your stay, you should contact the tourist office and visit the city and its monuments (c/ Major, 31 bis. Tel.: 973 700 319. www.paeria.es/turisme). Of Iberian origins, the city, which was well known to the Romans who named it Llerda, spent four centuries under Muslim influence. It was conquered by Count Ramón Berenguer in the middle of the twelfth century. Construction of the Romanesque cathedral of La Seu Vella, dedicated to Santa María, began in the thirteenth century on the same site where a large mosque had been located. The Romanesque church of Santa María de Gardeny and its tower are what remain of the 12th century monastery of the Knights Templar. Nearby are the ruins of the ancient walls that once surrounded the city and also the walls of the Zuda, a 9th century Arab fortress, rebuilt in the XIII century by the Catalan King, Jaime I. The Romanesque Town Hall in the plaza de la Paeria is from the thirteenth century. In the plaza de la Catedral, you will find La Seu Nova or New Cathedral (18th c.) and nearby is the Hospital of Santa María, a former convent with a stunning flamboyant Gothic interior courtyard from the fifteenth century. Also worth visiting is the Romanesque church of Sant Llorenç (12th and 13th c.) and the 12th century Church

of San Martí. Other highlights include the Main Casino (19th c.) and the Bishop's Palace. The pilgrim will be particularly interested in the chapel on calle Mayor which recalls a legend about the Apostle James: while preaching the gospel on his journey through Spain, James got a thorn in his foot and walking became impossible. He was unable to see where the thorn was because it was very dark. Sensing his desperation, some angels came from heaven with their lanterns lit, to help him out of his difficulty. Every 24th of July, Lleida's children process through the streets of Old Town with lanterns in honor of James the apostle.

Jesuit Fathers: Sant Ignasi' Parish is located in the plaza de Espanya, 4 (Tel.: 973 271 099). During opening hours (18:00 to 21:00), spiritual guidance and spiritual care to pilgrims is provided as well as a stamp for pilgrim passports.

◼ TAXI
Alcarràs:

Taxi Joan Alarcón	649 130 431
Taxi Alcarràs	973 791 027

Lleida:

Tele Radio Taxi Lleida	973 203 050
	680 203 050

◼ LODGING
ALCARRÀS: City Hall pilgrim's shelter. Tel.: 973 790 004. Can Peixan Hotel, Av. de Catalunya, 78. Tel.: 973 791 012. 2 km from town towards highway A-2, Restaurant Casa Miquel Hotel, Carretera Valmanya, km 2. Tel.: 973 791 627.

LLEIDA: Sant Anastasi youth shelter, Rambla d'Aragó, 11. Tel.: 973 266 099 (low season prices for accredited pilgrims). Hotel Real, Avinguda de Blondel, 22. Tel.: 973 271 031. Catalonia Transit Hotel, Plaza Berenguer IV, s/n. Tel.: 973 230 008.

LLEIDA – EL PALAU D'ANGLESOLA

(25.7 km)

«It is foolish to waste an immediate opportunity to serve God, hoping to do something greater in the future, since it may well be that we lose the one without ever seeing the other fulfilled.»

«The Lord assures the steps of man and cares for his ways. Though he stumbles, he will not fall, because the Lord takes him by the hand. I was young, now I am old: never have I seen the righteous abandoned...» (Ps 37:23-25).

The day may seem short after the long last stage, but we must not start late when we do the Camino during summertime when these Catalan lands usually suffer very high temperatures. As we have already seen many times, the «Camino Real» that Ignatius followed is nowadays national highways and freeways, so we are going to walk quite a lot of the time next to them.

We leave Lleida by way of the bridge of Pardinyes, which is the last bridge in the city uniting both banks of the Segre. We go through the park, following the river upstream and keep it on our left. Passing underneath the bridge, we go up to the level of the highway and follow the Camino Ignaciano waymarks towards the floodgates which regulate the river's flow.

We follow the asphalt road, which crosses an irrigation canal and skirts the wall of the Mitjana park, on the camino del Grenyana. At the park entrance we turn to the right, passing the train tracks, and reach the industrial park, which allows us to exit Lleida on the calle Enginyer Mies. We have to stay alert to find this street because we can easily get lost in the industrial park.

Once at the end, we take a dirt path in front of us and follow it until we reach a bridge over the freeway. Keep an eye on the signs because there are many intersections and turns. The paths between fields are not usually straight. The signs guide us along. Before arriving at the town of Bell-lloc d'Urgell we again cross the freeway.

At Bell-lloc, we cross the train tracks and follow carrer de la Mina to the town center. With a little luck, we will find the market along the village's streets but, alternatively, we can stop at one of the bars to freshen up. We leave the village next to the church of San Miguel and reach a roundabout; we follow a dirt road that leads us to the train tracks and then, after crossing them, to the A-2, which we will also cross by a bridge close by the El Molinet farm.

Beyond the bridge, we have to stay alert: the end of this stage is not easily distinguished and the farming roads intersect many times, potentially complicating our pilgrimage. We will pass a field with electrical generating solar panels. Staying on this path, we will arrive at El Palau d'Anglesola.

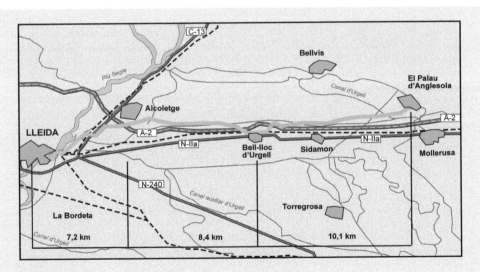

Total upward slope: 286 m. Total downward slope: 86 m.
Bicycles: easy.

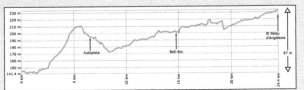

Lleida:	km 0
Autopista:	km 7.2
Bell-lloc:	km 15.6
El Palau d'Anglesola:	km 25.7

Description

To leave town, we follow the Segre River. Walking along the river path, with the Segre on our left, we pass under the railway bridge and, afterwards, under the Pardinyes bridge. After the bridge, stairs take us to street-level. Orange arrows and a signal post tell us that we are on the right path. We go on, parallel the Segre river taking the old camino de Granyena. Turn 90 degrees to the right and, after crossing the channel, turn to the left. We approach the river gates that are to our left. Go straight about 500 m, then turn right and cross the railroad tracks. Once we arrive at the Avenida de la Industria we take a left and after we turn right into calle Enginyer Mies. After 750 m, and crossing a road bridge, we find ourselves at the end of the industrial zone, once again surrounded by plowed fields.

We continue onto el camino de Alcoletge. We keep on the road, and we leave a stone and sand quarry. We carry on, without taking any diversion. There is a junction in our path: we turn to the right. We arrive at a bridge to cross A-2 highway. Once we have crossed the bridge, we turn right on a road, in a straight angle, and we carry on walking some meters

to find the path that turns left. We take it and continue walking straight on.

There are some long barns on the right. Reaching a transmission tower, our dirt path leads to another road but we continue straight on. We cross a path. We continue straight until we come across another asphalt road where we turn right. Our path continues on the left. We arrive at a junction, and we take the road to the right.

We cross a road perpendicular to ours. Going straight ahead and ignoring adjacent roads, we reach a crossroads and continue towards Mollerusa. We arrive at a bridge over the A-2. We cross and leave the A-2 behind. Our path leads to another that we take to our right and that leads us to Bell-lloc d'Urgell.

The road ends at calle Vilanova de la Barca. Fifty meters to our right there is a railway line.

Having reached the village of Bell-lloc, turn right to pass the train tracks.

We continue straight on calle Mina, diagonally across the plaza. Turn right down calle Pau Casals and then left down calle Urgell. We reach the end of the street and we find the N-II road. We see the church of San Miquel on our right and we continue straight. Next to the restaurant Bòria we find a water source. We go straight and, once in the roundabout, we cross it straight ahead and we take a dirt road, leaving the paved road to our right. At both the first and second forks, we go to the left and we approach the railway. We cross the tracks and continue straight, approaching the A-2. We join a dirt road on our right that runs parallel to the

highway and leads us to a farm (El Molinet) and a bridge to pass over the A-2.

After the bridge we turn right and in a few meters, again take a right turn to enter onto another dirt road. At the fork, once more, we go to the right. Continue straight on this road that takes us close to a solar power plant. Continuing straight ahead, leaving the solar panels on our left, at the next junction we go right. Within a few meters we turn left and we reach the Urgell water channel. We cross it and we continue walking straight.

Continuing straight, we will reach a roundabout that we cross at a little angle toward the left; we have already arrived at El Palau d'Anglesola. We enter on Avenida de Sant Roc, which becomes calle Font and leads directly to the main plaza.

■ Interesting facts

BELL-LLOC D'URGELL: This village of 2,350 inhabitants provides a restaurant, a supermarket, a pharmacy, a health center and a bank.

EL PALAU D'ANGLESOLA: This town of 2,000 inhabitants has its origin in an Arab palace that passed into Christian hands in 1085. The castle/palace was renovated in the seventeenth century. Here we can find a restaurant, supermarket, pharmacy, bank and health center.

■ TAXI
Bell-lloc d'Urgell
Taxi Miquel Bosch   636 213 070

El Palau d'Anglesola
Eurotaxi Albert   619 605 805

Church of San Juan Bautista, El Palau D'Anglesola.

■ LODGING
ALCOLETGE: Pilgrim's shelter, c/ Mayor, 19. Tel.: 973 196 011.

BELL-LLOC D'URGELL: City Hall usually offers some lodging. Plaza Mayor, s/n. Tel.: 973 560 100.

EL PALAU D'ANGLESOLA: Sant Antoni inn, c/ Sant Antoni, 7. Tel.: 973 602 158. City Hall. Tel.: 973 601 314. Pilgrim's shelter: amics.del.cami@gmail.com Tel.: 629 684 063. (Note: a very helpful, welcoming local group maintain this shelter!).

El Palau d'Anglesola – Verdú

(24.7 km)

«It should be our constant concern to see God in all things, not merely lifting our minds to him when we are praying.»

«Then I heard the voice of the Lord saying: "Whom shall I send? Who will go for us?" I answered: "Here I am, send me."» (Is 6:8).

The good pilgrim shelter we will find in Verdú will make today's effort worthwhile; furthermore, in the next stage we will have a day with only a few km that will make up for these last long stages.

We leave El Palau d'Anglesola, heading towards the highway LV-3321 in the direction of Vila-Sana but, just after passing the canal going out of town, we turn right to take the path which will carry us through the fields to Castellnou de Seana. Once again we have to pay attention to the signs because there are many forks and side paths. Luckily, signs are frequent on the Camino Ignaciano. We come into Castellnou on the street that goes to the church. Nearby is the Café Moderno whose owners are big promoters of pilgrimages: an excellent spot for a «knife and fork» breakfast. We leave Castellnou going by the schools and continue straight ahead on the same street, headed to the next town: Bellpuig. We run across many forks and other paths that can disorient us, but we always continue straight on towards the bridge over the A-2 freeway.

Crossing the freeway, we go down, following the train tracks, and cross them further on through a tunnel which brings us to the entrance of Bellpuig. We go into town and cross through it, going down Avenida de Urgell. Approaching the center of town we take calle Mayor. Lucky pilgrims will certainly enjoy the street market and some wonderful patisseries. We leave town on calle Balmes which connects with an asphalt road on which, in a few km, we pass by the rear of the Cataluña Motocross Circuit.

From there on, and until reaching Verdú, we pass through fields of olive trees, vineyards and grain which, with their changing colors, announce the seasons. In the spring, we are greeted with a special display of red poppies. On asphalt paths and then dirt, we come to an irrigation canal which we cross by a bridge, approaching a typical, though uninhabited, Catalan country house on the road to Preixana. We continue straight on the asphalt path, leaving the house to our right. In one km we leave the asphalt and turn right to take a dirt trail.

After a few crossroads, where we must pay attention to the signs, we arrive at a small chapel dedicated to la Madre de Dios del Remedio with a stone table where we can eat and relax. We cross the highway to continue on our way. At the

Café Moderno, Castellnou de Seana.

next intersection of five paths, we take the second to our left and head to the highway C-14. The hometown of St. Peter Claver is still hidden from our view but we are now very close. Crossing the C-14 and approaching the town, we run into a big water canal; after crossing over the canal bridge, we go up to the hermitage of Sant Miquel. Continuing straight on the same path, we arrive at calle Sant Pere Claver, the sanctuary and the pilgrim's shelter.

◼ Ignatian tip

We will not talk about Ignatius today but about a Catalan Jesuit, the patron of the Society of Jesus in Cataluña and in Colombia, South America: Saint Peter Claver (1580-1654). Pedro Claver was born in Verdú to a wealthy family. He wanted to become a priest and at the age of 17 he went to Barcelona. He met the Jesuits there and entered the Society of Jesus at the age of 22. Afterwards, he spent three years in the College of Palma de Mallorca. The saintly Jesuit porter there, Alphonsus Rodríguez, became Pedro's friend and mentor and deeply affected his life, encouraging him to work in the Americas, discovered just a century before. Pedro sailed from Seville on the 15th of April, 1610, and landed in Cartagena de Indias, in modern day Colombia. Cartagena was one of the transatlantic slave trading centers and received several thousand slaves every month. Up to a third of the slaves died during the trip from Africa and those who survived were treated horribly.

Claver would go below deck in the slave ships as soon as they docked and provide care for the hungry, frightened and often sickly slaves who had withstood the exhausting months-long journey. His ministry was controversial; he was criticized not only by the local officials who benefited from the slave trade but even by some of his fellow Jesuits. Although he lived over four centuries ago, Claver's life mission embodies the essence of modern ideals. His example eloquently goads us to raise our voices against injustice, to defend those who are stripped of their most fundamental rights, to persevere in honorable causes in spite of the opposition of the powerful, to care for the body as well as the soul of those who suffer, and to find the dignity and innate beauty in society's outcasts. Ignatian pilgrims can spend some time in the shrine which is devoted to this saint and ask for the strength, compassion and far-sightedness personified in Claver.

The extraordinary figure of Saint Peter Claver can be summed up in three stages.

1. He was baptized on the 26th of June, 1580, as recorded in the Baptismal Registry in the Parish Archives in the town of Verdú. The good pastor added to the inscription these words: «May God make him a good Catholic.» And thus it was.

2. This was a dark time in history, stained by the injustice and cruelty of slavery. Peter Claver was there when the slave ships arrived and could see how the slaves were treated. He began going to the port when a ship would arrive, welcoming the slaves with an open heart and a warm smile, while distributing clothing, food, drink and sweets. As he himself wrote, he spoke to them not with words but with his hands and his efforts. It was useless to speak to them any other way. He would kneel beside the sick, wash them, tend to them and try to make them happy with as many demonstrations of care as could help lighten the sick persons' burdens. His life was a beautiful example of human and evangelical love for his dear slaves. He cared for them materially, instructing them in the faith and baptizing them, always considering himself their servant. On April 3, 1622, he made a solemn commitment which he expressed

with the following words: «Slave of the Black Slaves forever.» He signed it and fulfilled it with his life.

3. He was canonized by Pope Leo XIII, who said that «since the life of Christ, no life had moved him so deeply as the life of Peter Claver.»

He lived on earth in poverty and freedom for 74 years, suffering with those who suffered, a white man among black men, always as a slave of the slaves. He was a Catalan of few words, but prodigious in heroism.

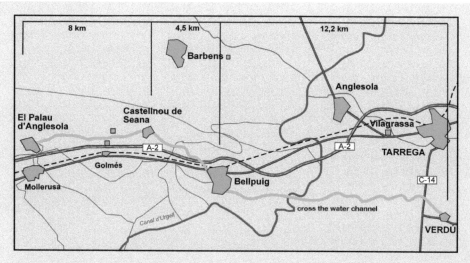

Total upward slope: 272 m. Total downward slope: 98 m.
Bicycles: easy.

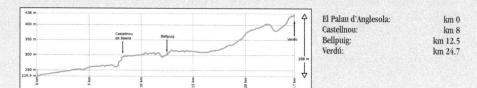

El Palau d'Anglesola:	km 0
Castellnou:	km 8
Bellpuig:	km 12.5
Verdú:	km 24.7

■ Description

From the plaza (Plaça) Major de El Palau, we take Carrer Sant Josep, passing by the Town Hall, and we keep straight toward the Carrer Nou. At the end of this street, we are already at the edge of the village: we cross over a canal via a small bridge and turn right at the first track that appears, just after the bridge and a house.

The road runs parallel to the canal which is on our right. In 400 m, we take the left hand fork, away from the canal and head for Castellnou de Seana. In 600 m we cross a road and in 1 km we cross another one.

We follow our path without veering left or right. Sometimes our camino crosses others but we continue straight ahead. After 1.7 km we cross another road. Take care here: after crossing the road, we do not take the first road on the right but the second, which is almost facing us.

We follow it and shortly we pass three farm buildings on our left. Continuing straight on, we can already make out

Castellnou de Seana ahead of us. The trail forks before reaching the village: take the left track, avoiding the roundabout, which orients us toward calle Mayor and the church plaza. The City Hall is nearby.

To leave the town, beginning from from the school building, we set off along calle Calvari which leads to a fork with calle Marius Tort on our left but we do not take this; instead, we continue along the same street. After leaving the town, we continue along the asphalt road which continues straight on, passing near fields and agricultural buildings. We pass a stone and sand quarry on our left, approaching the bridge that crosses the A-2 freeway. We cross the bridge and follow our road towards the railway tracks.

In 800 m we pass a bridge and, turning round to our left, we descend to the tunnel under the same bridge and pass through it to reach the other side of the tracks where we see the town of Bellpuig in front of us. We should have seen some Camino de Santiago signs guiding our turn under the bridge. At the first roundabout we turn left and then right at the second roundabout in order to enter the village. We continue straight down onto calle Avinguda d'Urgell until we reach Ramón Folch plaza. We cross it and at the roundabout we continue straight on to reach Sant Roc plaza and then we take calle Mayor on our right. At the end of this street, we turn 90 degrees to the left onto calle Balmes and then, after 80 m, we turn 90 degrees to the right, staying on calle Balmes, in effect, making a Z-turn. At this point calle Avinguda Preixana should be behind us and the church (which we will not reach) should be in front of us.

Walking straight ahead on calle Balmes, we leave town on a paved road and continue straight along until we come to a two-lane paved road. We cross it

and continue straight along the same path without deviating. At 1.5 km from the last junction, we see the Catalunya Motocross Circuit on our left. We keep walking on the same path and arrive in front of a farm that has two food containers, one labeled TEGAPOL. We take a dirt road that we find on our right, following the farm fence. We continue along the same path until we reach a bridge over a ditch. We cross it and continue straight along the road ahead of us.

The dirt road becomes asphalt when we reach a typical Catalan farmhouse. A signpost indicates the direction to Preixana. We do not turn in that direction but, instead, we continue straight ahead leaving the farm on our right. Then, 1.3 km from the farm, we turn right onto a dirt road and in another 100 m we turn left on the same road. We head straight on without deviating. In a few meters

we pass a sand quarry on our right and we keep walking straight ahead on the same road. We arrive at the LV-2021 road. To our right is a small religious shrine dedicated to la Madre de Dios del Remedio. Cross the road and continue straight along our dirt path. We come to a junction of five roads and we take the second on our left which is quite wide. We follow it down to the C -14 roadway. We cross the C -14 and continue straight on towards Verdú.

When we reach the ditch, we cross over it towards Verdú and the hermitage of Sant Miquel on the edge of town. We continue straight on, through the village streets. Following calle Sant Miquel, we reach a junction and straight ahead we find calle Sant Pere Claver. At the beginning of the street, on the left, is the Shrine and Birthplace of St. Peter Claver where the pilgrims' hostel is situated.

■ Interesting facts

CASTELLNOU DE SEANA: A village of less than 1,000 inhabitants which offers a restaurant, supermarket, pharmacy, health center and bank.

BELLPUIG: Population of about 5,000 inhabitants. Here, if we wish, we may stop to admire an impressive marble sarcophagus from Ramón Folch de Cardona - Anglesola (1525) in the parish church, which is dedicated to St. Nicholas (16th c.). The sarcophagus is a prominent example of the Catalan Renaissance style. The steps leading up to the church were built in 1792 in Baroque style. Bellpuig Castle was built in 1079 and during the twelfth century it was adapted to become the residence of the barons of Bellpuig. It was renovated again in 1472 and was fortified during the War of Spanish Succession. Part of the building was blown up during the War of Independence. In town, we can find restaurants, supermarket and pharmacy.

VERDÚ: This small village of 1,000 inhabitants has great significance for the Society of Jesus in Cataluña, as it is here that Pedro Claver was born and raised. He would become known as the «holy defender of the black slaves» in the port of Cartagena de Indias (Colombia). Although small, the Association of Friends of the saint (los amigos del santo) welcomes pilgrims with open arms. The most important religious monument is the parish church of Santa María (13th c.), with its Romanesque portal. Inside are the Gothic sculptures of the Virgin (15th c.), in polychrome stone, and that of Santa Flavia, the town's patron saint. In the nave, on the left, stands a Baroque altarpiece in polychrome wood, carved by Agustí Pujol. This is considered the masterpiece of this seventeenth century Catalan sculptor. The main altar contains a masterful fresco by Jaume Miguell. Beside the church stands the XII century castle, around which the community developed. Influenced by the nearby Cistercian monastery of Poblet, it

became the residence of the abbots when they were visiting Verdú. In the basement of the castle there was a wine cellar or bodega and an olive oil mill. L'Ermitage de Sant Miquel (14th century Gothic) is the other important religious building. The town's main plaza is surrounded by 17th and 18th century houses. The ceramics produced in this town are notable for their distinctive black color. The village has a restaurant, supermarket, pharmacy, health center and bank.

■ TAXI
Bellpuig
Taxis Bellpuig   629 321 623
Castellnou de Seana
Taxi Segarra   630 538 180
Tàrrega
Taxi Jaime Font   973 311 567

■ LODGING
CASTELLNOU DE SEANA: The City Hall provides shelter for 8 pilgrims (Tel.: 973 320 705). The Restaurant Café Moderno can provide information (c/ Sant Blai, 23. Tel.: 973 320 843). Casa rural Olivé, c/ Abat Carrera, 3. Tel.: 973 321 373.

BELLPUIG: Agustín Martín Mingot Hostel, Av. Catalunya, 32. Tel.: 973 320 076. Pilgrim Shelter (8 beds) Tel.: 973 320 408 (Note: you must call 2 days in advance or contact oficinaturisme@bellpuig.cat).

VERDÚ: Pilgrim's shelter of San Peter Claver, Asociación de Amigos de San Pedro Claver (30 beds), c/ Sant Pere Claver, 30. Tel.: 687 095 070. Apartments Cal Senyor Joan, Plaça Major, 21. Tel.: 636 990 493. Casa rural Ca N'Aleix. Arquebisbe Terés, 10. Tel.: 973 311 393 / 661 309 397. Casa rural L'Era de Can Roger. Sant Miquel, 34. Tel.: 973 311 393 / 678 640 343. Tourist Office, pl. Bisbe Comelles, 13. Tel.: 973 347 216. City Hall can also provide information on the shelter for temporary farmworkers. Tel.: 973 347 007.

Verdú – Cervera

(17 km)

«The more acutely you are able to notice the faults of others, the more likely that you overlook your own.»

«Because you took shelter in the Lord and dwelt with the Most High, misfortune will not approach you and the plague will not come into your tent. For he has ordered his angels to guard you on your ways. They will carry you in the palm of their hands so that your foot does not trip on a stone» (Ps 91:9-12).

Cervera.

Today's short stage allows us to get up later and to enjoy Verdú, or to arrive early in Cervera for a relaxed visit to this ancient university city. We leave Verdú from behind the church, looking for the old road from Verdú to Tàrrega.

The road descends towards fields of olive trees, vineyards and grain. After a small, wooded rest area around the fountain of the Magdalena, we continue straight ahead on the same road and soon the village of Tàrrega comes into sight ahead, in the valley. Going through the pretty historical center of the village of Tàrrega, and after coming to the Church of Santa María del Alba (Dawn), we make a ninety-degree turn to the right to leave Tàrrega on the Avenida de la Generalitat. A well-asphalted road which we find going out of town takes us directly to the next town: El Talladell.

In El Talladell, we always keep to the same road and cross town on calle Mayor, which leads us, as it did Ignatius, on the old Camino Real, directly to the end of our stage. We pass in front of the cemetery gate and further on, cross the same irrigation canal that we found in Verdú.

The town of La Mora is on our right and we continue straight ahead, passing another town, Fonolleres, perched on the hill above the road. Further on, we leave the ancient tower-house of Saportella behind on our right and, continuing straight ahead, we come to the ruins of the hermitage of Santa María Magdalena. We take the road to the left and, after some 800 m, taking the first street to the right we can walk up to the historic city center of Cervera.

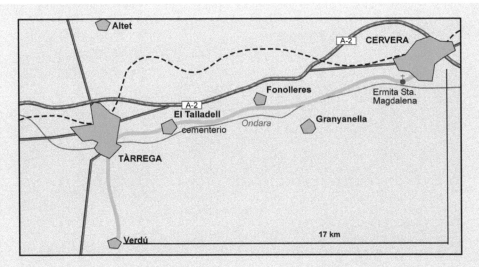

Total upward slope: 299 m. Total downward slope: 148 m.
Bicycles: easy.

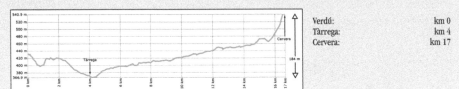

Verdú: km 0
Tàrrega: km 4
Cervera: km 17

■ Description

We leave this charming town starting from the church of Santa María de Verdú by way of calle de la Font and we come to a path that starts off in front of us, descending close to some houses which are next to cultivated fields. The dirt track where we start takes us from Verdú to Tàrrega, our next goal.

Our path is wider and more defined than others that we see but it is best to pay attention to the signs. We arrive at Tàrrega. We enter the town keeping to

Carrer major, Cervera

Cervera City Hall.

outskirts, we take the path that continues straight on, disregarding others that start on the left.

We are now on the «Camí Ral». We pass the cemetery on our left, continuing on this road, although at one point the road veers sharply to the right; we, however, continue straight on. We approach the small town of Fonolleres, which is partly on a height, but we pass it by on our left.

Maintaining the same direction, 900 meters past Fonolleres, on our right, we spot the fairly dilapidated Saportella «tower house». We continue on the track which is now wider and well-marked. Other roads meet ours, or we meet them, but we stick to our track.

The trail ends near the ruins of the hermitage of Santa María Magdalena. We take the asphalt road to our left to go to

Cervera. We follow the road for about 700 meters and on our right, amongst the first houses near the road, we see the hermitage of Sant Magí. We turn 90° to the right to take this street and enter Cervera city.

We are now in calle Castle which leads to the ruins of the old castle. Turning left, another street brings us into the old city center. We arrive at the church of Santa María. The pilgrim's shelter is not far away.

our path which leads us to calle Guardia Civil. We turn left and follow the same street until we reach the Ondara River. We cross over the footbridge and continue along calle Sant Agustí until we arrive at the plaza de Sant Antoni. Here, we take calle Mayor on our right which leads onto the main plaza and the church of Santa María del Alba.

Facing the church, we take a right down la calle Agoders. Going straight on, we walk along la calle Mossèn Jacint Verdaguer which becomes la Avenida de la Generalitat. We follow this avenue all the way and finally leave the town on the camino de Tàrrega for El Talladell.

We pass the church of El Pedregal on our left and after some distance enter El Talladell. We go through the village and, on the

■ Interesting facts

TÀRREGA: A city of more than 16,000 inhabitants and the capital of Urgell, famous for its Street Theater Fair (Feria de Teatro en la Calle), held in September, at which many artists perform. The town has restaurants, supermarkets, pharmacies, health centers, banks, a bike shop and a tourist information office (c/ Agoders, 16. Tel.: 973 500 707).

CERVERA: With more than 9,000 inhabitants, it maintains traces of eighteenth century splendor in its buildings and walls which are much older, having been repaired in 1368. The church of San Antonio dates from the Middle Ages and the Catholic monarchs, Ferdinand and Isabella, were engaged in the church of Sant Bernat. The impressive main plaza holds the church of Santa María and the 17th and 18th century palaces of the Paeria, used by the aristocracy. For political reasons, in the eighteenth-century Catalonia's only university was situated in this city. Cervera has restaurants, supermarkets, pharmacies, health centers, banks, a bike shop and a tourist information office (Tel.: 973 534 442 / 973 530 025).

■ TAXI
Tàrrega

Taxi Jaime Font	973 311 567

Cervera

Auto Taxi Sala 24h	608 608 130
Taxi Agramunt	973 923 327

■ LODGING
TÀRREGA: Pintor Marsà Hotel, Av. Catalunya, 112. Tel.: 973 501 516. Ciutat de Tàrrega Hotel, c/ Sant Pelegrí, 95. Tel.: 973 314 737. Ca N'Aleix de la Zarza shelter, Plaza del Carme, 5. Tel.: 973 314 635. City Hall. Tel.: 973 311 608.

CERVERA: Colegio Residencia – Pilgrim's shelter Sagrada Familia. c/ Sabaters, 6 (entrance next to n.º 51, calle Mayor; run by a religious order of sisters; meals can be arranged). Tel.: 973 530 805. Bonavista Hostel, Av. Catalunya, 14. Tel.: 973 530 027. La Sabina Hostel, Camí dels Horts, 2. Tel.: 973 531 393. Bona Teca Hostel, Av. Mil·lenari, 497. Tel.: 973 530 325. City Hall. Tel.: 973 530 025.

CERVERA – IGUALADA

(38.6 km)

«Do everything without expecting praise; but do everything such that you cannot be justly blamed.»

«When, for having sinned against you [oh, God], the sky closes and there is no rain, if they pray in this place, confess their sin to you and repent when you afflict them, listen from heaven and forgive the sin of your servant, your people, Israel, showing them the good path that they must follow and send the rain to the land which you gave as an inheritance to your people» (1 K 8:35-36).

Church of Santa Maria del Camí.

This is a very long stage that can be shortened to the pilgrim's taste. But pilgrims who have been building up their endurance over previous stages will have no trouble handling the walk. La Panadella and Jorba are two possible sites for spending the night. We will be going through small towns which will give us the chance to stock up on supplies.

We leave Cervera on the calle de la Muralla and by the gate, la puerta de la Muralla, with a magnificent view of the valley we are going to traverse today. Once at the bottom, we go to our right to follow the path which runs next to the Ondara River. We can also go up to the national road and take the asphalt to the town of Vergós. Both ways are good. On the river path we go by rest areas and an old mill. At Vergós, on the road that crosses through the village, we turn right passing the fountain and towards the old church of San Salvador along the Camino Real, where Ignatius would surely have stopped for a moment of reflection and prayer.

We leave Vergós in direction of the national road and go through the tunnel, then going to our right and keeping parallel to the freeway until a new tunnel which takes us straight to the town of Sant Pere dels Arquells. Coming to the fountain, we make a perpendicular turn to our left and cross the town. Leaving, we take the road to the left that leads us to the town of Sant Antolí i Vilanova.

We stay on the level, though the road rises bit by bit towards the height of La Panadella. We arrive at the town of Pallerols and, once through it, we continue straight, but be very alert to the double 90 degree curve, first to the left and then to the right: we are to leave the highway on the first path which appears to our left following this Z. It is a good idea to watch the signs at this point. We come to La Panadella and from there we can go down tranquilly on the old and now solitary highway National II, nowadays with hardly any traffic. We pass near the town of Porquerisses.

For a few km of the descent we encounter a bike path, separated from the highway, which accompanies us almost to the end of this stage. We cannot get lost because we always follow the N-II. We come to the town of Jorba and go through it, following the indications to the town of Sant Genís. Further on we come across a roundabout, in which we turn to the right in order to cross the freeway. We cross the next roundabout, after the bridge, to take the highway B-222 in front of us which leads to Santa Margarida de Montbui.

We arrive at Igualada and enter the city on the old «Camí Ral» which St. Ignatius took. The hermitage of Sant Jaume Sesoliveres (10th c.) is high on our left. We go ahead on Igualada's streets, without needing to follow the highway: we go parallel to the highway until coming to the bridge and cross the river to head to the center of the city. The pilgrim's shelter is found close to the first roundabout over the river.

■ Ignatian tip

It is thought that the town of Igualada is the place where Ignatius decided to buy his pilgrim garb, as described several years later:

«Arriving at a large village not far from Montserrat, he decided to purchase a garment to wear on his journey to Jerusalem. He therefore bought a poorly-woven piece of sackcloth, filled with prickly wooden fibers. Out of this he made a garment that reached his feet. He also bought a pair of shoes of coarse material often used to make brooms. He never wore but one shoe, not for the sake of the comfort he derived,

but because this leg would be quite swollen from riding on horseback all day since for mortification he wore a cord tied tightly just below the knee. For this reason he felt he ought to wear a shoe on that foot. He also bought a pilgrim's staff and a gourd to drink from. These he tied to his saddle.»

Let us pay close attention at this point. It may be helpful to reflect on all that we «carry with us» and anything else that is burdensome. What do I have in the way of «good-looking clothes» and other «valuables» that I could symbolically «leave» at

the feet of the Virgin of Montserrat? Is it possible for me to adopt a lifestyle more in keeping with the pilgrimage that we are making? For me, what would be the equivalent of a pilgrim's sackcloth and sandals? What can I leave behind and what do I not want to let go of? This journey has surely helped us to put many things into perspective and to question other realities. What might I want to leave behind Certainly not mere accessories, but rather anything that prevents me from following Jesus more closely – right?

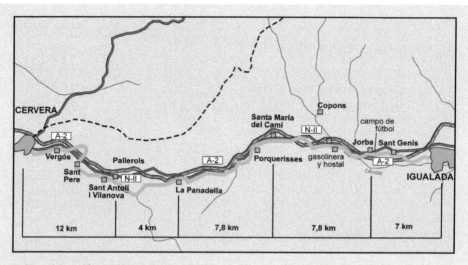

Total upward slope: 346 m. Total downward slope: 539 m.
Bicycles: easy and a wonderful ride down from La Panadella to Igualada.

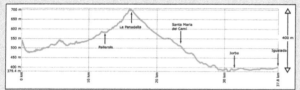

Cervera:	km 0
Pallerols:	km 12
Panadella:	km 16
Santa Maria del Camí:	km 23.8
Jorba:	km 31.6
Igualada:	km 38.6

■ Description

We say goodbye to Cervera and set off in search of the N-II. From the entrance of la Paeria, go down the calle Santa María and later turn left at calle Muralla. We come to our exit from Cervera, Muralla Gate and, after passing through, we go down to the left, following the wall.

We arrive at the drinking trough of Sant Francesc and we turn right to follow the Ondara river path. We pass picnic areas and an old watermill. The signposts show us the way to Vergós.

We arrive at Vergós center; we turn right and we pass the old church of San Salvador. We follow the road out of town and we reach the N-II. To our left is a tunnel that we go

through and we follow the road to our right, parallel to the A-2 highway. We always keep parallel to it. We find another tunnel, which we do not go through. We continue on this route for another 700 meters and then it turns left, taking us away from the A-2.

The road traces a wide curve to the right, taking us back to the A-2. We pass a traditional cement factory on our left. We cross under the highway A-2. We come to a roundabout which we go straight across and turn in the direction of the houses of Sant Pere dels Arquells. Entering the town, we are surprised to discover a few jets «parked» in the small field on our left. We keep going until we reach the fountain of Sant Pere. At this point we turn left at a ninety-degree angle.

At about 200 m from the fountain, once out into open country, the road forks. Our route is to the left. We follow its winding course without diverging from the road. At 1.6 km we come to the L-203, at which we turn left. We approach the N-II. Just before we get to the road, we take the street that lies 90° to our right and leads to Sant Antolí i Vilanova.

We cross through the town, exiting on the far side by the same road, heading to our next village, Pallerols. Once again, we follow our road straight through the village without diverting.

Pay attention at this point: the road makes a 90 degree left turn and in 100 meters turns right again. We continue for 150 meters before taking another trail

which starts 90 degrees to our left. On our right we pass a wooded area. We continue straight ahead, always keeping to our wide road. We pass through forested areas, maintaining the same route and disregarding the roads that join or split off from ours. At 1.7 km, we reach La Panadella service area.

When approaching the N-II, we pass the gas stations and restaurants in La Panadella and we continue as far as the roundabout which we cross in order to take the descending N-II. After 5 km along this road, we can see part of the town of Porquerises on our right.

We have no choice but to follow the N-II, the Camino Real of Ignacio de Loyola and of many other pilgrims who used this road in the past as we do today. Taking this route we arrive at Santa Maria del Camí.

We keep on the N-II and cross the bridge over the

A-2 motorway. After 600 meters, we cross the A-2 once again but this time we go underneath. We continue parallel to the A-2 and walk past a petrol station. Continuing on this road, we arrive at a roundabout at which we turn right, following the N-II.

We continue, walking parallel to the A-2, reaching a large roundabout. We enter the roundabout and once past the A-2 turn-off, we take the exit that connects to the N-II, going in the same direction. We reach

Jorba by the N-II, crossing through the village on this road. As we leave the town we take an asphalt road on our right. This is an old road, fairly parallel to the N-II. A football field greets us on our right. Do not leave the road, which takes us to the houses in Sant Genís, on our right.

We enter the village and cross the main road. We follow the same road towards Igualada, crossing over the A-2 on the bridge. We continue straight and on the other side of the A-2, at the roundabout, we go straight across towards Santa Margarida de Montbui and ahead lies the city of Igualada.

We are on the Sant Jaume Sesoliveres highway, the B-222. We press on, always on the road, down to Igualada. We pass a roundabout and come to the Avenida Àngel Guimerà. The hermitage of Sant Jaume de Sesoliveres is on our left, on top of a rise. We leave Av. Àngel Guimerà to enter calle Felicià Matheu and so we avoid the traffic. Go straight down the calle Jaume Serra Iglesias and then we zigzag, right and left, down on calle de Les Alzines. We go straight on and, just after the little bridge over the Anoia River, we reach a roundabout. We cross straight over and continue

along the same Av. Àngel Guimerà until we come across a petrol station on our right. We turn right on the la calle Prat de la Riba, which curves to the left. (Note: the pilgrim's shelter can be found by turning left in about 200 m. The small pilgrims hostel is inside an old factory on this same street.) We go straight over the roadway junction and find ourselves in la calle Sant Ignasi. We go straight on, noting the name change to calle Sant Domènec. We arrive at the plaza de la Creu. The calle de l'Argent leads off from here, which takes us to the church of Santa María.

▓ Interesting facts

VERGÓS: We can imagine that, like many other pilgrims, Ignatius visited the small 12th century church of San Salvador which was on the Camino Real. There is a bar in the town.

SANT PERE DELS ARQUELLS: A very unusual scene greets us: airplanes «parked» in a field at the village entrance. Also, note the detail that each house has its name printed on tiles and, noted under the names are the trades or professions to which each house was dedicated. No services offered for pilgrims.

SANT ANTOLÍ I VILANOVA: It has a restaurant, supermarket and pharmacy.

PALLEROLS: Here, pilgrims to Santiago can find a beautiful church dedicated to St. James dating from the 12th century. The «jacobean shells» are observed at different points, a testimony to the Jacobean tradition of the Camino Real. There are no facilities for pilgrims.

Cal Ratés, Igualada.

LA PANADELLA: A well-known service area on the old national road. It has a restaurant and a supermarket.

SANTA MARIA DEL CAMÍ: Here you will discover a 12th century Romanesque church that probably once served as a refuge for pilgrims and travelers. There are no facilities for modern-day pilgrims.

JORBA: The castle (crumbled but visible high above) dates from the 10th century. It has a restaurant and a supermarket.

SANT GENÍS: No services.

IGUALADA: A major city in the area, in which it is believed that Ignatius bought his «sturdy cloth robes.» Ignatius had already decided to spend a night in vigil at Montserrat, to cast aside his courtly identity and take up that of a pilgrim; he probably had a simple pilgrim's sackcloth made for him in this town known for producing clothing and shoes.
The church of Santa María dates from the 11th century but it was last renovated in the 17th century. The city has restaurants, supermarkets, pharmacies, health centers, banks, a bike shop and a Tourist Information Office (Tel.: 938 051 585).

■ **TAXI**

Igualada

Taxis Igualada	609 478 219
Marcial Pérez	938 045 503
Radio Taxi Igualada	983 070 308

■ **LODGING**

LA PANADELLA: Bayona Hostel (special rates for pilgrims, on request). Tel.: 938 092 011.

JORBA: Pilgrim's shelter (note: arrive before 6:00PM). Meals available (perhaps only for groups). Plaza de la Fuente, 3. Tel.: 938 094 101

IGUALADA: Pilgrim's shelter, c/ de Prat de la Riva, 47. Tel.: 938 045 515 (12 beds). Reception and key collection at the nursing home that is 150 m away, in Avenida Gaudí, 26 (reception hours: 8 to 22 h). América Hotel, Av. Mestre Montaner, 44-45. Tel.: 938 031 000. Canaletas inn, Av. Mestre Montaner, 60. Tel.: 938 032 750. City Hall. Tel.: 938 031 950. A brand new municipal shelter will be opened in 2018.

IGUALADA – MONTSERRAT
(27 km)

«No decision is to be made about anything when the mind is disturbed, whether by affection or by great distress; postpone the decision until the anxiety has abated so that it may be made according to mature and not impulsive reason.»

«Judge me, Lord, I act honorably, trusting in the Lord I do not falter. Scrutinize me, Lord, put me to the test, examine my bowels and my heart because I have your faithfulness before my eyes and I proceed according to your fidelity» (Ps 26:1-3).

Monastery of Santa María de Montserrat.

This is a difficult stage, with a steep climb to the *coll* of Can Massana. We are excited to be able to spend some time at the Benedictine monastery which houses the famous Black Madonna, the «Moreneta», the symbol of Montserrat and patroness of Cataluña. It is well worth the physical effort for the singular beauty of the landscape and the reward of visiting this monastery, closely associated with St. Ignatius's life story.

We leave Igualada passing near the train station. We go down to the industrial park which we are going to cross lengthwise. After 2 km, coming to its end in a roundabout with a bridge which raises

the highway above us, we take an asphalt path to the left which leads us to the next town. Tunnels and bridges help us to avoid the freeway, arriving finally at Castellolí. We have to pay attention to the signs so as not to end up on the freeway. At one point we are to turn to the right to enter on the road to Castellolí; if not, we will find ourselves on the acceleration lane of the freeway! The path is well-marked and takes us to a ramp which goes up to the bridge over the freeway. We continue up the El Bruc paved road. There is not much traffic but we have to be careful with the truck turns. It is good to watch for the mountain trails which serve as shortcuts and get us off the highway for periods. Signposts show us the entrances to the forest of Montserrat's natural park. The slope is steep but easy to climb. It is better for the cyclists to go up directly on the asphalt rather than push their bikes up the trails.

We come to the residential area of Montserrat Parc and go around it, keeping to the long Avenida Verge de Montserrat. Beyond the houses, we follow the signs to the hermitage and restaurant of Sant Pau de la Guàrdia. After Sant Pau, we continue straight ahead on the same path and keep our eyes on the signs, which are not too plentiful. A castle in ruins serves as a point of reference. Arriving almost to it, we are to descend following a little-marked path which takes us to the country house of Can Massana.

Next to the Can Massana house, we are going to take the road in the direction of Montserrat. We have a long walk before reaching the monastery but with gentle uphill and downhill slopes. We recommend keeping to the road in spite of the motorcycle traffic which can be quite disrespectful of walkers. The alternative of climbing the mountain to the monastery

not only takes longer and is more difficult but can be cut off at certain points by rock slides, caused by rain.

Seven km on, after passing the chapel/hermitage of Santa Cecilia and coming almost to the monastery's parking lot, we find a sign on our right which indicates «Camí dels Degotalls». We climb the stairs in the mountain and reach a good walking path which takes us directly to the monastery.

■ Ignatian tip

We are reaching a very special place for Ignatius of Loyola and many other pilgrims of his time. Montserrat is recognized by many as a place of great spiritual presence. Called «Magical/Marvelous Mountain» by some, tradition recounts it as a place where the presence of the Spirit is «natural». Let each of us be carried forward by the flow of this same spiritual force, as was Ignatius. Coming before the Black Madonna, let us offer ourselves to follow Jesus and serve him with great generosity and freedom of heart.

«He continued on his journey to Montserrat, thinking as usual of the great deeds he was going to perform for the love of God. As his mind was filled with the adventures of Amadis de Gaul and such books, thoughts about these adventures came to his mind. He determined, therefore, to spend the entire night in a watch of arms, without ever sitting or lying down, but standing a while and then kneeling before the altar of Our Lady of Montserrat. There he would lay aside his fine attire and clothe himself with the armor of Christ. When he arrived at Montserrat, he spent a long *time in prayer. With the consent of his confessor he spent three whole days writing a general confession of his sins. With the permission of his confessor he arranged to give up his horse and to hang up his sword and his dagger in the church, at the altar of Our Lady. This confessor was the first person he told about his resolution to devote himself to the spiritual life. Up to then he had not revealed this purpose to any confessor.*

On the eve of the Annunciation of Our Blessed Lady, March 24 in the year 1522, he approached a beggar. He removed his costly clothes and gave them to this man. He then put on the pilgrim's robe he had previously bought and went to kneel before the altar of Our Lady. Alternating between kneeling and standing, he spent the entire night with his staff in hand.»

Let us also spend a longer period in the chapel of the Virgin of Montserrat, praying in silent solitude with the text of 1 Corinthians 12:1-11, begging to receive the gifts of the Holy Spirit in our lives, all for the greater glory of God. Here we also change our old clothes and put on those which we «discovered» in Igualada: a new life needs new clothes! What, metaphorically, will I leave behind here in Montserrat? What am I going to bring back home?

The Basilica of Montserrat was destroyed and rebuilt on different occasions throughout its history, as wars shook the land. After Ignatius was named a saint, and wishing to preserve his memory at the site of the altar to the Virgin where he kept night-long vigil, a black stone was laid with a memorial carving. This stone, which marked the place, was moved in the successive reconstructions and renovations all the way to the entrance of the arched atrium of today's church. This round black stone can be seen today close to the statue of Ignatius on the floor beneath the arch. A weathered quote engraved in the memorial stone reminds us that it was there that Ignatius gave himself to the Virgin and began his new life.

Mare de Déu de Montserrat (Our Lady of Montserrat).

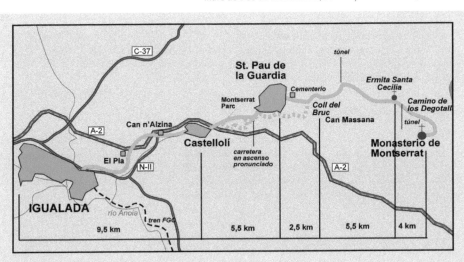

Total upward slope: 1,332 m. Total downward slope: 917 m.
Bicycles: medium difficulty. The climb up the hillside to Montserrat is somewhat steep. If the on-foot itinerary is followed, the bicycle will have to be pushed up. Therefore, it is preferable to ride up the El Bruc road and make your way to the monastery through the heights of Can Massana, following the paved road.

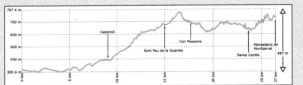

Igualada:	km 0
Castellolí:	km 9.5
Sant Pau de la Guàrdia:	km 15
Can Massana:	km 17.5
Santa Cecilia chapel:	km 24
Montserrat monastery:	km 27

■ Description

We leave Igualada from the Church of Santa Maria. We take the calle Santa Maria del Roser, which begins in the City Hall plaza where the church stands. We go straight along calle Soledad which then becomes Avenida de Caresmar and later, after a slight angle to the left, Avenida de Montserrat. We cross over the train tracks that link Igualada and Barcelona. We walk a bit further down Avenida de Montserrat and we take the first road that comes up on our right. It leads us to a great roundabout which we cross straight on. We leave behind a big restaurant, above us to our right, and we continue along the N-II highway.

Ahead of us we have 2 km of roadway that goes through an industrial park. After crossing two roundabouts, we bear left at the third one, on the first road that leaves the roundabout to our left and that allows us to go on a bit further away from the national road, without the distress of road traffic. A signpost shows us the way to Montserrat.

Always following the paved road straight on, we pass under the A-2. We keep parallel to it, keeping it now on our right. We reach a bridge and cross the A-2 once again, this time crossing over it. On the other side of the bridge, we turn to the left on the paved road. From the road, we take a paved track in front and to our right which takes us to Can Alzina. A signpost helps us orient ourselves. Following the same road which runs alongside the A-2, we get closer to Castelloli. We go into town and all the way through it along the same road. We leave Castelloli and carry on in the same direction. After a curve to the left, we see that the road rises to a bridge over the A-2. We do not

take it but instead follow the track that takes off to our right and runs parallel to the A-2. A signpost conveniently points it out.

We cross the A-2 and are already on the road that brings us up to the height of Can Massana. The arrows and the signposts show us the way. We can climb the whole way on the road, which will lead us to Can Massana. For those on foot, there are shortcuts that cut through the many bends on the way up. After the first and well-marked turn to the right, a path starts on the left, 100 m further on, which leads us away from the asphalt and into the woods. A post guides us.

We get back to the road and continue climbing on it. At the first bend we enter a path on our left which rises into the forest and which turns into a dirt trail that leads us to Montserrat Parc's residential area. Five

hundred meters after the road crosses the highway, we leave the dirt road and follow a path that takes us to the first residential homes. We are led onto the paved calle Castellolí. Just 100 m ahead we take a left along the Avenida Verge de Montserrat which, shortly after, begins bearing to our right in a slight curve. Continuing on down the same avenue which borders the residential area, without taking any of the adjacent streets, we reach its end at a crossroads. We take the road in front of us and arrive at Sant Pau de la Guàrdia.

We go through the town and exit by a dirt road which comes to a fork. We take the wide path to the left and follow it. We pass the cemetery of Sant Pau on our left. We continue the climb up the track which becomes a bit faint at times. We are getting closer to the highway and the summit of Can Massana. At last we see it from our path, rising over the highway. We go down to the highway and follow it towards our left until we reach the crossroads of Can Massana. We continue on the road in the direction of Montserrat (it is not recommended for pilgrims to take the mountain paths). The road takes us directly to the monastery. Before we get there, a sign to our right points the way to the monastery by the «Camí dels Degotalls». It is advisable for foot-pilgrims to climb up by this way as it lightens this last effort.

Once we arrive at Montserrat's complex of buildings, we go up to the plaza in front of the monastery: the pilgrim's service is there, inside a great door to the left.

■ Interesting facts

CASTELLOLÍ: small town. Its name comes from the ruins of the Castle of Aulí, dating back to the 10th century. There is a bakery/bar at our disposal.

MONTSERRAT: the mountain looks like an amazing frame, rightly named «Montserrat», which means «saw-toothed mountain». Although the history of the monastery's buildings is not known for certain, it seems there were already chapels there in the 9th century (San Acisclo's chapel, in the monastery gardens, is from the year 880).

The Benedictine monastery, founded in the 11th century, blossomed on the slopes of Montserrat as did the wild blooms we have been seeing along our Camino Ignaciano. The vitality of the Benedictine community is shown in their liturgies (monastery Eucharist at 11 o'clock) and in the spread of their influence throughout the whole socio-political landscape of Cataluña. Their presence and that of the Virgin of Montserrat have been a beacon of faith, hope and caring help to pilgrims for centuries. We too, standing before the effigy of the Virgin, give thanks to God for all that the Camino has accomplished until this point and we entrust ourselves to this last stage that will take us to Manresa, the Ignatian city.

According to tradition, the famous statue of the Black Virgin was sculpted by the evangelist St. Luke in the first century and was hidden for many long years from the Muslims in Montserrat's Holy Cave. Historians suggest that the statue is probably from the 12th century. Pilgrims have set off to the monastery—especially to this statue—for centuries, and there are records of many miraculous healings. Today, Montserrat is a well-known and highly popular destination for tourists and pilgrims, drawing over two million visitors each year. The great basilica was consecrated in 1592 and was almost entirely destroyed during the Napoleonic Invasion, being burned in 1811 and 1812. Once rebuilt, the monastery celebrated its millennial anniversary in 1880 and Pope Leo XIII declared the Virgin of Montserrat as patron of Cataluña in 1881.

The Black Virgin is not carved in black wood; rather, her dark shade comes from the smoke of the candles that has interacted with the statue's varnish over the course of centuries.

A long pathway down leads to the Cova Santa (Holy Cave), the place where tradition places the discovery of the Black Virgin. The vault, built in the 17th century, has a cruciform base. It is also possible to take a cable car which leaves us half way down to the cave. The view from some of the mountain paths are breathtaking, although pilgrims who have travelled the whole way from Loyola may not want to put in the extra work in search of a good panoramic view by climbing the steep slopes.

The Montserrat Museum's collection includes Gothic altarpieces and works by El Greco, Monet and Picasso. The Espai Audiovisual illustrates the life and spirituality of the monks through multimedia exhibitions. The basilica's façade, finished in 1968, shows Christ and the twelve apostles. Once inside, we follow the signs to the «Cambril de la Mare de Déu» to visit the Black Virgin's niche. On the other side of the basilica's entrance yard there is a hall where votive offerings and messages of thanks to the Virgin are exhibited, for favors granted by her intercession. The group of buildings offers restaurants, supermarkets, pharmacies, a health center, bank and tourist office (Tel.: 938 777 777).

■ TAXI
Montserrat:

Taxi Marcel	607 329 946
Castellolí:	
Taxi Castellolí	686 229 384

■ LODGING
CASTELLOLÍ: City Hall. Tel.: 938 084 000. There is a recently opened shelter.

SANT PAU DE LA GUÀRDIA: El Celler de la Guàrdia. It is a restaurant-hostel with rooms and pilgrim's shelter. Tel.: 937 710 323. (Phone ahead if you wish to stay here! May only accept pilgrims before 6PM).

MONTSERRAT: Abad Cisneros Hotel. Tel.: 938 777 701. Monastery's shelter for pilgrims in the Centre de Coordinació Pastoral (you must arrive before 17:30). Tel.: 938 777 766. Monastery information at: Tel.: 938 777 765, or check the website: www.abadiademontserrat.net.

MONTSERRAT – MANRESA

(24.6 km)

«Avoid all stubbornness but when you have gotten sufficiently started on something, stick to it and do not flee cravenly out of weariness or desperation.»

«In the morning let me know of your faithfulness, for I trust in you. Show me the path I am to follow, for I turn to you. Teach me to do your will, for you are my God. May your encouraging spirit guide me to level ground» (Ps 143:8-10).

Sanctuary of St. Ignatius' Cave (Santuario de la Cueva de San Ignacio / Santuari de la Cova de Sant Ignasi), Manresa.

We begin this last stage of our pilgrimage with great zest. We will walk these last kilometers with joy in our hearts and a spring in our steps though we still have a good long hike before reaching Manresa. Nevertheless, we will suceed. To know all that awaits us–the stone bridge over the Cardoner, the hospital of Santa Lucía, the sanctuary of the Cova and the grand church of the Seu–all this energizes our last effort towards this city where God graced Ignatius's heart and intellect with so many mystical visions.

We leave Montserrat in the direction of the Camí dels Degotalls and we backtrack along this last stage until reaching Santa Cecilia. Here we take the path which descends to our right, leaving the asphalt road. Pay attention: the path begins in a quite sharp curve to the left which will bring us down the mountain, steeply, to our first destination point: Sant Cristòfol.

The trail runs into a dirt path with a farmhouse in front of us on the other side of a stream. We follow the path going down towards the residential area of Can Prat and then towards the town of Sant Cristòfol, which we do not enter. Here, people recount the legend of a miracle San Ignacio performed, 500 years ago, saving the people from persistent drought. El Pozo del Milagro is 1 km away. We continue then in the direction of Sant Jaume de Castellbell. As we cross the fields, on our left, we are treated with an impressive vista of Montserrat, perhaps the best possible view of the sacred mountain.

We do not go into Sant Jaume either but, continuing on until we reach Marganell's asphalt roadway, we cross the river and, next to the restaurant on the curve, we go up to our left in the direction of Castellgalí and Manresa. The path takes us to a new, dry, stream which we cross and then turn to our right, always keeping an eye on the Camino Ignaciano trail signs.

We enter Castellgalí by the Montserrat road and go into the old town center. We head toward the church which can be seen on high. We pass in front of it and go down, leaving town by way of the old 10th century pilgrims' path. We descend on this path to the highway C-55. We have to walk for some 500 m along a path paralleling the highway, on the left, until we can cross the bridge and take the path which begins on our left once past the bridge.

Further on, a monument recalls the martyrdom of two nuns on this site in 1936. We follow this path until reaching the country house of Can Cornet where we do not enter. Before reaching it, we take a well-defined path which rises to the right towards an old stone quarry. A steep climb puts us to the test on the last 5 km of our pilgrimage. Once on top, we continue to our left in the direction of the castle of Oller del Mas and, on reaching the castle-house, we head towards a column on our right, which indicates the Roman road which leads us to Manresa.

Following the orange arrows, we go towards some houses and descend to the stream of Marganell which we are going to cross and go right back up to find the path which takes us to the tower of Santa Caterina. Watch for the orange signs: we have to turn to the right at the electrical tower and, further on to the left, to direct ourselves to the tower, marked by a Catalan flag which is visible from afar.

We go towards the tower and, once there, we see all of Manresa before us, where the Basilica of the Seu, and the Spirituality Center and Retreat House of the Cova of Sant Ignasi stand out. Below, spanning the Cardoner River, we see the old bridge and the hermitage of Nuestra Señora de la Guía (Our Lady of the Way).

Tradition maintains that, when Ignatius arrived at this point, he found the town in procession in honor of the Virgin. It is very likely that he entrusted himself to the Virgin de la Guía to guide him on his pilgrimage.

We go down directly to the river, going by the hermitage of La Guia and crossing the old bridge, following in the footsteps of Ignatius of Loyola. We cross it with the emotion of one who is coming to the end of a long journey, to a long desired destination. As Ignatius did in 1522, we also

head towards the hospital of Santa Lucía. Passing by the hermitage of San Marcos and going up calle San Marcos, we arrive at the hospital and at the Pilgrim Office. The sanctuary of the Cova is to the right and will also have to be visited in its turn.

We finish our walk on the Camino Ignaciano, celebrating our arrival and receiving our certificate as an Ignatian pilgrim in the Pilgrim's Office, fit for the final welcome in Manresa's City Hall.

■ Ignatian tip

Here, we find Ignatius already on the road to Manresa, with a new outfit and a deep inner desire to do everything for the greater glory of God. Yet we also experience quite strongly that good resolves are never easy, even when they are made with the heart's best intentions.

«After receiving the Blessed Sacrament, he left at daybreak. To avoid being recognized, he avoided the direct route that leads to Barcelona since he might have met those who knew him and honored him. Instead he took a byway that led him to a town called Manresa. Here he decided to stay a few days in the hospital and to write down some notes in a small book which for his own consolation he very carefully carried with him. About three miles from Montserrat, he was overtaken by a man who came after him in great haste. This man asked whether he had given some clothing to a poor man, as the man said he had. Ignatius answered that he had in fact given them to a beggar. When he learned that this man had been ill-treated because he was suspected of stealing the clothes, Ignatius' eyes filled with tears of compassion for this beggar. And no matter how much he tried to avoid praise and esteem, it did not take long in Manresa before people began telling great things about him because of what happened at Montserrat. His reputation increased day by day. It was not long before people were saying more than was true, declaring that he had given up a large fortune, and similar things that were not factual.»

«Every day, he begged alms in Manresa. He never ate meat nor drank wine, even though both were offered to him. On Sundays he did not fast and drank sparingly if wine were offered to him. Formerly he had been quite careful about his hair and wore it in the fashionable manner adopted by young men of his age. Now he made up his mind to neglect it and let it grow wild, without combing it or cutting it or covering it either day or night. For the same reason, he allowed the nails of his hands and feet to grow since here too his care had been excessive.»

The «some days» that Ignatius had first planned to spend in Manresa became more than ten months of personal growth. God was in no hurry with him and, thanks be to God, Ignatius was not overly eager to leave this city that welcomed him with open arms despite his eccentricities. The Ignatian pilgrim may well want to imitate some qualities of this «converted gentleman». Perhaps it is time to stop at a barber shop to get a good haircut.

The Tourist Office of the City and the «La Cova» (the Cave) Shrine in Manresa offer some leaflets and a small booklet so that pilgrims can continue this Manresa experience in their own personal journey.

Church of La Seo in Manresa.

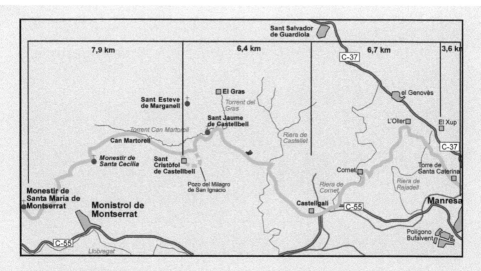

Total upward slope: 406 m. Total downward slope: 896 m.
Bicycles: medium difficulty. In order to go down from Santa Cecilia it is best not to take the narrow path posted for pilgrims on foot but continue straight on the dirt road, pass a house that stays on the left and, once across the dry river, find the point where the pilgrim's path joins the dirt road leading to Sant Cristòfol. And again, on the descent from Castellgalí, cyclists have to bring the bike to their side and walk carefully along the C-55 for about 400 m.

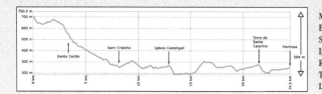

Montserrat:	km 0
Ermita de Santa Cecilia:	km 3.5
Sant Cristòfol:	km 7.9
Iglesia de Castellgalí:	km 14.3
Riera de El Xup:	km 21
Torre de Santa Caterina:	km 23.5
La Cova de Manresa:	km 24.6

◼ Description

We say goodbye to the Mare de Déu de Montserrat and take the same path (dels Degotalls) which took us up to Montserrat the previous day. As we return along this same road, we stay to the left, heading back towards the chapel/ hermitage of St. Cecilia. As we walk along this path, parallel to the road and, after passing the tunnel on the right side, we can see the shrine up at the top, next to the road.

At the St. Cecilia shrine we take a paved road down to our right. A sign indicates «GR-4 to Sant Cristòfol» and we follow it. We leave the shrine to the left and go down the paved road. The road we want to take runs parallel to the main road but below it. We pass the ravines which descend from the mountain.

For pilgrims on bicycles, it is best to follow the dirt road that continues to descend. It turns as we pass

some farms which we will notice on our left.

On each new trail we always proceed down to our right. At the bottom, we reach a dry stream and cross

to the other side. We then climb the dirt road and eventually come to the end of this road (an iron cross indicates the point) where we meet those pilgrims who have descended the mountain on foot.

The pilgrims on foot will follow the directions along the GR-4 road which lead to Sant Cristòfol. You will notice a sign which indicates a bend in the road. We take the mountain trail which descends steeply. We then follow the red and white GR-4 trails. We reach a wide dirt footpath which we take to the right. Cycling pilgrims join us. We can see yellow arrows going «opposite our direction».

We enter the neighbor-hood of Can Prat, along calle «Carrer de les Agulles». We follow the red and white signs along this same street. (Note that at times the signs on the light poles may be covered with pink paint.) Eventually we come to a hairpin turn on our right. Look for the sign which indicates the road to Manresa on our left. We follow the red and white signs of the GR-4. We find a vertical sign pointing towards Sant Cristòfol de Castellbell. At this point we can divert 2 km to the right, following the signs, to visit the village and the Pozo del Milagro de San Ignacio (the well/spring of St. Ignatius's miracle). Or, we can also go straight, following the direction towards Sant Jaume de Castellbell.

Following the path to Sant Jaume, we come to a crossroads and turn to the left, leaving Sant Cristòfol behind us. Descend to a stream, following the GR-4 trails. We cross the stream and pass a house on the left. At the next fork we turn right, following the red and white trail markings.

We reach the asphalt road and go left, down to the bridge. Just past the bridge,

and next to the restaurant, there is a path to our left which leads us up higher. A signpost indicates the direction to Manresa.

The dirt road joins another that comes from our right. Continue straight ahead and you will see a large pig farm on the left. Just past the farm buildings, we come to a fork. Take the road to the left as the sign indicates. We now leave the red and white GR-4 trail marks and begin to follow the blue and white markings. Take a right at the next fork. This road leads us across a stream and immediately past another path which crosses ours to the right. A sign on the right indicates the direction of Manresa and Castellgalí and so we take it to the right.

Our route crosses another one and we take a right. Soon a new road branches off to the left but we continue straight ahead. We reach the first houses of Castellgalí: an old Excursionista Union sign tells us that we still have two hours to Manresa. We take the first street on our left, following the white and blue trail markers. We are now on the road called «Camí de Montserrat» and we continue straight ahead.

We now approach the heart of Castellgalí; we can see the church in front of us, up higher. We approach the church on calle Sant Antoni. Here we say goodbye to the blue and white signs of the Catalan Camino de Santiago. Our Camino Ignaciano will continue ahead, past the church façade. Continue straight ahead; at the end of the village houses, look for a dirt road next to a utility pole. A sign indicates that we are now entering the old pilgrim road from Manresa to Montserrat. This 10th century path takes a steep descent down towards highway C-55. We go down to reach the road and then take it to our left. We continue for about 500 meters on a track that runs parallel to the highway, crossing a bridge over a river. After passing the golf course on the left, we take the middle asphalt road which begins at our left.

Church of San Miguel, Castellgalí.

We now border the golf course and follow the Can Cornet riverbed to our left. At the fork we go to the right to avoid crossing the stream. After 600 m we pass very close to La Masía (Can Cornet), a private house. We take the path that continues on our right and eventually this takes us up to an old stone quarry.

Our road has zigzagged while rising steadily. Large stones in the road help us imagine the presence of the old quarry which we do not currently see since the road continues to climb. Near the top, next to some fields, our road turns left. About 200 m farther on, this road meets another which we take to our left. After just a few

meters farther, we can see the city of Manresa.

We walk straight ahead, without taking any of the paths that emerge to the right and left. Soon we come to the castle of Oller del Mas. After about 1.5 km, another road meets us from the left. We arrive at 100 m from the castle gates. We turn right and we pass a column that indicates that we are on the old Roman road that Ignatius surely took to Manresa. We leave a path down to our right and continue towards some houses that we pass to our left. After a short descent, we arrive at the entrance to another house and at that point we turn left on a dirt road down to the

creek. We descend and cross a small bridge.

We pass the creek and we turn to our right about 50 m. We climb a path that we will follow, along with a stone wall. Once up, we take a left and we head towards some houses that we pass and continue straight until a new crossing, with a very

visible power poles. At the junction we take on our right, going away from the neighborhood of El Xup in front of us.

Keep walking straight ahead. After a while our road takes a sharp turn right to enter a farm but we continue straight, by an old lane, not very well marked, passing between fields. At about 200 m it forks. We take the narrow path to go straight to our right.

Soon this path crosses a paved road. We continue straight ahead towards the Tower of Santa Caterina, a former lookout tower. We head directly to this tower.

We leave the Tower on a path that runs to the right before heading to La Cova. A steep descent takes us almost to the foot of the shrine of la Virgen de la Guía, which we can see to our right. We take the road to our left and cross the bridge over the railroad tracks. We continue down to the road along Cardoner River and turn right as we head to the Old Bridge. In front of us, up above, we behold the building holding St. Ignatius' Cave. The Camino Ignaciano ends at San Llúcia's hospital, also known as the Shrine of Rapture. To get there, we must walk up calle San Marcos, the one that goes by the chapel on the other side of the bridge. We climb up until we reach la plaza de San Ignacio and the old Manresa Jesuit college, now the Regional Museum (Museu Comarcal). In the Pilgrim's Office our credentials will be signed and the final certificate of the Ignatian pilgrimage will be awarded.

◼ Interesting facts

CASTELLGALÍ: is a small town of 1,700 citizens yet it is rich in the pilgrim tradition. Its origins are very old, dating from the times of the Iberians. It has a privileged location on a mountain-side with a broad overview of the Cardoner river valley. The Roman settlers gave the name «Boades» to this settlement. During the Middle Ages, with the influx of pilgrims who travelled the Camino Real to the monastery of Montserrat, Castellgalí was known for its hospitality and its blacksmiths. We can suppose that Ignatius, during his long stay in Manresa, may have travelled back to Montserrat, and, if he did, surely stopped in Castellgalí. Very close to our final destination, this town offers restaurants, supermarkets, a pharmacy and a bank.

SANTA CATERINA: watchtower.

MANRESA: This Ignatian city welcomed its first Jesuits in 1602. Since then, the city has maintained a constant Ignatian presence which, today, receives a boost with the arrival of so many «Ignatian pilgrims». In order to visit the many Ignatian historical locations in Manresa, it is worth planning a longer visit. (Check the tourism website: www.manresaturisme.cat)

El Santuario de La Cova de Sant Ignasi is a perfect place to end our pilgrimage. Here we attend to our inner experience and discern the lights and shadows that we will surely have experienced along our Camino Ignaciano. Let us not be in a hurry to leave this holy place, so emblematic of Ignatian spirituality. At La Cova you can get all the information you need to plan your stay (see website www.covamanresa. cat). The city of Manresa offers restaurants, supermarkets, pharmacies, a health center, a bike shop, banks and an information office (Tel.: 938 784 090).

Note: Manresa, end of the way. Manresa, together with Montserrat, constitutes the culmination of the Camino Ignaciano. It is

impossible to overestimate its importance in the life of Ignatius, in the spirituality of the Society of Jesus, and in the development of the Spiritual Exercises. Manresa embodies

a central maxim of Ignatian spirituality: one finds God «in all things», not only in tranquil spaces, but also in modern and heterogeneous cities. Modern Manresa is full, nevertheless, of historical reminders of the pilgrim's stay. One can imagine Ignatius, before he crossed the river during his own journey, praying in the small hermitage of the *Virgin de la Guía* (the hermitage was moved some meters in 1856 to make room for the train tracks), and at the nearby elevated cross. There can be no doubt that Ignatius crossed the graceful Puente Viejo, of Roman origin and medieval design. He also knew the tiny *Capilla de Sant Marc* in which, in the testimony of some witnesses in the canonization process of Ignatius, he frequently prayed; and in which he may even have had, mystical visions. The exquisite *Seu de Manresa*, the collegiate basilica of Santa María, one of the most spacious churches of Europe, was finished some three decades before Ignatius' arrival and testifies to the great prosperity that Manresa enjoyed in that historical era. One of the witnesses who was questioned during the canonization process declared that Ignatius prayed in the basilica for more than two hours as soon as he arrived in Manresa, before going to the *Hospital de Santa Lucía* where he lodged. Tradition maintains that Ignatius composed some of the key passages of the

Spiritual Exercises in the small cave known as the Santa Cova, situated today within the *Santuario de la Cova de Sant Ignasi*. The inhabitants of Manresa associated this cave site with Ignatius and the first chapel was constructed there in 1603, still quite proximate to the residents' «living memory».

The autobiography of Ignatius also relates that, while contemplating along the Cardoner River, he experienced extraordinary spiritual illuminations, which ended up changing his life. Where exactly did this happen? The river runs through the city, so pilgrims can imagine other places, aside from the Cova, where Ignatius may have rested and savored mystical consolations. According to one tradition, it was on the way to the Iglesia de San Pablo, a kilometer and a half from the center of Manresa, when Ignatius experienced that key illumination on the banks of the Cardoner River. This site is marked at present by a modern work of art and can be reached by going up behind the Retreat House/Spirituality Center on the old road of Santa Clara and, before reaching the convent of Santa Clara, turning right and taking la calle del Peix to a park where there is a bench indicating the spot.

The modern pilgrim can easily find many traces of Ignatius because he stayed in different places, visited various churches and convents, helped in caring for the sick and poor and paused here and there to pray. For several weeks he lived on the ground floor of a house, now marked as number 25 on *calle Sobrerroca*. (The remains of one of the town's medieval gates can be seen at the end of this street.) For a period of time, when Ignatius was ill, he was put up by the well-to-do Amigant family; and today the *Capilla de Sant Ignasi Malalt* commemorates this site. The current plaza of *Sant Domènec* is located in what was a residence of the Dominicans in Manresa, another of the places where Ignatius lived while he regularly visited the churches of Manresa.

In addition to those already mentioned, one of his favorite places to visit was the Iglesia del Carme, a Carmelite church built on the Puig Mercadal, the town's highest hill. The church was destroyed during the Spanish

Iglesia de Nuestra Señora de la Salud (Church of Our Lady of Health), Viladordis.

Tower of the Cathedral in Barcelona.

Civil War but the reconstruction conserves some parts of the old cloister. Santa María de la Salut de Viladordis, situated outside the original city walls, dates from the 10th century and was another of Ignatius' favorite prayer spots. There is a stone in this church on which he was wont to kneel to pray to the Virgin. Ignatius also liked to stop and pray next to the Cruz del Tort—and to enjoy the view from there—in his walks to the Convento de Santa Clara.

The office of tourism of Manresa is an excellent resource for obtaining maps and orientations on how to get to the mentioned Ignatian sites, as well as other information. The office is located in the Town Hall plaza.

■ TAXI
Castellbell i el Vilar

Asociación Taxistas del Valle   938 282 475

Manresa

Taxis Manresa   938 770 877
Manuel Artero   630 918 900
Radio Taxi Manresa   938 744 000

■ LODGING
CASTELLGALI: Pilgrim Shelter: Contact Town Hall: 938 330 021.

MANRESA: Alberg (shelter) del Carme, Pl. Milcentenari, s/n. Tel.: 938 750 396. Apartaments Grup Urbi, c/ Codinella, 9, entresol 2.ª. Tel.: 938 768 241 / 606 993 537. Apartaments la Farola, c/ Canyelles, 5. Tel.: 938 731 300. Casa d'Exercicis La Cova de Sant Ignasi, Pasaje de la Cova. Tel.: 938 720 422. Turó de la Torre Hostel,

Sallent, s/n, Polígon Els Dolors. Tel.: 938 733 286. 1948 Hotel, Carretera de Santpedor, 54-58. Tel.: 938 748 216. Els Noguers Hotel, Avinguda Països Catalans, 167. Tel.: 938 743 258. La Masia inn, Plaça Sant Ignasi, 22. Tel.: 938 724 237. Roser Manila Sant Andreu inn, Carrer Sant Andreu, 9. Tel.: 938 725 908. Apartamentos Somiarte. Tel.: 630 538 838. Manresa Apartaments. Tel.: 660 551 333.

Note: Ignatian Barcelona. Upon finishing the Camino Ignaciano, many pilgrims will go through Barcelona on their way home. Barcelona, too, has considerable importance for the life of Ignatius. After his long stay in Manresa, he spent some weeks in Barcelona preparing for his upcoming trip to the Holy Land. The odyssey of Ignatius does not stop here: he embarked from Barcelona, first to Rome and then later to the Holy Land. When the Franciscan Friars who supervised pilgrims in the Holy Land, made him return after only three weeks, Ignatius found himself back in Barcelona where he undertook two years of basic studies of Latin grammar.

Alltogether, Ignatius visited Barcelona on five occasions, and in the city made many friends and found benefactor-families who helped him generously in his student years and in the early years of the Society of Jesus. That is why he wrote: «It seems to me, and I do not doubt it, that I am indebted and owe more to that populace of Barcelona than to any other town in my life.»

Ignatian sites in Barcelona: the city is full of Ignatian and Jesuit history. On the web page of the Camino Ignaciano, in the section «On pilgrimage in Ignatian Spain», there is a link to the very detailed and erudite study by Miguel Lop, SJ, *Ignatian memories in Barcelona*. There is also a guide on the Jesuits' website which corresponds to this study (http://www.jesuites.net/es/sant-ignasi-i-barcelona).

In your visit, keep in mind that the Barcelona of Ignatius had a population of around 40,000, instead of the 1,600,000 of today. The city center was in what today is called, the barri Gòtic. Since he spent more than two years in Barcelona, we can assume that Ignatius passed along most of the streets of the old city. Wandering through the neighborhood of the Ribera, the economic center of the city in his time, by Santa María del Mar, or around the Gothic quarter, we can steep ourselves in the neighborhood's atmosphere, which still maintains many of the buildings and streets from 1500.

The gate into the walled medieval city was in the plaza of Sant Agustí Vell, where calle del Portal Nou enters. Ignatius assuredly would have stopped by the *Capella d'en Marcús* (from the 12th century, in the intersection of the calle de Carders and calle de Montcada), where travelers venerated an image of the Madre de Dios de la Guía. Parallel to the vía Laietana runs a small, short street named calle de Sant Ignasi. In Ignatius' day, Inés Pascual, his great friend and benefactor from Manresa, lived in a house which stood where the calle de Sant Ignasi meets calle de la Princesa. The house was torn down to build the new street.

Ignatius studied Latin with a gentleman named Jeroni Ardèvol, who lived in the Ribera district, on calle *dels Mirallers*. The *Basílica de Santa María del Mar* (14th c.) is another important Ignatian site. Next to the left lateral door there is a chapel dedicated to St. Ignatius and also a plaque which recalls the place where the saint would usually beg for alms. Another important church is the *Basílica de los Santos Mártires Justo y Pastor*, where Ignatius liked to sit, often accompanied by children, to listen to the sermons of the Franciscans. His devotion attracted the attention of Isabel Roser, who in time became a good friend and an important benefactor. Her house was in front of the basilica, in the building with floral motifs on the façade.

Other Ignatian sites can be found in the city but we will only mention two more. The first is calle Casp 27, where the Jesuit church of the Sagrado Corazón is found. On the altar dedicated to St. Ignatius, the sword Ignatius offered to the Moreneta in the sanctuary of Montserrat is displayed. And the second, a bit out of the way since it was outside of the city in the time of Ignatius, is the place where today the great waterfall is found in Ciutadella Park. There was a convent of Dominican sisters here, whose moral behavior Ignatius attempted to reform, earning him a good drubbing which almost killed him.

As the pilgrim can well imagine, a city like Barcelona is not simply known for Ignatian memories. Here, Catalan modernism and the works of Gaudí, among other things, will surely fill the pilgrim's final days in Cataluña.

Church of the Sacred Heart of Jesus, Barcelona.

PART THREE

Guide to the interior way

As was already said at the start of this guide, this third part is linked to the second, day by day. For those who do not know the workings of the *Spiritual Exercises* of St. Ignatius, it is recommended that they look into the corresponding explanations on the Camino Ignaciano webpage (www.caminoigna ciano.org), which can help explain the depth and meaning of St. Ignatius' spirituality. On the webpage's window entitled «Peregrination» there is helpful advice on the spiritual path proposed. Do not hesitate to consult the pages when preparing.

You will see that each day has its own meditation, together with texts taken from the New Testament and some from the Old Testament; the latter are included on these pages, while the ones from the New Testament are not. This choice was made to encourage the pilgrim to carry a small, light edition of the New Testament, as a kind of travelling companion. Thus the pilgrim will always be able to freely broaden his or her readings and find other texts. One can never know where God might surprise us with meaningful inspirations.

For those pilgrims who are not doing the whole Camino Ignaciano at once and wish to do it in parts, perhaps year-by-year, it is still advisable to follow the four-week structure that Ignatius introduced and take up a whole "week" of the Exercises, in order, during each successive week-long trek of the camino. In this manner, the Exercises can reveal their true meaning. If you are only planning to make a short pilgrimage, you can always adjust the meditations to your own needs.

One last quick contribution, to help understand Ignatian vocabulary: the *annotations* are very short instructions that help the retreatant get into a prayerful mood; the *petitions* are what the person wishes to receive from God, or, as Ignatius would say, "that which I wish to obtain as the result of prayer"; the *reflections* are meant to help the person place him or herself into the day's theme; the *texts* are the main body of the meditation; the *colloquy* at the end is a conclusion to the prayer time, the moment when the soul lets itself be taken into the final contact with the Creator.

There is no need for anything else and may the Lord walk in pilgrimage beside us.

Stage 1: Loyola – Zumarraga

Preparatory Prayer:

- Annotation: Let us begin our journey calmly, taking up our subject seriously. It is very useful to spend some time reflecting on the Preparatory Prayer: Beg God for the grace that all my intentions, actions and works will be directed solely for the praise and service of His Divine Majesty. If you find «spiritual nourishment» in any word or at some point, it is better not to move on, but to remain there, asking what the Spirit is saying and allowing it to speak to you in your heart. Ignatius tells us that «to know and taste something interiorly» is more important than knowing a great deal about it.

- Petition: Lord, grant me the grace to feel your love in my life interiorly and to be profoundly grateful for it.

- Reflections: Spirituality has been defined as «turning one's journey through life into a journey towards God.» We hope to transform our journey through Spain into a spiritual journey.

We begin by contemplating what surrounds us in these beautiful places near Loyola. We walk slowly, aware that it is a gift to be able to dedicate time to this encounter with God, with the world and ourselves. It is a privilege to be able to do these «exercises!» Let our hearts leap in gratitude as we begin our pilgrimage. The One who has loved us from the beginning and leads us in our lives is the One who has brought us here. With this conviction, we begin our walk. God who is Father and Mother to us comes to meet us in every person and thing we see. May His presence fill us with gratitude.

- Texts

Isaiah 55:1-11. God, in his love for me, invites me to come to Him.

«All you who are thirsty, come to the water! You who have no money, come, buy grain and eat. Come, buy grain without money, wine and milk without cost! Why spend your money for what is not bread; your wages for what does not satisfy? Only listen to me and you shall eat well, you shall delight in rich fare. Pay attention and come to me; listen, that you may have life. I will make an everlasting covenant with you, the steadfast loyalty I promised to David. As I made him a witness to peoples, a leader and commander of peoples, so shall you summon a nation you knew not, and a nation that knew you not shall run to you because of the Lord, your God, the Holy One of Israel, who has glorified you. Seek the Lord while he may be found, call upon him while he is near. Let the wicked forsake their way, and sinners their thoughts; let them turn to the Lord to find mercy; to our God who is generous in forgiving. For my thoughts are not your thoughts, nor are your ways my ways–this is the oracle of the Lord. For as the heavens are higher than the earth, so are my ways higher than your ways, my thoughts higher than your thoughts. Yet just as from the heavens the rain and snow come down and do not return there till they have watered the earth, making it fertile and fruitful, giving seed to the one who sows and bread to the one who eats. So shall my word be, that goes forth from my mouth. It shall not return to me empty, but shall do what pleases me, achieving the end for which I sent it.»

Psalm 63. I respond to God by expressing my desire to meet him.

«O God, you are my God; early in the morning I will begin my search for you: my soul is dry for need of you, my flesh is wasted with desire for you, as a dry and burning land without water; to see your power and your glory, as I contemplate you in the holy place. Because your mercy is better than life, my lips will give you praise. So will I go on blessing you all

Cervera.

my life, lifting up my hands in your name. My soul will be comforted, as with good food; my mouth will give you praise with songs of joy when I remember you, on my bed and when I give thought to you in the nighttime. Because you have been my help, I will have joy in the shade of your wings. My soul keeps ever near you: your right hand is my support. But those whose desire is my soul's destruction will go down to the lower parts of the earth.

They will be cut off by the sword; they will be food for jackals. But the king will have joy in God; everyone who takes an oath by him will have cause for pride; but the false mouth will be shut.»

● Final Colloquy: Sum up what I have thought about or felt during my prayer, talking to Jesus as one friend does to another. Be frank with him about what you have experienced and felt (or not felt) during this stage of your walk with him.

Stage 2: Zumarraga – Arantzazu

● Annotation: We insist that it is very useful to devote some time to the introductory prayer, which expresses the fundamental objective of our inner pilgrimage. Remember that if you find «spiritual nourishment» in some a word or idea, it is better not to go further, but to remain there, allowing it to talk to us more deeply. Today, we recommend that you spend a long time in prayer on arrival at Arantzazu sanctuary, just as Ignatius did. Pray with gratitude for everything in your life, for the gifts that you have received up to now and, last but not least, for being here!

● Petition: Lord, grant me the grace to feel your love interiorly with profound thanksgiving.

● Reflections: As we approach the sanctuary of our Lady of Arantzazu, we devote a second day to delving prayerfully into the happy points in our life's story. As you walk and pray, recall moments of happiness and grace, especially those you now see as turning points in your life. Were there moments when you particularly felt God's presence as you made a major choice, or moments in which you endured a major tribulation that you overcame with the help of God? Were there moments when you felt God was absent, times when you could not believe that God could be with you? Nonetheless, God was always there, as your best friend, as a tender Fa-

Arantzazu.

ther, as a nurturing Mother. Take into your heart all those moments and feel filled with great gratitude for the persons and events in your past life: God is always at work in our surroundings. Why not present those moments and all those people to God and give thanks that they were God's hands and arms that held you?

● Texts

Luke 1:46-55. With Mary, my soul glorifies the Lord.

Luke 12:22-34. Lord, You know all my needs. I am not to worry.

● Final Colloquy: Sum up your meditation in a spirit of prayer, talking to Mary as a son or daughter does to her or his mother. Now that you are close to her shrine, be open with her about what you have discovered during this stage of your journey.

Stage 3: Arantzazu – Araia

- Annotation: We would like to insist on the importance of devoting some time to reflection on the introductory prayer. Remember what Ignatius tells us, that «to know and savor something interiorly» is more important than knowing a great deal. So do not be in a hurry. Today we begin to consider our Principle and Foundation, by reflecting on the purpose for which we were created, because an overall vision of life is essential before going into detail later on.

- Petition: Lord, grant me the grace to feel your love internally in my life, with profound thanksgiving. Help me, O Lord, to discover the foundation of my life, according to your will.

- Reflections: We begin by recalling that our whole life has been a spiritual journey. As you walk today, devote some time to remembering again your own life story and letting your mind wander over it prayerfully. Recall your past and let God show you a sort of photo album of key moments in it, some painful, others joyful, which have brought you to this present stage of your life. Who am I? How have I reached this point in my life? What people, events or places have been influential in moulding the person I am now? Let these images surface, along with whatever grateful, painful, or prayerful feelings go with them.

In contrast with the good ones, are there moments, people, or aspects of your life that cause feelings of embarrassment, which you want to disown and which you cannot imagine God accepting either? Present those moments to God, with a prayer for acceptance and growth. You do not have to feel you have become completely reconciled or to «settle» anything today; the people and moments you have recalled and the feelings that have welled up can become matters for consideration and prayer as you walk with God on this pilgrimage. We are experiencing the process of «holding our whole life up to God», which may at times fill us with joy and gratitude, and at others with regret and shame. The graces we seek will be gratitude, understanding and acceptance of oneself and realization that we are accepted by God. Think of yourself as «panning for gold», sifting through the multitude of ideas that first come up until you find the «nugget», the aspects of life where you may have something to learn or where you need to grow. God may be leading you to spend time reflecting on them.

- Texts

Hosea 11:1-9. His love for me is a tender love.

«When Israel was a child he was dear to me and I took my son out of Egypt. When I sent for them, then they went away from me; they made offerings to the Baals, burning perfumes to images. But I was guiding Ephraim's footsteps; I took them up in my arms, but they were not conscious that I was ready to make them well. I made them come after me with human cords, with the bands of love; I fostered them like those who raise an infant to their cheeks; I bent down to feed them. He will go back to the land of Egypt and the Assyrian will be his king because they would not come back to me. And the sword will go through his towns, wasting his children and causing destruction because of their evil designs. My people are given up to sinning against me; though their voice goes up on high, no one will be lifting them up. How may I give you up, O Ephraim? How may I be your savior, O Israel? How may I make you like Admah? How may I do to you as I did to Zeboim? My heart is overwhelmed, my pity is stirred. I will not put into effect the heat of my wrath; I will not again send destruction on Ephraim; for I am God and not man, the Holy One among you; I will not put an end to you.»

Psalm 139:1-14.17-18. In awe and reverence I remember how God has cared for me in times of joy and pain, in times of success and failure, in times of faithfulness and infidelity.

«O Lord, you know me, searching out all my secrets. You know when I am seated and when I stand, you see my thoughts from far away. You keep watch over my waking and my sleep, and have knowledge of all my ways. For there is not a word on my tongue which is not clear to you, O Lord. I am shut in by you on every side, and you have put your hand on me. Such knowledge is a wonder greater than my powers; it is so high that I may not come near it. Where may I hide from your spirit? How may I flee from you? If I go up to heaven, you are there: or if I make my bed in the underworld, you are there. If I take the wings of the morning, and go to the farthest parts of the sea; Even there, will I be guided by your hand, and your right hand will keep me. If I say, only let me be covered by the dark, and the light about me be night; Even the dark is not dark to you; the night is as bright as the day: for dark and light are the same to you. My flesh was made by you, and my parts joined together in my mother's body. I will give you praise, for I am wonderfully and intricately formed; your works are great wonders, and of this my soul is fully conscious. […] How dear are your thoughts to me, O God! how great is the number of them! If I made up their number, it would be more than the grains of sand; when I am awake, I am still with you.»

Spiritual Exercises [5]:

«It is very helpful if those who do the exercises begin them with great courage and generosity towards their Creator and Lord, offering Him all their love and freedom, so that his Divine Majesty may dispose of their person and all they have according to His holy will.»

● Final Colloquy: Sum up what has come to mind in your prayer time, talking to Jesus as one friend does to another. Be honest with him about what you have discovered on this stage of your journey.

Urbia.

177

Stage 4: Araia – Alda

● Annotation: We insist again on the need to devote some time to reflection on the introductory prayer. Remember as well what Ignatius tells us: that «interior knowledge and savoring» are more important than knowing much. So do not be in a hurry. Today we continue our consideration of our Principle and Foundation.

● Petition: I beseech you, Lord, to direct all my actions by Your inspiration, to carry them on by Your gracious help, so that every intention and action of mine may begin always from You and through You be happily completed.

● Reflections: The previous meditations reminded you where you have been in your life and that God has been and always will remain a faithful presence in your life journey. Today our meditation shifts focus. We reflect on the wider panorama, the bigger and fuller picture of your life, the meaning of our human journey through life. What is God's plan for us humans? What is the purpose of our pilgrimage through this world? In the Spiritual Exercises, Ignatius gives a straightforward yet profound answer to those questions: «God created us to praise reverence and serve Him and in this way to save our souls. God created all other creatures to help us achieve this purpose.»

This statement is simple yet profound. God created us for union with Him (to «save our souls,» as Ignatius puts it). In this earthly life, we draw close to God by praise and gratitude for the wonders of this planet, by reverencing and showing deep respect for the persons and gifts God has created, and by serving God in our fellow men and women.

I attain full spiritual freedom when I am seized so completely by the love of God that all the desires of my heart and every action, affection, thought and decision which flows from them are directed to God my Father/Mother and His service and praise.

We begin by reflecting on the purpose of our lives: we know what a coffeemaker is for. What are human beings for?

● Texts

Psalm 104. The God who calls me is the God who created me and who made everything else because He loves me.

«Give praise to the Lord, O my soul. O Lord my God, you are very great; you are robed with honor and power. You are clothed with light as with a robe; stretching out the heavens like a curtain: The arches of your house are set on the waters; you make the clouds your carriage; you go on the wings of the wind: You make the winds your messengers and flames of fire your servants. You have made the earth strong on its bases, so that it may not be moved for ever and ever; Covering it with the sea as with a robe: the waters were high over the mountains; At the voice of your word they went in flight; at the sound of your thunder they went away in fear; The mountains came up and the valleys went down into the place which you had made ready for them. You made a limit over which they might not go, so that the earth would never again be covered by them. You sent the springs into the valleys; they are flowing between the hills. They give drink to every beast of the field; the wild asses come to them for water. The birds of the air have their resting-places by them and make their song among the branches. You send down rain from your heavenly chambers: the earth is full of the fruit of your works. You make the grass come up for the cattle and plants for the use of man; so that bread may come out of the earth; And wine to make glad the heart of man and oil to make his face shine and bread giving strength to his heart. The trees of the Lord are full of growth, the cedars of Lebanon of his planting; where the birds have their resting-places; as for the stork, the tall trees are her house. The high hills are a safe place for the mountain goats and the rocks for the small beasts. You made the moon for a sign of the divisions of the year; teaching the sun the time of its going down. When you make it dark, it is night, when all the beasts of the woods come

Zezama – Parzonería de Entzia – Mountain pass of Opakua.

quietly out of their secret places. The young lions go thundering after their food; searching for their meat from God. The sun comes up and they come together and go back to their secret places to take their rest. Man goes out to his work and to his business until the evening. O Lord, how great is the number of your works! In wisdom you have made them all; the earth is full of the things you have made. There is the great, wide sea, where there are living things, great and small, more than may be numbered. There go the ships; there is that great beast, which you have made as a plaything. All of them are waiting for you, to give them their food in its time. They take what you give them; they are full of the good things which come from your open hand. If your face is veiled, they are troubled; when you take away their breath, they come to an end and go back to the dust. If You send out your spirit, they are given life; you make new the face of the earth. Let the glory of the Lord be for ever; let the Lord have joy in his works: At whose glance the earth is shaking; at whose touch the mountains send out smoke. I will make songs to the Lord all my life; I will make melody to my God while I have my being. Let my thoughts be sweet to him: I will be glad in the Lord. Let sinners be cut off from the earth and let all evildoers come to an end. Give praise to the Lord, O my soul. Give praise to the Lord.»

Genesis 22:1-18. This text, about Abraham's faith and freedom, questions my own faith and freedom.

«Now after these things, God put Abraham to the test and said to him, Abraham; he said, Here am I. And he said to him, Take your son, your dearly loved only son Isaac and go to the land of Moriah and give him as a burned offering on one of the mountains which I will identify for you. And Abraham got up early in the morning and made ready his ass and took with him two of his young men and Isaac, his son and, after the wood for the burned offering had been cut, he went on his way to the place of which God had told him. And on the third day, Abraham, lifting up his eyes, saw the place a long way off. Then he said to his young men, "Stay here with the ass; the boy and I will go on and give worship and then return to you." Abraham put the wood for the burned offering on his son's back and he himself took the fire and the knife in his hand and the two of them went on together. Then Isaac said to Abraham, "My father;" he said, "Here am I, my son." And he said, "We have wood and fire here, but where is the lamb for the burned offering?" And Abraham said, "God himself will give the lamb for the burned offering."

So they went on together. And they came to the place of which God had told him; there Abraham made the altar and put the wood in place on it and then, making tight the bands round Isaac his son, he put him on the wood on the altar. Stretching out his hand, Abraham took the knife to put his son to death. But the voice of the angel of the Lord came from heaven, saying, "Abraham, Abraham," and he said, "Here am I." And he said, "Let not your hand be stretched out against the boy to do anything to him; for now I am certain that the fear of God is in your heart, because you have not kept back your son, your only son, from me. And lifting up his eyes, Abraham saw a sheep fixed by its horns in the brushwood: and Abraham took the sheep and made a burned offering of it in place of his son. And Abraham gave that place the name Yahweh-yireh: as it is said to this day, on the mountain the Lord is seen. And the voice of the angel of the Lord came to Abraham a second time from heaven, saying, I have taken an oath by my name, says the Lord, because you have done this and have not kept back from me your dearly loved only son, that I will certainly give you my blessing and your seed will be increased like the stars of heaven and the sand by the seaside; your seed will take the land of those who are against them; your seed will be a blessing to all the nations of the earth, because you have done what I gave you orders to do.»

Mark 12:28-34. My Principle and Foundation is the Love of God.

- Final Colloquy: Sum up what has come to mind during your prayer time, talking to Jesus as one friend does to another. Be honest with him about what you have discovered on this stage of your journey.

Stage 5: Alda – Genevilla

- Annotation: We know already that it is very important to reflect on the introductory prayer. We should also bear in mind that we should not be in a hurry while meditating. Today we want to consider all the «means» that God employs to show us His Love and the use to which we should put these «means».

- Petition: I beseech you, Lord, to direct all my actions by Your inspiration, to carry them on by Your gracious help, so that every intention and action of mine may begin always from You and be happily completed through You.

- Reflections: Today we reflect further on our human life and how to live in order to better achieve its purpose. Specifically we consider more deeply this sentence from the Spiritual Exercises of St Ignatius: «The other things on the face of the earth were created for humans, to help them in pursuing the end for which they were created.» Here is how Ignatius reveals some of the challenging implications of that sentence: «We ought to use these things to the extent that they help us towards our end and free ourselves from them to the extent that they hinder us from it. To attain this it is necessary to make ourselves indifferent to all created things, so that we do not to seek wealth rather than poverty, honor rather than dishonor, a long life rather than a short one and so on. Rather, we ought to desire and choose only that which is most conducive to the end for which we were created.»

Being «indifferent», in Ignatius's words, means being «free»: that is we are free from being so attached, addicted, enslaved or bewitched by any created or merely human thing that it gets in the way of living according to our purpose. That is, we do not want to become so obsessed with living a successful earthly life that our life becomes about serving ourselves and not serving God and following His plan. We want to be free from anything that could prevent us from being available for our true purpose. We want to put the love of God above any merely human love. We want to live a balanced, ordered life: a life in which we have a proper relationship with other persons, with money and with things, so that we do not become enslaved by an attachment to things. While created things can help us achieve our purpose, they can also distract us from it if we become focused on them rather than on our greater purpose. We should not confuse earthly ambitions with the purpose of life and allow them to take the place of God.

Make a list of people you admire in this regard. What is it that you admire in them? Perhaps you can picture holy people from the past or people you know now, whose lives show this healthy balance and freedom. This is not the time to judge yourself on where you may be falling short (you will reflect on your own performance later). For the moment, we are trying to develop a clear sense of purpose and a clear sense of the ideals we want to aspire to in our lives.

● Texts

Psalm 8. What is a frail human, that you should be mindful of him?

«O Lord, our Lord, whose glory is higher than the heavens, how noble is your name in all the earth! You have made clear your strength even out of the mouths of babies at the breast. You have established a bulwark against your foes;

that you may put to shame the cruel and violent man. When I see your heavens, the work of your fingers, the moon and the stars, which you have put in their places; what is man, that you keep him in mind? The son of man, that you take him into account? For you have made him only a little lower than the gods, crowning him with glory and honor. You have made him ruler over the works of your hands; you have put all things under his feet; all sheep and oxen and all the beasts of the field; the birds of the air and the fish of the sea and whatever goes through the deep waters of the seas. O Lord, our Lord, how noble is your name in all the earth!»

Romans 8:5-6.12-18. All who are led by the Spirit of God are children of God. Those who live according to the Spirit set their minds on the things of the Spirit.

Philippians 1:21-26; 3:7-16; 4:10-13. Here and now, how closely can I identify with the attitude of San Paul?

● Final Colloquy: Sum up what has come to mind in your prayer time, talking to Jesus as one friend does to another. Be honest with him about what you have discovered on this stage of your journey.

San Vicente de Arana.

Stage 6: Genevilla – Laguardia

- Annotation: Today we begin to consider the presence of evil in our lives. We are called to feel the pain of our sinful ways. It is a «gloomy day», when we discover that serious reality. Ignatius asks us to be in that mood during our meditation, our walk, our day. The Jesuits have defined themselves as follows: «What is it to be a Jesuit? It is to know that one is a sinner, yet called to be a companion of Jesus as Ignatius was. What is it to be a companion of Jesus today? It is to engage, under the Standard of the Cross, in the crucial struggle of our time: the struggle for faith and the struggle for justice which it includes» (General Congregation 32, [11-12]).

- Petition: Aware of the end for which I was created and of the call which God makes to me, I beg Him for a deeply felt understanding of my sins and of the disordered tendencies in my life, so that I may feel shame and confusion and turn to Him for healing and forgiveness.

- Reflections: We have been reflecting on God's plan for humans and the harmony that results when our relationships with other people and the world are in good order. Today we reflect on the reality of sin: namely that there is gross disorder in our world. Sin is not just an accident or a mistake. Rather, sin means that people are deliberately choosing to bring disorder and chaos into their own and others' lives because of some disordered attachments: the salesperson who cheats customers to enrich himself, the pimp who sells children into sex slavery, the government official who steals money and allows citizens to live in squalor, the parent whose children do not get the love they deserve.

Let us reflect today not so much on our own personal history as a sinner (that will be tomorrow), but on the harsh, cruel reality of sin in our world and the disorder, pain and chaos it causes. Sin has consequences. Reflect as well on the reality of Christ hanging on the cross, an image that is enshrined at the center, above the altar in every Catholic Church. Christ entered history and suffered in response to human sinfulness, to redeem humans and show them a better path. Try to appreciate what our culture has lost today: an awareness of the reality of sin. Call to mind images of our World in Pain, suffering because of the injustice that is at work in nearly every relationship and human interchange. Go through the economic crises and their causes. Think of the roots of sin and selfishness in the World. As you walk along, pray for a clear vision of Sin, at work throughout this suffering world and which, until now, you have not felt any shame for. Then pray that you will feel the disorder in your own life and the shame of it.

- Texts

Jeremiah 18:1-10. The clay vessel he was making was spoiled in the potter's hand and he reworked it into another vessel.

Lapuebla de Labarca.

«The word which came to Jeremiah from the Lord said, Up! Go down to the potter's house and there I will let my words come to your ears. Then I went down to the potter's house and he was doing his work on the stones. And when the vessel, which he was forming out of earth, got damaged in the hand of the potter, he made it again into another vessel, as it seemed good to the potter to make it. Then the word of the Lord came to me, saying, O Israel, am I not able to do with you as this potter does, says the Lord? See, like earth in the potter's hand are you in my hands, O Israel. Whenever I say anything about uprooting a nation or a kingdom and smashing it and sending destruction on it; If, in that very minute, that nation of which I was talking turns away from its evil, my purpose of doing evil to them will be changed. And whenever I say anything about building up a nation or a kingdom and planting it; If, in that very minute, it does evil in my eyes, going against my orders, then my good purpose, which I said I would do for them, will be changed.»

1 John 1:5-2:2. If we say: «We are without sin,» we deceive ourselves and the truth is not in us. But if we acknowledge our sins, he who is faithful and just will forgive our sins and cleanse us from every wrongdoing.

- Final Colloquy: «Imagining Christ our Lord before me, nailed to the Cross, I ask why the Creator became human and turned from eternal life to accept temporal death, so as to die for my sins. Likewise, looking at myself, ask what I have done for Christ, what I am doing for Christ, what I should do for Christ; seeing Him like this hanging on the cross, I reflect on what occurs to me. The Conversation/Prayer is made speaking as one friend speaks to another, or a servant to his Master, asking for some grace, or blaming myself for some wrong, or bringing my concerns before Him and asking for advice about them. Conclude by saying an Our Father.»

Stage 7: Laguardia – Navarrete

- Annotation: We continue considering the presence of evil in life, but now we look at the evil in our own lives. We try to become aware of our own faults. Ignatius advises us to keep a «gloomy day», as an aid to discovering the sin in our lives and experiencing its reality. So we maintain that «sad mood» for meditation, to help us more efficaciously enter into this consideration of evil.

- Petition: Having become aware of the purpose for which I was created and of the vocation to which God invites me, I beg Him for a deeply felt understanding of sin in myself and of the disordered tendencies in my life, so that I may feel shame and confusion and turn to Him for healing and forgiveness.

- Reflections: Yesterday we prayed for the grace of a deeper understanding of the reality of a sinful world. Today we take on another uncomfortable,

awkward reality: My own sin. That we are sinners is true not only of accursed convicted criminals, but each of us is a sinner, starting with the Pope down to whatever wretched soul occupies this morning's news. Each of us has habitual patterns of rebellion against God's plan: what are mine? One psalm declares: «The Lord hears the cry of the poor.» What about me? Are there ways in which I have habitually not listened to «those in need» who have crossed my path: the poor, the elderly, «friends», the unpopular, the outcasts, etc.? Have there been ways in which I have used or abused other people or situations in order to satisfy my own needs: for attention, to obtain money dishonestly, to abuse and misuse sex, to seek approval without earning it, to look for selfish comfort, to neglect others, to avoid getting involved in the responsibilities of life?

Fuenmayor Church.

Today we seek the grace of understanding our own sinfulness. Too often, our culture «anesthetizes» us from taking responsibility for our own false way of thinking and our wrongdoing. Aristotle once declared that «the unexamined life is not worth living.» We need to scrutinize our shortcomings and habitual failings: the pockets of darkness in our lives, the habits which have become «normal». The ones which drag us down and hold us back from living in proper relationship with God, with others and with God's world. We might pray to God for the courage to discover our blind spots, to confront ourselves and our sinfulness in order to abhor it!

Be sure to talk to God and Jesus. Feeling abandoned in our sin is exactly the opposite of the grace we seek for this day. Our sinfulness should not leave us depressed or wallowing in self-pity; rather, we pray for exactly the opposite grace— a sense of wonder and gratitude that I am a «sinner who is loved», so loved by God that He gave His only begotten Son for me, so loved that, although He knows fully the extent of my sins, His love remains undimmed and His desire for partnership and friendship with me is utterly unchanged. Ignatius invites me to experience genuine shame for my sinfulness, coupled with great wonder that I am still here and alive: the wonder that I am a sinner but also loved and redeemed. I seek an in-

ner healing, knowing that I am a sinner who is loved.

- Texts

  Luke 15:1-7. Jesus receives sinners and eats with them.

  Luke 5:1-11. I say to Jesus: Depart from me, Lord, for I am a sinner!

  2 Cor 12:8-10. When I am weak, then I am strong.

- Final Colloquy: «Imagining Christ our Lord before me, hanging on a cross, I speak to Him, asking Him how the Creator became human for me and left his eternal life to accept temporal death and so died for my sins. Likewise, looking at myself, I ask what have I done for Christ, what am I doing for Christ, what should I do for Christ; so, seeing Him like this, hanging on the cross, discuss what occurs to me. The dialogue is held as one friend speaks to another, or a servant to his Master; sometimes asking for some grace, sometimes blaming myself for some wrong, sometimes discussing my affairs and asking advice about them. Conclude by saying an Our Father.»

Carravalseca Lagoon, Laguardia.

- Annotation: We are still considering the presence of evil in our lives but, today, in an entirely different way. We now open ourselves to the mercy of our Father. Ignatius invites us to experience the wonder to be felt when, in spite of the reality of our own sin, we come face to face with the infinite mercy of God. Today our attitude on our Walk is that of a repentant sinner but, above all, of a sinner who is immensely loved.

- Petition: Dear Father, I ask you for the gift of an interior, felt, knowledge of my sinfulness so that I may also experience your love for me, as well as a growing desire to turn towards you and a renewed enthusiasm for following Jesus.

- Reflections: You have reflected on the reality of human sin and your own sinfulness. Today you are invited to reflect on the awesome reality of God's mercy. You are loved and forgiven, completely. «Repent and believe the Good News.» The two go hand in hand. That is, we first accept the reality of our sinfulness and repent truly that we have brought disharmony and disorder to our own life and to the world. We then believe the Good News: God is merciful, always has been and always will be. What ultimately matters is not that we are faithful to God (none of us is capable of complete fidelity) but that God is faithful to us. It is the same God who accompanies you: at your best moments, when you behave well and earn praise from all sides and in your most shameful moments, when you know there is good reason for you to be disgraced. You cannot earn God's love and you do not have to! God's love is freely given, so freely given that it seems impossible to us! The father in the parable that follows, though he has every reason to be angry, harbors no resentment. His younger son has offended him and squandered what he worked so hard to accumulate, a thing we humans find almost impossible to accept. Indeed, the elder son cannot accept the forgiving attitude of the father.

In your life as a sinner, you are not alone. You are forgiven. You are loved. This is what drives us to repentance, to the desire to make amends. But we must know that we need God's grace to repent and have the desire to do so: we neither know nor follow the right way by our own wisdom and strength. Ask Jesus. Pray that you may be willing and able to accept fully what God offers so freely: forgiveness. We humans often go through life saddled with crippling guilt. God asks us, instead, to walk in freedom.

- Texts

Luke 15:11-32. This son of mine was dead and has come back to life; he was lost and is found.

Luke 5:17-26. When Jesus saw their faith he said (to the paralytic): «Your sins are forgiven.»

John 8:2-11. And Jesus said: «Neither do I condemn you. Go and do not sin again.»

Romans 5:1-8. God shows his love for us in that while we were still sinners Christ died for us.

- Final Colloquy: I talk to Jesus as one friend does to another, experiencing with growing feeling the wonder of being alive at this moment and feeling that I live in a world that is called to be saved by the love of God. I contemplate its creation and history. Then, after meditating on the destruction of sin, I speak with Jesus about the grace of the forgiveness I have received. It is a dialogue about mercy, in which I reflect and give thanks to God our Lord because has given me life until now; I propose with His grace to amend my life from now on. To conclude, I say a heartfelt Our Father.

Stage 9: Logroño – Alcanadre

- **Annotation:** Today we begin the «second week» of the Spiritual Exercises. Our entry point is through a meditation that invites us to follow Christ the King. We are walking through a big earthly city so we can see the wonders of a «worldly kingdom» and imagine the Kingdom of God. Today we meditate on how our life is oriented: are we walking with Jesus or are we following other leaders?

- **Petition:** Despite my limitations, yet aware of the Father's love for me, I ask for the grace to feel personally called to journey alongside Jesus as his companion and co-laborer.

- **Reflection:** A deep awareness of God's merciful love (yesterday's grace), often leads to a desire to respond to that love. Today we begin to meditate on Jesus' invitation to walk beside him in his work. In the Spiritual Exercises, Ignatius places God's call to work with him just after the meditations that touch on our own human sinfulness. The juxtaposition is important: God calls us to work closely with him while he knows us fully yet loves us as we are. He calls us as «loved sinners», just as St Paul tells us: when he asked the Lord to help him, the Lord replied: «My grace is enough for you, for my power is made perfect in weakness.» So Paul said: «I will all the more gladly boast of my weaknesses, that the power of Christ may rest upon me» (2 Cor 12:9). So, despite being sinners, today we feel called to work in that same world which is touched by our sin; work for peace and justice with the support of the merciful love we have received. We believe in a God who is justice because He is love. The road to justice and the road to faith in our world are inseparable. In the Gospel, Faith and justice are undivided. We are deeply conscious of how often and how grievously we ourselves have sinned against the Gospel yet it remains our ambition to proclaim it worthily: that is, in love, in poverty and in humility. This is what the 32nd Jesuit General Congregation said.

In his famous meditation, «The Call of the King», Ignatius imagines how compelling the call of a truly worthy king would be, one who is striving for faith and justice. After that consideration of an admirable earthly king, we turn to Jesus, whose call is still even more worthy because Christ our Lord, the eternal King, calls each person in particular and says: «My will is to bring together the best in the whole world and build the Kingdom of Eternal Love.» Ignatius sees that all those who wish to throw in their lot with Christ the King must labor with Him so that, following Him in pain, they may also follow Him in the glory of his Kingdom.

The call of the King is the call to become His companion, to learn more about Him, to experience His loving care and to join Him in serving His people. And this King comes to us as one who shares our human state, all the more able to share our lot. Today we focus on the marvel of being called and on the nature of the call; tomorrow you can begin to focus on your response to this call.

- **Texts**

Psalm 102. The Lord is kind and full of compassion.

«Hear my prayer, O Lord; let my cry come to you! Do not hide your face from me in the day of my distress! Incline your ear to me; answer me speedily in the day when I call! For my days pass away like smoke and my bones burn like a furnace.

But you, O Lord, are enthroned forever; you are remembered throughout all generations. You will arise and have pity on Zion; it is the time to favor her; the appointed time has come. For your servants hold Zion's rocks dearly and have pity on her dust. Nations will fear the name of the Lord and all the kings of the earth will fear your glory. For the Lord builds up Zion; he appears in his glory; he regards the prayer of the destitute and does not despise their prayer. Let this be recorded for a generation to

Ebro river.

come, so that a people yet to be created may praise the Lord: that he looked down from his holy height; from heaven the Lord looked at the earth, to hear the groans of the prisoners, to set free those who were doomed to die, that they may declare in Zion the name of the Lord, and in Jerusalem his praise, when peoples gather together, and kingdoms, to worship the Lord.

Of old you laid the foundation of the earth, and the heavens are the work of your hands. They will perish, but you will remain; they will all wear out like a garment. You will change them like a robe, and they will pass away, but you are the same, and your years have no end. The children of your servants shall dwell securely; their offspring shall be established before you.»

Luke 5:27-32. Follow me.

Micah 5:1-3. A mighty king will come to free his flock with the power of Yahweh.

«But you, Beth-lehem Ephrathah, the least among the families of Judah, out of you one will come to me one who is to be ruler in Israel; whose origin is of old, from time past, from the eternal days. For this cause he will give them up until the time when she who is with child has given birth: then the rest of his brothers will come back to the children of Israel. And he will take his place and give food to his flock in the strength of the Lord, in the glory of the name of the Lord his God; their resting-place will be safe: for now he will be great to the ends of the earth.»

● Closing Colloquy: As a friend speaks to a friend, so we speak with Jesus. We bring together our thoughts and emotions from our meditation on the Kingdom and on the value of following Jesus. We discuss with Jesus and, if we so feel, we ask Him to invite us to walk with him.

Stage 10: Alcanadre – Calahorra

● Annotation: Do not forget the «Introductory Prayer» which speaks to the final outcome of the entire experience. We should not forget that important prayer. This «second week» of our inner pilgrimage is characterized by intimacy: we want to know our Lord and King better, in order to follow him more closely. Intimacy is required! We try to find that intimacy as a grace.

● Petition: I ask the Father for three things that I need and only He can give: a more intimate knowledge of Jesus who has become one of us; a more personal experience of His love for me so that I may love Him more tenderly; and have

Tudela.

a closer union with Jesus in His mission of bringing salvation to humankind.

● Reflection: The companion of Jesus the King grows in awareness of who the King is, what He stands for, who His enemies are and what His aspirations and plans are. One grows in intimacy by experiencing the loving presence of this King who calls, teaches, heals, challenges, nurtures and accepts His followers as they are. The companion of Jesus the King yearns to bear with Jesus all wrongs, abuse and poverty if that is

what is required for intimate fellowship with Him. We know that we are never alone in this enterprise. We are in constant communion with the King in work, prayer and rest. The follower of the King shares totally in the mission of Jesus: to bring the good news of salvation, liberation, justice and peace to all people. Consider that Jesus' call to us is of such a kind that no one can predict where our life journey will take us as we go through the twists and turns of our careers and relationships, unexpected death or remarkably good luck. Likewise, we do not know where our journey by Jesus' side will lead us any more than we know whom we might meet at today's journey's end. And so, you are invited to join Jesus with generosity and great faith in Him.

This intimacy and generosity is also God's deep desire for humankind. God looks at humanity and feels that desire for intimacy crying out inside Himself. The incarnation is the answer to God's desire for generous intimacy. Ignatius invites us to look at the Holy Trinity, which itself is looking at humankind, and so share God's vision with Him: «I will see the various persons on the face of the earth, so diverse in dress and behavior: some white and others black, some in peace and others at war, some weeping and others laughing, some healthy and others sick, some being born and others dying and so forth.» Then, I will see and consider the three Holy Persons, seated, so to speak, on their royal thrones of Divine Majesty. They are gazing upon the whole surface of the earth. They see all the peoples in such great blindness and how they are suffering and dying in the absurdity of sin «I will hear what the Divine Persons are saying, that is: "Let us commit ourselves to the redemption of the human race."»

Earlier, we reflected on the reality of sin and on its rebellion against God's plan.

Now we reflect on God's compassionate and free choice regarding this sinful world: that Jesus would come into human history, show us a new way of living, redeem us and bring God's love into our hearts of stone.

- Texts

Luke 1:26-38. God invites Mary to collaborate in the mystery of the Incarnation. Though free to say «no», Mary chose freely to say «yes». We feel the hope and wonder present in the scene: anything is possible with God. Elizabeth, who thought she was barren, is now in her seventh month; for nothing is impossible for God. If God can bring this about in the world, What can God not do?

Philippians 2:5-11. As I see myself in the presence of the Holy Trinity who determine that the Son is to become one of us, and as I contemplate Jesus, present in Mary's womb, I let this ancient Christological hymn express the awesome mystery of God, the infinite being who has become finite, the unlimited become limited, pure spirit become enfleshed.

John 1:1-14. Let us pray using the prologue of John's Gospel and let God fill us with awe and wonder at the gift of Himself to me and to all His people.

Luke 1:39-55. Contemplating Mary's visit to Elizabeth, let us try to be aware of the human and divine drama that is taking place. Let us be particularly attentive to Jesus, present in Mary's womb. Note that the humanity in John the Baptist welcomes Jesus, the Son of God.

- Closing Colloquy: Make a summary of what we have meditated on in our prayer time, talking to Jesus as a friend does to a friend. Be honest with him regarding the points that struck you as you meditated during this stage of my camino. End with the «Our Father».

Stage 11: Calahorra – Alfaro

- Annotation: This second week, Ignatius introduces a new kind of prayer: the contemplation of the mysteries of the Gospel.

The goal is not to gather facts about Jesus but «to see Thee more clearly, love Thee more dearly, follow Thee more nearly». Again, let us not forget the «introductory prayer», which is the ultimate fruit of the entire experience.

Ignatius asks us to immerse (exercise) ourselves in contemplative prayer, a kind of imaginative prayer where all our senses are involved. Here is a little guidance: «Read the account of the story and then leave the text aside. We begin by slowly picturing the scene as completely as we can. Where is it happening? Notice all the things in and around the scene. Who is there? What is everyone wearing? How hot or cold is it? What smells come to me? I then enter more fully into the scene by becoming a character in it. I might just let myself be a member of the crowd or I might become one of the principal characters in the story. When I feel I am in the scene, I let the story unfold in my imagination and go wherever it goes. Once inside the scene, the words and actions are no longer merely a videotaped replay of the text. Inside the scene, I can back up and fill in how the scene began, I can let what is revealed to me be played out in the words and gestures of the participants and I can speak or simply experience my own reactions. The details of the text cease to be important as it is the experience of the story that moves my heart. Finally, I would end with a prayer, speaking to Our Lord, heart to heart, friend to friend, in whatever way comes to me, expressing my gratitude for the graces I have just received.»

We begin this type of spiritual exercise by contemplating the mystery of the Incarnation. Do not be disappointed if you find this kind of prayer somewhat difficult: we are asked to pray from our own life, so everyone has their own way of finding and relating to God! Ignatius found this kind of prayer very useful and we encourage you to try it also!

- Petition: We ask for a lasting appreciation of the miracle of the Incarnation through the persons and responses of Mary and Joseph; we beg for the grace to believe and accept the almost incredible good news, that Jesus is among us and how that good news affects us. We beg for a deeper gratitude for the wonder of God being born in human form.

- Reflection: Focus today on the miracle of the Incarnation, trying, as the cliché goes, to «keep it real». The Nativity crèche in a church typically figures a cherubic Jesus, smiling at his parents and surrounded by clean shepherds and kings. In fact, tradition tells us that Jesus was born, after a long, uncomfortable trip, in a place that must have been neglected and filthy. His parents, exhausted from travel, likely felt desolate and worried, delivering a child in an unsanitary, unfamiliar place, without the support of relatives. The Prince of Peace has come among us but not in a way that any of us would have imagined. Feel all the same travails that you do as a pilgrim-traveler: will I get lost? Will something go wrong en route? Will adequate accommodation be available? What if I get sick? But now multiply these a thousand times, imagining yourself alongside a pregnant loved one.

Ignatius invites us to: «see Our Lady, Joseph and the infant Jesus after his birth. I will make myself a poor, little, unworthy slave, gazing at them, contemplating them and serving them in their needs, just as if I were there, with all possible respect and reverence ... Consider what they are doing: for example, journeying or toiling, in order that the Lord may be born in the greatest poverty; that after so many hardships of hunger, thirst, heat, cold, injuries and insults, he may die on the cross! And all this for me!

- Texts

Matthew 1:18-25. Contemplating the mystery of the Incarnation, we enter into the feelings of Joseph and his struggle with law and love.

Luke 2:1-20. She gave birth to her firstborn son and wrapped him in swaddling clothes and laid him in a manger, because there was no room for them in the inn. Present at His birth, with a sense of inner peace, I receive Jesus with joy and gratitude as the Father's gift to me and to His people.

- Closing Colloquy: «Finally, I end with a prayer, speaking to Our Lord, heart to heart, friend to friend, in whatever way comes to me, expressing my gratitude for the graces I have just received.» Conclude with an Our Father.

Alfaro.

Stage 12: Alfaro – Tudela

● **Annotation:** Remember that the goal of these second week meditations is to see Jesus more clearly, to love Him more deeply and follow him more closely. Let us not forget the «Introductory Prayer»: the ultimate fruit of this entire exercise. Use this prayer of contemplation to enter into the gospel account of the Baptism of Jesus.

● **Petition:** I ask the Father for three things that I need and that only He can give: a more intimate knowledge of Jesus who has become one of us; a more personal experience of His love for me so that I may love Him more tenderly; and a closer union with Jesus in His mission to bring salvation to humankind.

● **Reflection:** At around thirty years of age, Jesus left his work and home to begin his public ministry. Try to imagine what thoughts he might have had.

Tudela.

Jesus' public life began with a journey, a kind of pilgrimage. He left his home in Nazareth and travelled southeast to the Jordan river where he was baptized by John the Baptist. John's ministry was calling sinners to repentance. John was well known and respected: certainly Jesus knew of John's message as a prophet of God, sent to the Jewish people. Jesus knew what John was doing. Ponder the message that Jesus, the sinless one, chooses in order to launch his ministry by placing himself in solidarity with sinners. The symbolism of these early verses from the gospel summons up rich imagery of a pilgrimage toward a new way of life. John the Baptist's ministry is introduced with Isaiah's words: «Prepare the way of the Lord, make his paths straight.» John calls sinners to repentance and to conversion. It is a message with roots that suggest a «turning point». John is inviting us to turn in a new direction and to follow a new path in life.

At some point, Jesus makes a conscious and deliberate choice to begin his ministry, to change his worldly life in Nazareth; imagine what might have been going through his mind, what he saw around him to make him feel this was the right moment. Consider too how he chooses to begin his ministry, not with a speech or a miracle, but by travelling to be baptized by John. And also consider the experience of Jesus at the Jordan, His discovery, His understanding of the mission which the Father invites Him to carry out fully.

You can beg the Father to place you with Jesus, His Son, alongside John the Baptist. Imagine that you are one of His companions and that you are right behind Him because you want to know Him better, love Him more and be more faithful in serving Him and all humanity.

Try to contemplate the gospel scene. What is John telling us?

● Texts

Romans 6:3-4. Christ was raised from the dead by the glory of the Father so that we too might walk in newness of life.

Luke 3:1-22. «Then what are we to do?» At the moment of His baptism by John, God's voice confirms His sonship and His mission.

Matthew 3:13-17. Jesus, having pondered in His heart the mystery of the Fatherhood of God and the mission given Him by the Father, decides to leave Nazareth. I try to be present to Him as He reaches this decision, shares it with His mother, makes His farewells and leaves all that has helped to form Him as an adult, responsible human being. Let us walk with Him towards the Jordan River and remain on the riverbank contemplating His baptism. What is it that I hear? What should I understand?

● Closing Colloquy: Make a summary of what I have meditated upon during my prayer time, talking to Jesus as a friend talks to a friend, being candid with him about the items found at this stage of the journey we have made. End with the Our Father.

Stage 13: Tudela – Gallur

● Annotation: Again we persist in making the introductory prayer. Today we enter into a fundamental meditation of the Spiritual Exercises: «The Two Standards». Here, Saint Ignatius proposes an exercise in contrasting goals to enable us to more definitively choose our fundamental option in life as we consider how we want to follow Jesus. Throughout this day, we can be considering how Jesus is asking us to go on pilgrimage with Him and asking for the grace of this meditation: to be able to feel what Jesus wants of us and what we most deeply want. The typical «Triple Colloquy» that St. Ignatius proposes in this exercises can be undertaken as the book sets it out below ... or done as your heart tells you, following the manner of pilgrimage you are making.

● Petition: As a friend of Jesus, I ask God to allow me to share the gift of being able to recognize the deceits of the devil so that I can guard against them. I also ask for a true knowledge of Jesus Christ, my true Leader and Lord, and the grace to imitate Him.

● Reflection: Over the coming days we will reflect on Jesus' earthly ministry and on his way of living and working in accordance with the values of the Kingdom. Today we take a meditation commonly known as the «two standards» (standard as in a flag or banner). We can imagine Jesus, prepared to set out on his own journey, poised at a critical fork in the road. He has no doubt which way he is going and he (figuratively) asks us to join him. Jesus' values and Jesus' «Camino» is the way of simplicity (even of poverty), leading often to dishonor and humility: in other words, it is the way of those who share their life with God and hope for everything from Him. The other way is the worldly choice of riches, honor and pride: in other words, to have the things and prestige that makes us feel important in the world, to turn ourselves into the gods of our own life and be «the only ones in the world». Earlier in this spiritual pilgrimage, Ignatius invited us to make a fundamental choice: to be faithful to our Principle and Foundation. Today's is not a new choice, or a «do-over»; rather, it is a reminder, a deeper insight into Jesus's Camino and a check on our desire to follow Him, choosing a way that is fundamentally different from the ways of the world. Who are we: is our essence simply comprised of our possessions and reputation? Or, are we God's beloved creation? Why are we important? Is it because others know us? Or because God has chosen us? Jesus is inviting us to lighten our load so as to be able to walk beside him freely on our spiritual pilgrimage through life.

The purpose of this meditation is to become aware of the strategies of Jesus and of the Evil One so that I may accurately discern the spirits which I often experience when I have to make a decision in my life: In what direction am I going? Am I going with Jesus? As Ignatius says: «We shall in our next exercise observe the intention of Christ our Lord and, in contrast, that of the Evil One, the enemy of human nature... Imagine the leader of all the enemies of human nature, seated in that great plain of Babylon and calling all his supporters... and sending them to tempt people to covet riches, so that they may more easily gain the empty, vain, honors of the world and be filled with overflowing pride. Then, from this, all the fulfillment of all human-caused disasters in the world will be guaranteed. Similarly, in contrast, gaze in your imagination on the supreme and true leader, Christ our Lord, summoning all His people... sending them to attract all persons, first, into the most perfect spiritual poverty and, also, if the Divine Majesty should be served and should wish to choose them for it, even to a state of actual poverty; second, by attracting them to desire of reproaches and contempt, since from these humility results. And from there true humility will follow.» We should consider these two banners and make a choice from our heart: Shall I go with Jesus? Do I really feel that? Is that what I desire?

● Texts

1 Tim 6:6-10. Those who desire to be rich fall into temptation, into a snare, into many senseless and hurtful desires that plunge men into ruin and destruction.

Galatians 5:16-25. I pray to know what it is like to be with and without the Spirit.

Ephesians 6:10-20. War of the spirit.

● Final Triple Colloquy: «1st. A discussion with Our Lady that she obtain for me from her son and Lord, the grace to be received under his banner, first in spiritual poverty and, if His Divine Majesty would be served and He wishes to choose me, to be received in no less than actual poverty and second, to experience insults and slander in order to imitate him, only if that could happen without sin on the part of any person or displeasure of His Divine Majesty. Finish with a Hail Mary. 2nd colloquy: Ask the same of the Son, that he may obtain it from the Father and, with this, say an Anima Christi. (See below.) 3rd colloquy. Ask the same of the Father, that he grant it to me, and finish with an Our Father.»

«Anima Christi» prayer. It is a prayer from around the 14th century. It is still prayed widely after receiving the body and blood of Our Lord, Jesus Christ in Holy Communion. Certainly St. Ignatius prayed with it often and that is why he included it in the Spiritual Exercises.

Soul of Christ, sanctify me.
Body of Christ, save me.
Blood of Christ, inebriate me.
Water from Christ's side, wash me.
Passion of Christ, strengthen me.
O good Jesus, hear me.
Within Thy wounds hide me.
Suffer me not to be separated from Thee.
From the malicious enemy defend me.
In the hour of my death call me.
And bid me come unto Thee.
That I may praise Thee with Thy saints
and with Thy angels
Forever and ever. Amen.

Imperial Canal.

Stage 14: Gallur – Tudela

● Annotation: We keep walking with Jesus in order to see Him more clearly, love Him more deeply and follow Him more closely. Do not forget the «preparatory prayer» both before we pray and throughout the day. Starting today, the final colloquy becomes even more

Former Jesuit College in Alagón.

important: we enter more deeply into this interior knowledge of Jesus who will strengthen our life commitment. We talk about this with our «friend» at the end of our prayer and during the day.

● Petition: I ask the Father for three things that I need and that only He can grant: a more intimate knowledge of Jesus who has become one of us; a more personal experience of His love for me so that I may love Him more tenderly; and a closer union with Jesus in His mission of bringing salvation to humankind.

● Reflection: Jesus as a person who heals people may be the image that stands out most clearly from His public life.

The healing ministry of Jesus is also a saving ministry. Jesus heals bodies, spirits and broken relationships with God and with others by means of forgiveness. Jesus tells a paralytic to get up and walk, rubs mud over a blind man's eyes. But His concern is not just for the withered limb or the non-functioning organ. It is also that the one whom He heals may turn from sin and believe in Him. We know His wonderful compassion, his willingness to touch and engage with the outcasts and untouchables of ancient society. Today we will use the Ignatian practice of contemplation to pray with these healing scenes: imagine one or more of these scenes from Jesus' ministry and imagine yourself in the scene, perhaps as a companion travelling with Jesus or, perhaps, others bring you to Jesus. What is it that I want Jesus to do to heal me? On entering into these mysteries in my pilgrimage, I present myself to Jesus as one in need of healing in body, mind and spirit. I should repeatedly keep asking for the grace of this day.

● Texts

Luke 18:35-43. «Jesus, Son of David, have mercy on me!»

John 5:1-9. Jesus' question to a sick and crippled man is, in my contemplation, addressed also to me: «Do you want to be healed?» I tell the Lord my need for healing: from my pettiness, my pride, my ambition, my need for security and control, my self-deception. Yes, Lord, I want to be healed.

Luke 8:40-56. I beg Jesus to come to my home. I try to touch the hem of His cloak.

● Closing Colloquy: Make a summary of the things I have meditated upon during my prayer time, talking to Jesus as a friend talks to a friend. Be honest with him about the items you dealt with at this time. Ask Him to accept you under His banner and to become a healer like Him. End with the «Our Father».

Stage 15: Alagón – Zaragoza

● **Annotation:** We continue to walk with Jesus in order to see Him more clearly, love Him more deeply and follow Him more closely. There is no further need to remind you to say the «introductory prayer» before you begin and throughout this day. Remember also that the final colloquy is becoming more and more important as we grow in this interior knowledge of Jesus who is strengthening our life commitment. Continue to discuss this with our «friend» Jesus in our colloquy at the end of our prayer and during the day.

● **Petition:** I will ask the Father for three things that I need and that only He can grant: a more intimate knowledge of Jesus who has become one of us; a more personal experience of His love for me so that I may love Him more tenderly and have a closer union with Jesus in His mission of bringing salvation to humankind.

● **Reflection:** After watching Jesus' healing, another great image of Jesus to admire is His preaching: He was a real innovator as well as a really free man! Admire the clarity and purity of Jesus' message and his courage in proclaiming it, even though he was well aware of the danger he was courting. Jesus maintains his unyielding focus on the justice of God's kingdom. He accepts no hypocrisy, no double-dealing. He rejects legalistic or ritualistic positions that raise the letter of law above its true spirit.

Jesus promulgates his new alliance, his plan for living, his plan of action for how we, his followers, will help restore this world to what God originally planned for how human beings would treat one another. The famed «Sermon on the Mount» or «the Manifesto of the Kingdom» comes early in Jesus' ministry. We have heard these words before, but do not let their familiarity detract from their radical appeal. Listen reverently to this discourse and allow the seed of Jesus' word to be implanted in

you and take root. Imagine yourself sitting among the impoverished people who gathered on a hillside to listen to Jesus comprehensively laying out his path, his «Camino». Then as now, his way is highly counterintuitive; he is inviting us to be and to live for values that are exactly the opposite of what

Paseo de la Independencia, Zaragoza.

contemporary culture and advertising tell us to do. In His time, Jesus was in contradiction to His world.

● **Texts**

Matthew 23:11-12.23-24. He who is greatest among you shall be your servant; whoever exalts himself will be humbled and whoever humbles himself will be exalted.

Matthew 5:1-48. Seeing the crowds, he went up on the mountain, and when he sat down his disciples came to him. And he opened his mouth and taught them, saying …

John 12:44-50. I prepare myself to listen to Jesus, for when I hear His message, I hear the Father.

● **Closing Conversation:** Make a summary of the things I have meditated on during my prayer, talking to Jesus as a friend talks to a friend. Be candid with him about the things I have just found at this prayer time. If that is how I feel, ask Him to be accepted under His banner. Finish with the Our Father.

Stage 16: Zaragoza – Fuentes de Ebro

● Annotation: We continue our journey with Jesus so we may see Him more clearly, love Him more deeply and follow Him more closely. We now enter into the «third week» of our interior pilgrimage. Remember the «introductory prayer» before the beginning prayer as well as during the day. Remember that the final colloquy with God at the end of prayer becomes very important. We beg to grow in our interior knowledge of Jesus who strengthens our life-commitment. We discuss all of this with our «friend» Jesus, in the dialogue at the end of prayer, as well as throughout the day.

● Petition: I beg the Father to draw me closer to Jesus so I may hear and understand His challenge, thrill to the adventure he invites and ardently desire to serve Him and His people, all the while sharing His lot and His suffering.

● Reflections: The gospels tell us that, as Jesus walked along the Sea of Galilee, He called two disciples who were casting their nets into the sea. «Follow me,» he said, «and I will make you fishers of all people.» They immediately left their nets and followed Him. So mysteriously compelling is this Jesus, we are told, that the two fishermen simply dropped their nets, leaving the past behind and following Jesus toward a new life, a new pilgrimage. We pray to know this Jesus better and to have deeper insights into the attractiveness of His call. We also beg for a growing desire to be with Jesus so that an important criterion in my life choices will become less, «what would please me», but, rather «what will help me to walk with and to become like Jesus?»

Much will be asked of the King's followers. There will be the challenge to discover «the one thing necessary» and the «one thing more». Pondering these challenges, I pay attention to the interior movements that are taking place within me during this pilgrimage. Do I know where I am headed? Does this matter to me?

● Texts

Luke 9:57-62. I pray not to be a half-hearted follower of Jesus.

Luke 10:1-9. After this the Lord appointed seventy others and sent them on ahead of Him.

Luke 10:38-41. Jesus says to me: «One thing alone is required.» My challenge is to include both «Martha and Mary» in my life, as I become the contemplative-in-action whose work for the Lord is animated by constant intimacy with Him.

Mark 10:17-27. As Jesus looks with love on a good man whose life has been a model of goodness and fidelity, Jesus challenges him—as He also challenges me—with these words: «There is one thing more you must do.» I know what He said to the man in the gospel. I listen now as Jesus tells me in my own heart what one thing more is asked of me.

Burgo de Ebro.

● Final Colloquy: Make a summary of your thoughts in this prayer time, speaking to Jesus as one friend does with another. Open your heart to Him about what you have discovered within yourself during this pilgrimage. As you are able, invite Jesus to accept you under His banner. End with the «Our Father».

Stage 17: Fuentes de Ebro – Venta de Santa Lucía

- **Annotation:** Pay attention to the «introductory prayer». We are in the «third week» of our Spiritual Exercises. Ignatius invites us to become aware of the growing hardships Jesus encounters in His own «life pilgrimage». We also enter into a more «arid» part of our pilgrimage. As we do so, keep in mind the cost and courage of Jesus' commitment for each of us. Our hearts become sad as we walk with Jesus towards Jerusalem for the last time. In our final colloquy we enter into this interior understanding of Jesus who suffers death on the cross, even though innocent. We speak of this sadness with our «friend» Jesus, during the colloquy at the end of this prayer, as well as throughout the day.

Pina de Ebro, Monegros Desert.

- **Petition:** I beg the Father to draw me closer to Jesus so that I may hear and understand His challenge, thrill to the adventure He invites and ardently desire to serve Him and His people, all the while sharing His lot and His suffering.

- **Reflections:** In the gospel, Jesus makes a pilgrimage from Galilee to Jerusalem where He will celebrate the Last Supper and undergo His passion. He has spent nearly three years in the company of His disciples, yet this final journey with them shows that they still do not fully grasp His message. They argue, for example, about who will be greatest in God's kingdom. Jesus tries once again to help them understand that leadership in God's kingdom involves service to others. They do not understand—or perhaps cannot bring themselves to hear and accept—that Jesus' way involves both suffering and sacrifice. Imagine yourself on this long journey to Jerusalem with Jesus. Bring Him your own questions and pray that your eyes will be open to seeing his message more clearly and that your ears will be ever more open to hear his call.

Jesus feels weak and tired along His journey. The disciples go to fetch food and water but He stays outside the village. The sun is high and it is hot in Samaria. In John's gospel, Jesus encounters a Samaritan woman—remember that there was deep enmity between Jews and Samaritans. Jesus meets her at a well as she comes to draw water. Jesus is very thirsty so He asks the woman for water. In the ensuing conversation the woman comes to know who Jesus is and accepts Him as the Christ, even as she discovers Him as a tired and thirsty man who needs help!

Who am I? Who is Jesus? In encountering Jesus, God helps us to understand ourselves more deeply. In the process, we also come to understand God more deeply. The Ignatian journey passes through «Los Monegros», Spain's desert-like region. Walking through this hot, arid and dusty landscape, one can imagine how vital water became in the reality and imagination of Jesus' listeners. Without food and water, there is no life. Thus we find one of the most evocative and enduring gospel images: Jesus is the water of eternal life, the wellspring that never runs dry, water always abundant. A true personal encounter with Jesus is inevitably transforming:

it changed this woman's life, the same as it transformed the lives of the many disabled people Jesus met. Meet Jesus yourself at the well as this Samaritan woman did. Who am I... really? And who is Jesus for me? What is Jesus asking of me? And what is my response?

- Texts

Mark 10:32-45. «If anyone would be the first, he must become last of all and servant of all.»

John 4:6-15. «Everyone who drinks of this water will thirst again, but whoever drinks of the water I shall give will never thirst.»

John 6:30-44. I believe that Jesus is living bread and life-giving water. I beg the Father to draw me closer to Jesus so that, eating and drinking with Him, I may have new life.

- Final Colloquy: Make a summary of your thoughts during this prayer time. Speak with Jesus as one friend does with another. Open your heart to Him about what you have discovered within yourself during this pilgrimage. As you are able, invite Jesus to accept you under His banner. Conclude with the «Our Father».

Stage 18: Venta de Santa Lucía – Bujaraloz

- Annotation: We walk with Jesus in His ascent to the Cross. Do not neglect the «introductory prayer»: now more than ever we ask that our lives be directed to God's will, our only source of salvation and happiness. Recall that the final colloquy is very important: we enter deeply into an inner knowledge of the suffering Jesus who strengthens our personal life commitments. We discuss all this with our «friend» in the colloquy at the end of the prayer, as well as during the day.

- Petition: I ask the Father for this gift: to feel sorrow with Christ in sorrow; to experience anguish with Christ's own anguish; even to experience tears and deep grief because of all the afflictions Christ endures for me at the end of His life.

- Reflections: After so many days walking with Jesus, we know already that His life is in danger. He knows this as well, even though people do not understand. The Kingdom of God is fighting for survival but the enemy is powerful. As the prophet said, our hearts are made of stone and we are not prepared to change this. Our hearts are difficult to break into. In the core of our being we even feel that the tender merciful heart of God is not attractive. Jesus confronts us on this but we do not want to hear.

Jesus feels angry but He cannot change our hearts. As His disciple, I feel awkward in this situation. I do not understand either and I feel tired. Jesus sees me and asks me to go with Him without fear. Things are not going to be easier in Jerusalem.

In Jerusalem, Jesus celebrates His last supper on earth with His disciples. Through a powerful, almost shocking gesture, Jesus, again, reinforces the nature of servant-leadership in God's kingdom. Jesus, the Lord, takes upon Himself a household servant's task by washing the dirty feet of the supper guests. Can you imagine Jesus washing your feet? During the meal, Jesus breaks bread and shares wine with his disciples, inviting them to «do this in memory of me». Picture in how many places and by how many varied peoples throughout history this Eucharistic moment has been repeated over the past two millennia. This is not only the manner in which Christians remember Jesus, but also their linking of themselves to His life, their intimate connection with Jesus: the bread and wine Jesus offers us are His own body and blood, given by each of us to each o us.

Recall that Ignatius invites us to pray by mentally inserting ourselves into the various scenes as they unfold, filling in the blanks of the basic gospel stories. The passion narratives especially lend themselves to this type of contemplative prayer. For example, regarding the Last Supper, Ignatius speaks to us of Jesus who, «after eating the Paschal lamb and finishing the meal, washed their feet and gave his most Holy Body and Precious Blood to his disciples.» Ignatius says further: «See the persons at the supper and, then, as I reflect on myself, draw profit from them. Listen to what they are saying… see what they are doing.»

● Texts

Mark 8:34-38. «Anyone who wants to be my follower must renounce him or her-self. Then he/she must take up his/her cross and follow me.»

Matthew 11:2-30. Only the simple can recognize the Messiah. The world cannot understand. With my heart longing for companionship and intimacy, I welcome the invitation of Jesus to share His rest as He shares my burden. I ardently desire to give myself totally to the love and service of Jesus and His people.

Matthew 26:26-31. As they were eating, Jesus took bread and He blessed and broke it and gave it to the disciples saying: «Take, eat; this is my body.»

John: 13:1-17. When He had washed their feet and put back on His garments, He resumed His place and said to them: «Do you know what I have done for you?»

Hermitage of Saint George, Bujaraloz.

● Colloquy: As in human situations, taking care of the sick and dying, our personal presence is often more important than our faltering words or awkward actions. It is the same as if we were to follow Jesus Christ in word and action. We previously described the colloquy as an intimate conversation between friends. Expand that description now to include the depth of feeling, love and compassion which allows us just to be present with Jesus. Ask Him once more, as you wish, to be accepted under His banner, the standard of the Cross. End with the «Our Father».

- Annotation: We walk with Jesus on the way to His death. Pay attention to the «introductory prayer»: we ask once again that our lives be directed to the will of God, the only source of our happiness and Resurrection. Recall that the final colloquy is very important: we draw closer to the suffering Jesus and ask Him to strengthen us for our personal life commitments. Make this colloquy at the end of the prayer and often during the day.

- Petition: I ask the Father for this gift: to feel sorrow with Christ in sorrow; to experience anguish with Christ in anguish; even to experience tears and interior grief because of all the sufferings Christ endures for me at the end of His life.

- Reflections: After His last supper, Jesus experiences agony while praying in the garden. He seems to wish that he could avoid the suffering He is about to undergo. He is betrayed by Judas. He is abandoned by the very friends and disciples who had been his closest companions for the last three years. He is publicly humiliated. His life mission seems to end in failure and ridicule. None of this is an «act» on his part. Christians do believe that Jesus, though always God, actually became «fully human» in nature. Thus, this particular moment reveals Jesus' total solidarity with the human condition. Each of us suffers humiliation, rejection, doubt, as well as our own personal agonies. While inserting yourself into this narrative, pray to experience great solidarity with Jesus and great compassion for Him. Take special note of Jesus' ultimate and utter faithfulness to His mission, to His Father and, by extension, to us. Jesus is the one who remains faithful to what He is called to accomplish. He also remains faithful to each of us in our personal moments of grief, pain and uncertainty.

Use Ignatian contemplation as you follow Jesus with the disciples to Gethsemane. Stay with them as they wait for Jesus. Or just go there and watch Jesus praying to His Father. We follow Jesus in embracing the Father's will, experiencing His humiliation, darkness and doubt. Look at Judas arriving with astonishment and pride, not really understanding the role he is playing. Feel the emotion of this situation. Stay close to Jesus in the house of Caiaphas. Keep your eyes on Jesus: What is He feeling? What is He thinking? How does He respond in this moment? Stay close to Jesus and look at the people who are speaking. What are they saying? What do you feel in this moment? Move forward and follow Peter outside of the house. Watch Jesus here since He knows that Peter will betray Him. Experience the pain of betrayal through some sign of affection. Notice how Jesus regards Peter. Jesus has been denied by the very one whom Jesus had called «Rock». This is Jesus's lot, which I am invited to share. For me, this is a moment of personal truth. How do I feel?

- Texts

Matthew 26:30-75. «Then Jesus came to the disciples and said to them: "Still asleep? Still resting? The hour has come."»

Isaiah 42:1-9. «Here is my servant whom I uphold.»

«See my servant, whom I uphold, my beloved one, in whom I take delight: I have put my spirit on him; he will give knowledge of the true God to the nations. He will make no cry, his voice will not be loud: his words will not come to men's ears in the streets. He will not let a crushed stem be broken and he will not let a feebly burning light be put out: he will go on, sending out the true word to the peoples. His light will not be put out, and its wick will not be crushed until he has given the knowledge of the true God to the earth; the sea-lands will be waiting for his teaching. Thus says God the Lord who made the heavens, measuring them out on high, stretching out the surface of the earth and giving it its produce; he who gives breath to his people on earth and spirit to those who walk on it: I the Lord have called you to bring justice, I have taken you by the hand and kept you safe, and I have set you as a covenant for the people and a light to the nations: To give eyes to the blind, to free the prisoners from the dungeon, to let out those who are shut up in the dark. I am the Lord; that is my name: I will not give my glory to another nor my praise to idols. See, the things said before have come to pass, and now I give word of new things: before they come I give you news of them.»

Psalm 54. «Save me, God!»

«Let your name be my salvation, O God; let my cause be judged by your strength. Let my prayer come before you, O God; give ear to the words of my mouth. For men who are going after me have come out against me, violent men are purposing to take my soul; they have not put God before their eyes. (Selah.) See, God is my helper: the Lord is the great supporter of my soul. Let the evil works of my haters come back on them again; let them be cut off by your good faith. Freely will I make my offerings to you; I will give praise to your name, O Lord, for it

Candasnos.

is good. Because it has been my savior from all my trouble; my eyes have seen the punishment of my haters.»

● Colloquy: We stay with Jesus, just as we did yesterday. Our presence is more important than any of our faltering words or awkward actions. We bring our personal depth of feeling, love and compassion into our prayer. This allows us to accompany Jesus at a greater depth. End with the «Our Father».

Stage 20: Candasnos – Fraga

● Annotation: We walk with Jesus, accompanying Him in His final moments as the disciples take his Body down from the cross for burial. Take time with the «introductory prayer»: once again we ask that our lives be always directed to God's will, the only source of our happiness and resurrection. Remember that the final colloquy is always important: we draw closer to the suffering Jesus and ask Him to give us strength for our personal life commitments. Make the colloquy at the end of the prayer and often during the day.

● Petition: I ask the Father for this gift: to feel sorrow with Christ in sorrow; to experience anguish with Christ in anguish; even to experience tears and profound grief because of the suffering Jesus endures at the end of His life, for my sake.

● Reflections: The crucifix, suspended over the altar of every Catholic Church, reminds us that the Mass is a remem-

brance and re-living of Jesus' own offering of Himself for each of us–Jesus poured out for us, unto death. At times we can over-intellectualize the crucifixion, pondering the theological mystery of Jesus' death. Sometimes we have changed the Crucifixion into a «golden cross», even with gemstones. Today we mean to live the passion as the harsh reality it is. In your imagination spend time with the human Jesus who died a painful, slow and humiliating death, hanging between two criminals. Spend time beside His mother who had to watch her son die. We current-day Christians know that this drama ends in Jesus' resurrection. Mary and the apostles did not. In our Ignatian contemplation, we accompany Mary, Jesus' mother, as she moves away from the tomb, back to the house where she is staying. We stay with her; we wait with her. We listen to her as she shares with us all those realities she has pondered in her heart since Jesus was just a boy. We listen to the memories of her Son. We weep with her; we hope with her. And we tell her who we are—companions and followers of her Son!

Ignatius invites us to identify as closely as possible with Jesus by experiencing «sorrow with Christ in sorrow»: a broken spirit with Christ, also so broken and to feel interior strain because of the great suffering which Christ endured for me. Consider also Our Lady's personal loneliness, along with her deep grief and fatigue. I can also ponder the fatigue of the disciples. Everything has finished. It is the end.

Christ our Lord and King continues to labor in our world to save all men and women. Jesus continues to be tortured in His brothers and sisters. He continues to be led to His cross. Take some moments of reflection about the situation of our personal humanity. Ask the Father to place you with Christ crucified in the world today.

- Texts

Matthew 27:1-66. «Crucify him!» «Why, what harm has he done?» «Crucify him!»

Psalm 22. «My God, my God, why have you forsaken me?»

«My God, my God, why have you turned away from me? Why are you so far from helping me and from the words of my anguish? O my God, I make my cry during the day and you give no answer; in the night, but I find no relief. But you are enthroned as the holy one, O Lord; you are the glory of Israel. Our fathers had faith in you: they had faith and you were their savior. They sent up their cry to you and were made free: they put their faith in you and were not put to shame. But I am a worm and not a man; cursed by men and looked down upon by the people. I am laughed at by all those who see me: curling their lips and shaking their heads they say, He put his faith in the Lord; let the Lord be his savior now: let the Lord be his savior because he had delight in him. But it was you who took care of me from the day of my birth: you gave me faith even from my mother's breasts. I was in your hands even before my birth; you are my God from the time when I was in my mother's body. Be not far from me for trouble is near; there is no one to give help. A great herd of oxen is round me: I am shut in by the strong oxen of Bashan. I saw their mouths wide open, like lions crying after food. I am flowing away like water and all my bones are out of place: my heart melts like wax, it has become soft in my body. My throat is dry like a broken vessel; my tongue is fixed to the roof of my mouth and the dust of death is on my lips. Dogs have come round me: I am shut in by the band of evil-doers; they made wounds in my hands and feet. I am able to see all my bones; their looks are fixed on me: They make a division of my robes among themselves by casting lots for my clothing. Do not be far from me, O Lord: O my strength, come quickly to my help. Make my soul safe from the sword, my life from the power of the dog. Be my savior from the lion's mouth; let me go free from the horns of the cruel oxen. I will give the knowledge of your name to my brothers: I will give you praise among the people. You who have fear of the Lord, give him praise; all you seed of Jacob give him glory; go in fear of him all you seed of Israel. For he has not been unmoved by the pain of him who is troubled; or kept his face covered from him; no, he has given an answer to his cry. Your praise I will give in the great assembly: I will fulfill my vows before your worshippers. The poor will have a feast of good things: those who search for the Lord will give him praise: their hearts will have life forever. All the ends of the earth will remember and be turned to the Lord: all the families of nations will give him worship. For the kingdom is the Lord's; he is the ruler among the nations. All who live on the earth will give him worship; all those who go down to the dust will kneel before him, even he who has not enough for the life of his soul. A seed will be his servant; the doings of the Lord will be made clear to the generation which comes after. They will come and make his righteousness known to a future people because he has done this.»

Psalm 31. «In you, Lord, I have found refuge.»

«In you, O Lord, have I put my hope; let me never be shamed; keep me safe in your righteousness. Let your ear be turned to me; take me quickly out of danger; be my strong Rock, my place of strength where I may be safe. For you are my Rock and my strong tower; go in front of me and be my guide; because of your name. Take me out of the net which they have secretly made ready for me; for you are my strength. Into your hands I give my spirit; you are my savior, O Lord God of truth. You hate those who serve false gods; but my hope is in the Lord. I will be glad and have delight in your mercy; because you have seen my trouble; you have had pity on my soul in its sorrows; And you have not given me into the hand of my enemy; you have set my feet free from confinement. Have mercy on me, O Lord, for I am in trouble; my eyes are wasted with grief, I am wasted in soul and body. My life is worn out in sorrow and my years in weeping; my strength is almost gone because of my sin and my bones are wasted away. To all those who oppose me, I have become a word of shame to my neighbors; a horror to my friends: those who saw me in the street shied away from me. I have gone from men's minds and memory like a dead man; I am like a bro-ken vessel. False statements against me have come to my ears; fear was on every side: they were talking together against me, designing to take away my life. But I had faith in you, O Lord; I said, You are my God. The prospects of my life are in your hand; take me out of the hands of my haters and of those who pursue me. Let your servant see the light of your face; in your mercy be my savior. Let me not be shamed, O Lord, for I have made my prayer to you; let the sinners be shamed and let their mouths be shut in the underworld. Let the false lips be shut which say evil against the upright, looking down on him in their pride. O how great is your grace which you have put in store for your worshippers and which you have made clear to those who had faith in you before the sons of men! You will keep them safe in your house from the designs of man; in the secret of your tent will you keep them from angry tongues. May the Lord be praised because he has made clear to me the wonder of his grace in a fortified town. And as for me, I said in my fear, I am cut off from before your eyes; but you gave ear to the voice of my prayer when my cry went up to you. O have love for the Lord all you his saints; for the Lord keeps safe from danger all those who are true to him and gives the arrogant their just reward. Put away fear and let your

Cinca valley, Fraga.

heart be strong, all you whose hope is in the Lord.»

Isaiah 50:4-9. «The Lord God is my helper.»

«The Lord God has given me a well-trained tongue so that I might know how to answer the feeble-hearted: every morning my ear is open to his teaching, like those who follow him: and I have not put myself against him or let my heart be turned back from him. I was offering my back to those who gave me blows and my face to those who were pulling out my beard: I did not keep my face covered from marks of shame. For the Lord God is my helper; I will not be put to shame: so I have made my face

like a rock, and I am certain that he will give me my right. He who takes up my cause is near; who will go to court with me? Let us come together before the judge; who is against me? Let him come near to me. See, the Lord God is my helper; who will give a decision against me? Truly, all of them will wear out like an old garment; they will be food for the worm.»

● Colloquy: We spend time with Jesus, just as we did yesterday. Our personal presence is worth more than any faltering words or awkward actions. We experience in our colloquy the depth of feeling, love and compassion which allows us simply to walk with Jesus in His suffering. Conclude with the «Our Father».

Stage 21: Fraga – Lleida

● Annotation: We now enter the final stage of our pilgrimage: the «fourth week» of the Spiritual Exercises. The mood shifts as we enter into the contemplation of God's life in all its fullness. We experience with Jesus and the disciples that the final door has been opened. There is nothing now that can stop us in our journey to freedom and eternal happiness in the Love of God. This final week is a time full of grace and light. We rejoice in each small flower, bird, smile and extended hand. Remember the «introductory prayer» as you enter into prayer, use it as well throughout the day. Pay attention to the final colloquy: we draw more deeply into this interior knowledge of the risen Jesus who strengthens our life-commitment forever. We discuss this desire with our «friend» Jesus, at the end of the prayer and as the day moves along.

● Petition: I ask the Father for this gift: to enter fully into the joy of the risen and victorious Christ. To be able to grasp the fullness of life that Jesus has achieved for us. To rejoice deeply with Christ, with Mary and all his disciples.

● Reflections: Today, and in the days to follow, Ignatius invites us to «ask for the grace to be glad and to rejoice intensely

because of the great glory and joy of Christ our Lord» who is risen from the dead. No one could imagine what was going to happen, even though Isaiah the prophet had already announced that «My servant will prosper; he will be raised high and greatly exalted.» But the last days of Jesus were so hard to endure. His death was so incomprehensible that it was impossible to imagine how God was still present. Everyone was perplexed and demoralized. More than once throughout the Bible a barren, elderly, woman found herself with child, unbelievably against all odds. Yes, Scripture writers remind us that «nothing is impossible with God»; but the Resurrection was still difficult to believe. Even though the guards explained all the details to the chief priests and elders, nobody accepted their story. We believe that the resurrection is the ultimate truth of God's extraordinary power and goodness. God has the power to liberate us from death, every kind of death.

Sometimes our faith is all too weak, however. The God who transformed Jesus from death to life can surely transform us as well. Still we are often tempted to feel discouraged and even hopeless in the face of whatever problems, fears, sinfulness, or grief take hold of us. The risen Jesus is transformed forever; by this same fact, each of us is also transformed interiorly since we hold the seeds of Resurrection within us. Jesus is alive and with us forever, even though we sometimes find it hard to believe this. The disciples going to Emmaus were given that message.

It is also the experience of Mary, the mother of Christ. She understood from the very beginning that Jesus was alive. As Ignatius tells us: she was certainly the first person to experience His Resurrection. And, from that moment, she drew closer to the disciples, helping them overcome their own sadness and disappointment. Yes, the Risen Lord is with us as He promised, consoling us and offering His gifts so that we in turn may console those suffering throughout the world.

When the women approached the empty tomb, unable to accept the possibility that Jesus had risen, the watchman simply said: «Why do you look for the living among the dead?» The same is said to us: often, we too cannot believe the good news about ourselves and our world. Once again Jesus confounds our expectations in so many ways! Today we recognize that the Risen Jesus does not, first, show himself to the apostles like Peter, Matthew or John but rather to the women, the most courageous and faithful of all the disciples.

In this contemplation let us enter into the scene personally and experience vividly Jesus' resurrection from death. I listen, I observe, I speak, I entreat, I touch… I am actually inside the event. We pray for the resurrection of every death within us and among all those we love. Today Mary understands us very well!

- Texts

Isaiah 52:13-53:12. «Who could have believed what we have heard?»

«See, my servant will do well in his undertakings, he will be honored and lifted up and be greatly exalted. Even as peoples were amazed at him, so marred was his face by disease, neither attractive nor desirable like those of other people; his form was no longer that of the sons of men. So will nations give him honor; kings will keep quiet because of him: for what had not been made clear to them they will see; they will give their minds to what had not come to their ears. Who would have believed the word which has come to our ears; to whom has the arm of the Lord been unveiled? For his growth was like that of a delicate plant before him and like a root out of a dry place: he had no grace of form to give us pleasure; Men made sport of him, turning away from him; he was a man of sorrows, marked by disease; like one from whom men's faces are turned away, he was looked down upon and we put no value on him. But it was our pain he took and

Segre river, Lleida.

our diseases were put on him: while to us he seemed as one diseased, on whom God's punishment had come. But it was for our sins he that was wounded and for our evil doings he was crushed: he bore the punishment through which we find peace; by his wounds we are made well. We all went wandering like sheep; every one of us following our own desires; the Lord laid upon him all of our guilt. Men were cruel to him but he was gentle and quiet, as a lamb taken to the slaughterhouse and as a ewe, before those who take her wool; makes no sound, so he said not a word. Without trial or arrest, they got rid of him; who gave a thought to his fate? For he was cut off from the land of the living: he came to his death for the sin of his people. They put his body into the earth with sinners and his last resting-place was with evildoers, though he had done no wrong and no deceit was in his mouth. Yet the Lord gave thought to his oppressed servant and healed him who had given himself as a sacrifice for sin. He will enjoy long life and see his children's children and in his hand the Lord's purpose will prosper. By his humiliation, my servant will justify many; after his suffer-ing he will see light and be satisfied: it is their guilt he bears. For this cause he will have a heritage with the great and he will have a part in the spoils of war with the strong because he gave up his life and was numbered with the evil-doers; taking on himself the sins of the people and making prayer for the wrongdoers.»

Matthew 28:1-15. «Do not be afraid; I know that you seek Jesus who was cruci-fied. He is not here; he has been raised.»

Luke 24:13-35. Jesus, my companion, all along this pilgrimage explains to me how He has been part of my history and even my pre-history. Consoled in this way, I want to proclaim to others just as the Emmaus disciples did: «The Lord has been raised!»

● Final Colloquy: At this point in our in-ner pilgrimage, we are already accus-tomed to walking with our friend and Lord, Jesus Christ, speaking freely as one friend does to another. If in your heart you feel the strength and grace to do so, invite Jesus to accept you for service under His banner, joining at His side to build the Kingdom of God. Conclude with the «Our Father».

Stage 22: Lleida – El Palau d'Anglesola

● Annotation: Throughout the «fourth week» of the Spiritual Exercises we keep up the same positive spirit, especially because we now contemplate God's life in all its fullness. There is nothing that can hinder our journey to freedom and eternal happiness since we are grounded in God's love. Live this final week filled with grace and light. We rejoice in eve-ry flower, bird, smile and shaken hand. Remember the «introductory prayer» before each prayer period and continue it during the day. Pay attention to the final colloquy: we enter into the inte-rior knowledge of the risen Jesus who strengthens our commitment to eternal life. This we discuss with our «friend» Je-sus in the colloquy at the end of prayer as well as during the day.

● Petition: I ask the Father for this gift: to be able to enter into the joy of the risen and victorious Christ. To contem-plate the fullness of life that Jesus has achieved for us. To rejoice deeply with Christ, with Mary and all his disciples.

● Reflections: We focus our contemplation today on the wonder of the Resurrection. It took the disciples many days to under-stand the experience of Jesus' full risen Life. Stay close to Mary Magdalene, the woman who loved Jesus so deeply. Expe-rience her distress. Try to feel as she did, once she has lost the only purpose for her life. And be there with her at the moment of her discovery. The world rejoices with her. Feel the fear and guilt of the disciples when the risen Jesus returns to the upper

El Palau d'Anglesola.

room where they used to gather together. See the place and be one of them. Experience the wonder of the Resurrection.

Jesus comes today to our personal desperation, to that dark room where we have enclosed our most difficult moments. He wants to heal all our personal deaths and losses, restoring us to life. Jesus no longer permits our suffering. He is Life and He wants to release us from our personal tomb. Listen to the voice of Jesus calling you to come forth as Lazarus did. Be conscious of His presence, walking with you and telling you: «Awake from your death for I am indeed alive!»

As always, Ignatius invites us to put ourselves inside these incredible scenes. Allow these familiar resurrection stories to play out within your own heart as you put yourself into the scene. Make use of nature's many delights to help you. As Ignatius wrote his Spiritual Exercises, he no doubt recalled the most enjoyable days of his pilgrimage to Montserrat and everything there that brought him joy. In this fourth week, «I will make use of light and the pleasant features of the seasons, like refreshing coolness in summer or the sun's warmth in winter, as far as I think or imagine that this will help me rejoice in Christ my Creator and redeemer.»

● Texts

John 20:11-18. With Mary Magdalene I hear my own name and respond with joy.

John 20:19-23. The fear, guilt and confusion of Jesus' ten companions in the upper room are familiar since I have felt them all. It is into just such a personal place that He wants and needs to come. I welcome Him and receive His gifts: peace, joy, mission, His life-giving Spirit, His forgiving heart.

John 11:17-44. Jesus said: «I am the Resurrection and the life do you believe this?» Jesus called: «Lazarus, come out!» Lazarus heard himself called from death to life, from being bound up to being set free. Lying on the ledge in the tomb, I ponder my own small deaths and all that limits my freedom.

● Final colloquy: At this stage of our inner pilgrimage, we are accustomed to walking with our Lord and friend, Jesus Christ, speaking freely as one friend does to another. If you honestly feel the strength and grace to do so, invite Jesus to accept you under His banner, and thus to build God's Kingdom at His side. Finish with the «Our Father».

Stage 23: El Palau d'Anglesola – Verdú

- **Annotation:** We maintain the same positive spirit as we continue to contemplate the life of God in all its fullness. There is nothing that can hinder us on our path to freedom and eternal happiness in God's love. Live this last week full of grace and full of light. We rejoice in every flower, bird, smile, extended hand. Remember the «introductory prayer» as we enter into prayer, as well as throughout the day. Pay attention to the final colloquy: we ask an interior knowledge of the risen Jesus who strengthens our eternal life-commitment. We discuss this with our «friend» Jesus in the colloquy at the end of prayer and during the day. At this point, pay attention to the Ignatian tips referring to St. Peter Claver (pp. 141-142). Peter Claver was a follower of Jesus Christ and a Jesuit missionary in Latin America; he was often called the «slave of slaves».

- **Petition:** I beg the Father for this gift: to enter into the joy of the risen and victorious Christ. To be able to contemplate the fullness of life that Jesus has achieved for us. I ask to rejoice deeply with Christ and to be sent into the world to serve in Jesus Christ's mission.

- **Reflections:** The grace of being alive, the grace of experiencing the resurrection within you is not just a personal gift. Rather, with great energy, this grace must be shared with others and placed at the service of Jesus' Mission: to spread the Good News of the Kingdom of God. Today we feel renewed as in the same moment we commit ourselves with Jesus, our best «friend», to help realize His mission on earth. The Father continues to pour out the Spirit of Christ upon the men and women of our day. Jesus consoles us always and sends us forth on mission to console the suffering, the poor and all who long for salvation. As it is written: «When you send forth your spirit, they are created, and you renew the face of the earth» (Ps 104:30). We pray today to our God that we may enter into the joy and consoling mission of the Risen Jesus.

In Matthew's gospel, we find Jesus asking the disciples to go to Galilee and assist him there. The disciples were those sinners He had invited to become His companions, the same ones who were traitors at the very end. We are now one with them, as disciples in our pilgrimage to the Kingdom. We are also united with

Saint Peter Claver Sanctuary/Shrine, Verdú.

others, whether more sinful or more faithful than ourselves. But this does not really matter since our strength and wisdom is centered in Christ. Do not be afraid to answer His call. We gather now at the mountain, that meeting place between God and His people. For us, this place can be a slum, a lab, a church, a clinic, an office, a parlor, a classroom. Jesus gives us our mission: go forth, baptize, teach, love and bring God's compassion as reconciliation for all of humanity. We are invited to fulfill this mission in every moment and circumstance of life. Now, Jesus speaks the most wonderful words to us: He promises that He will be with us always, in each joyful and painful moment. Even though I may not feel worthy to accept His presence, Jesus will always stay close to me. Even if I am a sinful person, unfaithful and limited, Jesus is going to send His Spirit to transform every human situation as an experience of growth.

Even though our faith may be weak, Jesus counts on us. Thomas had to recognize his lack of faith before being sent to the world. We pray to answer the call of Jesus, inviting us to follow him to the beach and stay with Him. We join the disciples there in receiving His commission and His blessing.

● Texts

Matthew 28:16-20: «I will be with you always, until the end of time.»

John 20:24-29: Tolerant of my darkness and unbelief, as He was of Thomas, Jesus delights in consoling me with the gift of renewed faith. In His loving presence, I say: «My Lord and my God!»

John 21:1-17: A moment of joy – «It is the Lord!» A moment of companionship – «Come and eat your meal.» A moment of intimacy and decision – «Do you love me?» A moment of mission – «Feed my sheep!»

● Final Colloquy: At this point in our interior pilgrimage, we are accustomed to walking with our friend and Lord, Jesus Christ, speaking freely just as one friend does with another. If you honestly experience the strength and grace within you, beg Jesus to accept you under His banner, thus to build the Kingdom of God at His side. Finish with the «Our Father».

Stage 24: Verdú – Cervera

● Annotation: Although we meditate today about Jesus' temptations, we keep our same positive spirit since we continue to contemplate the life of God in all its fullness. Nothing can deter us on our journey to freedom and eternal happiness in the love of God. Remember the «introductory prayer» as well as the final colloquy at the end of the prayer and recall it throughout the day. Today, rejoice in Christ's Resurrection! Light, flowers, water and friends are all welcome!

● Petition: I pray to rejoice deeply with Christ since I am now sent into the world to serve His mission. I pray that I can recognize the deceits of Evil and guard myself against them, as Jesus did in the full confidence of God's Love.

● Reflections: Yesterday we were called to return to Galilee, to our «regular life» and usual habits. We have a mission: to work for the Kingdom. Today we consider the beginning of Jesus' mission and the discernment He went through before beginning His work. The purpose of this meditation is to gain insight into the strategies of Jesus and of the Evil One, knowing that we are called to work for the Kingdom in our ordinary daily living.

How will you use your power, gifts, talents and resources? This is the fundamental question of Jesus' temptation in the desert. We are told that the Evil One showed Jesus all the kingdoms of the world and said: «All these I will give you, if you will fall down and worship me.» The answer was: «You shall worship the Lord your God and Him alone shall you serve.» This moment of crisis in the wilderness is the same moment of crisis that we all face constantly. Can we restrain our desires and wanton need for praise, adulation, power and comfort? Will our lives be all about using our talents to serve ourselves or will our lives focus on contributing to society and the world we have inherited? Call to mind the temptations that beset you. Realize that Jesus—fully human like you—may likewise have suffered any of these same temptations, shameful as they may be. Jesus' solution to temptation was to recognize it and to rely totally on God. In the same way, we can bring our temptations to Jesus, proclaiming our confidence in Him. Let us pray that we find ourselves so close to Jesus that we want to choose what He chooses.

As we already said, Jesus does not choose «perfect men and women» to become His disciples. He knows us very well. Understanding the kind of persons Jesus chose, Ignatius invites us to ponder first «how they came from such a rude and lowly condition of living, and then to realize the dignity to which they were so gently called.» This is our mystery as well: we are born very low, yet called to such lofty service. Temptation is at our door. It is normal.

Ignatius proposes a meditation on three kinds of response to Jesus' invitation to follow this mission. Ignatius challenges us to reflect on just what it means to find that true spiritual freedom to embrace Jesus' mission. We are speaking about true freedom, freedom that brings about God's action in the world. All of us experience attractions that can get in the way of our serving God within

the world: we may love money, sex, power, our good looks, appearing well-clothed, having expensive cars or other things. Some folks have good intentions but they never manage to change their ways of living until the day before their deaths. Others, deep down, know that something is not quite right but they keep finding excuses and rationalizations to keep doing the same thing and even try to convince God that it is really not that bad. Others are free: they can be rich and well-satisfied, if this is God's will and for God's service. But they can also be happy and poor, giving up what they are involved with. They can graciously accept prestige insofar as it helps serve Jesus' mission but they do not crave and chase prestige for its own sake and can easily live without it.

It is entirely human to have attachments which crush our freedom May we be able to accept graciously any prestige that helps to serve the mission of our King. At the same time may we not shrink from persecution or loss of prestige if this will produce some greater good and allow us live without positions of power. Perhaps it is sufficient for today's meditation to simply recognize such harmful attachments and to avoid them. For this grace we beg for God's light.

● Texts

Matthew 4:1-11. The tactics of his adversary are not to tempt Jesus to evil, but rather to become a Messiah of possessions, prestige and power instead of a Messiah of poverty, persecution and powerlessness, as the Father has called Him to be.

Ecclesiastes 3:1-22. Humans cannot understand God's ways. Thus we should definitely stay close to Him. Since everything has its own time, I should hold onto the times of God in my life.

«For everything there is a fixed time, and a time for every business under the sun. A time for birth and a time for death; a time for planting and a time for uprooting. A time to put to death and a time to make well; a time for pulling down and a time for building up. A

Tàrrega.

time for weeping and a time for laughing; a time for sorrow and a time for dancing. A time to scatter stones and a time to gather stones together; a time to embrace and a time to keep from embracing. A time to seek and a time to lose; a time to keep and a time to give away. A time to rend and a time to stitch; a time for keeping quiet and a time for talk. A time for love and a time for hate; a time for war and a time for peace. What profit has the worker in the work which he does? I have seen the work which God has given the sons of man. He has made everything right in its time; but he has made men's hearts ignorant of the mysteries of time, so man is unable to see the works of God, from the start to the finish. I am certain that there is nothing better for a man than to be glad, and to do good while life is in him. And for every man to take food and drink, and have joy in all his work, is a reward from God. I am certain that whatever God does will be forever. No addition may be made to it, nothing may be taken from it; God has done it so that man may be in awe before him. Whatever is has been before, and what is to be is now; because God brings back the things which are past. And again, I saw under the sun, in the place of the judges, that evil was there; in the place of righteousness, that evil was there. I said in my heart, God will be judge of the good and of the bad; because a time for every purpose and for every work has been fixed by him. I said in my heart, It is because of the sons of men, so that God may put them to the test and that they may see themselves as beasts. Because the fate of the sons of men and the fate of the beasts is the same. As is the death of one so is the death of the other, and all have one spirit. Humans have no preeminence over the beasts; that is simply vanity. All go to the same place, all are of the dust, and all will be turned to dust again. Who is certain that the spirit of the sons of men goes up to heaven, or that the spirit of the beasts goes down to the earth? So I saw that there is nothing better than for

a man to have joy in his work--because that is his reward. Who will make him see what will come after him?»

Proverbs 3:1-12. Put your loyalty and faith in God and you will never fail.

«My son, keep my teaching in your memory and my rules in your heart: for they will give you increase of days, years of life and peace. Let not mercy and good faith go from you; let them be hanging round your neck, recorded on your heart; So you will have grace and a good name in the eyes of God and men. Put all your hope in God, not looking to your reason for support. In all your ways give ear to him, and he will make straight your footsteps. Put no high value on your wisdom: let the fear of the Lord be before you, and keep yourself from evil: This will give strength to your flesh and new life to your bones. Give honor to the Lord with your wealth,

Bellpuig.

and with the first-fruits of all your produce: So your store-houses will be full of grain, and your vessels overflowing with new wine. My son, do not make your heart hard against the Lord's teaching; do not be made angry by his training: For to those who are dear to him the Lord says sharp words, and makes the son in whom he has delight undergo pain.»

Wisdom 3:1-12. Those who trust in God will understand that His Truth is real, and the faithful will abide with God in Love.

«But the souls of the upright are in the hands of God, and no torment can touch them. To the unenlightened, they appeared to die, their departure was regarded as disaster, their leaving us like annihilation; but they are at peace. If, as it seemed to us, they suffered punishment, their hope was rich with immortality; slight was their correction, great will their blessings be. God was putting them to the test and has proved them worthy to be with him; he has tested them like gold in a furnace, and accepted them as a perfect burnt offering. At their time of their judgment, they will shine out; as sparks run through the stubble, so will they. They will judge nations, rule over peoples, and the Lord will be their king for ever. Those who trust in him will understand the truth, those who are faithful will live with him in love; for grace and mercy await his holy ones, and he intervenes on behalf of his chosen. But the godless will be duly punished for their reasoning, for having

neglected the upright and deserted the Lord. Yes, wretched are they who scorn wisdom and discipline: their hope is void, their toil unavailing, their achievements unprofitable; their wives are reckless, their children depraved, their descendants accursed.»

Matthew 6:24-34. No one can serve two masters; either he will hate the one and love the other, or he will be devoted to the one and despise the other. You cannot serve both God and material wealth.

- Final Colloquy: At this stage of our inner journey, we are accustomed to walking with our friend and Lord, Jesus Christ, speaking freely with Him as one friend does with another. If you honestly experience the strength and grace within you, invite Jesus to accept you under His banner, joining at His side to build the Kingdom of God. Conclude with the «Our Father».

Stage 25: Cervera – Igualada

- Note: We maintain the same positive spirit as we continue in our «fourth week», since we feel more and more united with Jesus Christ in His mission. Indeed nothing can hinder our progress towards freedom and eternal happiness in the love of God. Remember the «introductory prayer» and the final colloquy—at the end of the prayer as well as during the day. Rejoice in Christ's Resurrection! Songs, light, flowers, water and friends are welcome!

- Petition: I beg God to rejoice deeply with the Risen Christ since I have been sent into the world to serve His mission. I pray to recognize His transfigured presence in my life, accompanying Him on his mission to reconcile and give life to all people.

- Reflections: Jesus needs our hands to welcome those men and women who need care, reconciliation, Love and Life. Jesus needs our wills, our desires to move forward and build, to continue creating

the Kingdom among us. The Risen Jesus calls us to follow Him and to participate with Him in the [gospel] transformation that has already begun in the World. In the gospels, Jesus explicitly calls several people by name. As we contemplate the mysteries proposed today, we hear our own name and discover that our hearts are also stirred. How do I feel, as I am called by name today, just as Zacchaeus was? How do I feel, invited to climb the mount of Tabor with Jesus? What does it mean for me to feel close to Jesus?

The story of Jesus' transfiguration on Mount Tabor proclaims the truth hidden deep within our own humanity, unclear as this may be. The Light is certainly within us. The Divine Essence inhabits us and is noticeable from the first moment of our conception. Our human condition sometimes acts as a «dark filter», dimming the Divine Light. But nonetheless we must turn «black holes» into «bright stars». The suffering, the injustice, and the absurdity that surround us in so many situations   these create the «filter» that can switch off the smallest spark of light. But in the Risen Jesus we discover that, despite all the turmoil in which we live, the Light of Jesus still burns within us—and this experience transforms us. Nothing indeed can separate us from God's Love. Everything can be transfigured in His Love.

The Risen Jesus is God alive within us. Whoever communicates this message with their time and talents will not fail. What needs to be transformed in my life? What prevents the divine light from shining through me?

- Texts

Luke 19:1-10. Jesus calls out to Zacchaeus and invites him to «descend» from his concerns and lifestyle. If you want to see Jesus, leave behind the fabrications you have made. If you want to meet Jesus in your life, return to your home. He awaits you there. Open your heart to Him so that this reunion will be generous and transforming.

Romans 8:31-39. Nothing can separate us from the love of God.

Matthew 17:1-13. Jesus calls his disciples and invites them to accompany him on his journey of transfiguration. I also need to go up the mountain with Him. So much pain and so many difficulties can undermine our faith and determination but if we believe in the Resurrection, we also believe that Life has no ending. Nothing can hide the Light within us. Nothing can silence the Word [of God] within us.

Matthew 17:14-21. Called to serve Jesus Christ and to share together in mission, our faith cannot be weak. If we believe in Jesus we will not fail. If we believe only in ourselves and our possibilities, we will achieve nothing—even if we bear His name.

- Final colloquy: At this point in our interior pilgrimage, we are accustomed to walk with Jesus Christ, our friend and Lord, speaking freely with Him as one friend does with another. If you are personally able to find the strength and grace within you, beg Jesus to be accepted under His banner and thus to build the Kingdom of God at His side. Conclude with the «Our Father».

Sant Pere dels Arquells.

Stage 26: Igualada – Montserrat

● Annotation: Easter joy continues within us. Remember to begin with the «introductory prayer»; to conclude with the final colloquy and to pray it throughout the day. Live the joy of Christ's Resurrection! Songs, light, flowers, water and friends are welcome! Our Ignatian journey invites us today to do as Ignatius did: spend some special prayer time with the Black Virgin of Montserrat.

● Petition: I beg God that I may rejoice deeply with the Risen Christ since I have also been sent into the world to serve His mission. I pray to receive the Holy Spirit so I can better accompany Jesus in His mission to reconcile the world and bring life to all persons.

● Reflections: the Spirit of God confirms us in the mission we have received from Christ. Moreover, the same Spirit remains with us and strengthens us in any difficulties that come our way. We follow the dynamics of previous weeks: the true King invites us to accompany him in his conquest of good against the absurd destruction of all that is human. The Spirit strengthens us in our journey across the world, preaching the Good News.

The Spirit breaks down barriers and opens pathways. The Spirit creates fraternity, creates community and brings

Montserrat Basilica.

forth the Image of God in the world. The Spirit awakens us, enlightens us and removes our deafness and blindness. The Spirit launches us and pushes us forward and does not allow us to sit still for very long. The Spirit challenges us, pulls us away from our creature comforts and breaks through our well-planned schemes. The Spirit fills us with compassion, love and the desire for solidarity. The Spirit raises us up, helps us to dream and exalts us. In the Spirit we can hope for everything, we can bear everything, we can accomplish everything. The Spirit is the actual presence of God in our daily lives.

Throughout our pilgrimage we have been «breathing in» the Spirit. Today we beg for a deep awareness of the Holy Spirit, present within us. Where do I find the Spirit working within me? Within others? Do I recognize the «action» of the Spirit within the world? Remember to beg for this important grace.

● Texts

John 16:5-15. I recall the words of Jesus about the work of the Holy Spirit.

Acts 2:1-21. The promise of the Spirit's coming is fulfilled on the day of Pentecost.

Acts 10:44-48. While Peter was speaking, the Holy Spirit came down upon all those who were listening. The work of evangelization had begun. I ask to embrace this challenge with energy and commitment.

Luke 4:14-20. Jesus returned to Galilee, filled with the power of the Spirit. I pray that my return home will also be filled with the Spirit. I need God's Holy Spirit to fulfill the mission of God's Kingdom.

● Final colloquy: At this stage of our interior pilgrimage, we are accustomed to walk with our friend and Lord, Jesus Christ, speaking freely as one friend does with another. Conclude with the «Our Father».

Stage 27: Montserrat – Manresa

- Annotation: Great joy stays with us during this final stage of the «outer» journey. The long cherished goal of Manresa is at hand! Remember the «introductory prayer» and the final colloquy, both at the end of the prayer and also during the day. May our hearts be filled with the strength of the Holy Spirit and may the Spirit's strength go with us on this milestone day in our lives. The Ignatian path for today invites us to continue our inner pilgrimage.

- Petition: I beg God to give me an intimate knowledge of the many gifts I have received. Filled with gratitude for these many gifts, may I love and serve the Divine Majesty.

- Reflections: The Father, Son, and Holy Spirit are always at work, sharing themselves with us. This sharing empowers us to be contemplatives-in-action, finding God in all things. The Jesuits decreed in their 32nd General Congregation that «each member of every Jesuit community must be mindful of what St. Ignatius says about love–that it consists in sharing what one has, who one is, and all those whom one loves. Today we will focus our meditation on this experience of love as an exchange of who one is and what one shares with the beloved. In the Spiritual Exercises, Ignatius invites us to understand just how God's Love is given to us and shared so generously out of God's great goodness. With this cascade of gifts and graces, we must also respond in a generous and loving way. We will follow the directions of Ignatius to let our hearts expand in the Love of God. The steps of this Ignatian contemplation are as follows:

- CONTEMPLATION TO ATTAIN LOVE

Two things should be noted: The first is that love is expressed more in actions than in words.

The second is that love is a communication between two persons. It is to know, to give, and to communicate from the lover to the one loved, and vice versa, whatever one has or is able to have. So, if one has wisdom, he shares this with the one who has not, or honors and riches from the one who has to the one who does not.

El Xup, Manresa.

Then I return to the introductory prayer and ask that everything be directed to God's will.

Next I center myself within the prayer. I imagine that I stand before God the Father, Jesus the Son, and the Spirit of Love who created me in my humanity. I call to mind today's conscious desire: I ask the Father to give me an intimate knowledge of the many gifts I have received so that, filled with gratitude for all of them, I may love and serve the Divine Majesty in every way.

As I begin my contemplation, *the first point* is *to call to mind the benefits received from God*: the fact of being born and of being saved by Jesus, as well as for all those personal gifts I enjoy. I consider all that God our Lord has done for me and how much of Himself God has shared with me. Aware of this reality, I ponder with much reason and justice what I might offer and return to His Divine Majesty, that is to say all my possessions and all of myself.

Then, as you wish, consider that anyone who desires to be more responsive to God will make the following self-offering: «Take, Lord, and receive all my liberty, my memory, my understanding and my entire will, all I have and call my own. You have given all to me. To you, Lord, I return it. Everything is yours; do with it what you will. Give me only your love and your grace. That is enough for me.»

Completing the first point, Ignatius proposes a *second point*: *notice how God dwells in all of creation* and in all living creatures: giving life to all natural elements, bringing vegetation to the plants, sense to the animals, and understanding to humans. God also gives me life, encouragement, direction, and understanding. God also makes me a holy temple, created in His likeness and Divine image. I then reflect on myself --how I live, what I accomplish, and how I may serve. I end this point by returning to the previous prayer of self-offering: «Take, Lord, and receive …»

The third point is *to consider how God actually works and labors for me in all*

created things: everything in the heavens and the elements, plants, fruits, animals, etc. God gives and preserves all life, giving awareness, vegetation, etc. Then I think about myself: what can I do to return this love I have received. I finish this point by returning to the previous prayer of self-offering: «Take, Lord, and receive …»

The fourth: *notice how every good gift descends from above*, and my own strength comes only from God's infinite power. Thus, justice, goodness, mercy, all other good gifts that I recognize in myself as well as in the world (like the rays from the sun, our water supply, etc.), all come from God. After considering the origins of all that is good, I consider myself and the way I will make a return for all that I have received. I end this reflection by returning to the self-offering prayer above: «Take, Lord, and receive …» Finish with the usual colloquy and the «Our Father».

- Final colloquy: At this point in our inner pilgrimage, we are accustomed to walking with our friend and Lord, Jesus Christ, speaking freely as one friend does with another. Conclude with the «Our Father».

Castellgalí.

Stage 28: Manresa

We propose one last meditation on the Spiritual Exercises, now that we have arrived at our outer pilgrimage's destination. The inner pilgrimage might carry on for some more time. After these thirty days, the retreatant will have had enough experience to go on with his or her pilgrimage back home.

● Annotation: The practice of these spiritual exercises has already given each of us a personal experience. Each pilgrim has found his or her own way forward along this «inner pilgrimage». At the «Cave of Manresa» you will find a multitude of materials that can help you continue to grow in Ignatian spirituality. Seeking such advice is always helpful!

● Petition: I ask the Father to give me an interior knowledge of the many gifts I have received from God. Filled with gratitude for these blessings, I pray that in all things I may love and serve the Divine Majesty. I also pray that the spiritual

Well of Enlightenment (*Pozo de la Iluminación*), Manresa.

experience of St. Ignatius of Loyola will help guide me along my own path of life.

● Reflections: Today we repeat the same meditation as yesterday, focusing this time on the pilgrimage we have completed. The Camino Ignaciano has certainly offered us an experience of God's love in its many forms. So we spend our prayer time using this contemplation of God's love to review the various stages of our journey. We thank God for so many experiences and blessings as we prepare to return to our everyday routine.

● CONTEMPLATION TO ATTAIN LOVE ON YOUR PILGRIMAGE

As yesterday, two realities should be noted at the outset: The first is that love is expressed more in actions than in words.

The second is that love is a communication between two persons. It is to know, to give, and to communicate from the lover to the one loved, and vice versa, whatever one has or is able to have. So, if one has wisdom, he shares this with the one who needs it, or honors and riches from the one who has to the one who does not.

Then go back to the introductory prayer and ask that everything can be directed to God's will.

Next I center myself in the prayer. I imagine that I stand before God the Father, Jesus the Son, and the Spirit of Love that created me in all my humanity.

Today I ask the Father to give me an intimate knowledge of the many gifts I have received so that, filled with gratitude for all of these, I may love and serve the Divine Majesty in everything I undertake.

I begin the prayer. The first point is *to call to mind all the blessings I have received from God* throughout this time of pilgrimage. I recall both the ones that seemed good to me from the very beginning and others that I now realize were really not so bad after all.

Aware of this personal reality, I consider with much reason and justice what I must give of myself as an offering to His Divine Majesty—that is to say all my possessions and all of my life.

Also, as you wish, consider that anyone wanting to be more responsive to the Lord will make the following loving response: «Take, Lord, and receive all my liberty, my memory, my understanding and my entire will, all I have and call my own. You have given all to me. To you, Lord, I return it. Everything is yours; do with it what you will. Give me only your love and your grace. That is enough for me.»

Completing the first point, Ignatius proposes a second point: *notice how God is present and alive in each meeting and experience*, around me and inside of me as I think about myself and the way I live, in all that I accomplish and in those I serve. Finish this point by returning to the previous prayer of self-offering: «Take, Lord, and receive ...»

In the third point, I consider how God has labored for me in all created things

and persons I have met on this pilgrimage. After considering this point, I ask myself what I can do to become a more loving person. I conclude this third point by returning to the prayer of self-offering: «Take, Lord, and receive »

The fourth: *notice how every good gift descends from above*, and my own strength comes only from God's infinite power. Thus justice, goodness, mercy, all other good gifts that I recognize in myself as well as in the world (like the rays from the sun, our water supply, etc.) all come from God. After considering the origins of all this goodness, I consider myself and the way I will make a return for all that I have received during this pilgrimage. I end this reflection by returning to the self-offering prayer above: «Take, Lord, and receive...»

● Final Colloquy: Summarize your thoughts during this prayer time, speaking with Jesus as one friend does with another. Be honest with him about the desires and decisions you found in your heart during these days of pilgrimage and prayer. Conclude with the «Our Father».

GLOSSARY

abadía: abbey
agua: water
agua potable: drinking water
albergue: (pilgrim's) shelter, hostel
alto: heights, summit, top
arco: arch
avenida, av.: avenue, ave., boulevard
ayuntamiento: city hall
bosque: forest, woods
bus: bus
calle, c/: street, st.
calle Mayor: Main street
camino: (pilgrim's) way, path, road
campanario: belltower
canal: canal
capilla: chapel, shrine
carretera, ctra.: road, rd., highway, asphalt
    road
casa: house
casa rural: cottage, farmhouse (for guests)
castillo: castle
catedral: cathedral
cementerio: graveyard, cemetery
centro: city center, downtown
centro histórico, casco histórico: old town
ciudad: city
colina: hill
convento: convent
cruce: cross, crossroads
empresa: business
ermita: chapel, shrine
escalera: stairs
estación: (bus, train) station

fortaleza: keep, fort
fuente: well, spring, fountain
gruta: cavern, grotto
iglesia: church
lago: lake
laguna: lagoon
llanura: plain, flatland
molino: mill
monasterio: monastery
montaña: mountain
monte: hill
muro: wall
palacio: palace
parque: park
paseo: boulevard, promenade
peregrino: pilgrim
piedra: stone, rock
plaza: village or town central square, plaza
posada, pensión: inn, hostel
prado: meadow
pueblo: town, village
puente: bridge
puerta: door, gate
puerto de montaña: mountain pass
refugio: refuge, shelter
río: river
salón columnario: columned hall
santuario: sanctuary
sendero: path, way
torre: tower
torrente, arroyo: stream, brook
tren: train
valle: valley

CPSIA information can be obtained
at www.ICGtesting.com
Printed in the USA
FSHW01n1435061018
52708FS

9 781944 418731